No Way Ray and Stone Dancer at the Mexican border
April 16, 2006

A THRU-HIKER'S HEART
Tales of the Pacific Crest Trail

"No Way" Ray Echols

Edited by Alice Tulloch (Mrs. No Way)

Tuolumne Press

Mariposa, CA

A Thru-Hiker's Heart: Tales of the Pacific Crest Trail
by Ray Echols

Front and back cover photos, interior photos and illustrations copyright © 2009 by Alice Tulloch. Ray Echols photographer.
Book, cover and map design: Wild Pete Publishing, Coarsegold, CA
Book Editor: Alice Tulloch

Library of Congress Cataloging-in-Publication Data

Echols, Ray 1942-2006
    A Thru-Hiker's Heart: Tales of the Pacific Crest Trail / by "No Way" Ray Echols
    p. cm.
    ISBN 978-0-9814722-0-1 (pbk.)
    1. Backpacking—Pacific Crest Trail. 2. Echols, Ray, 1942 – Travel—Pacific Crest Trail. 3. Pacific Crest Trail – Description and travel. 1. Title

Library of Congress Control Number: 2008912130

ISBN: 978-0-9814722-0-1

Manufactured in the United States of America

Published by :   Tuolumne Press
                  P O Box 273
                  Mariposa, CA 95338
                  209-742-6963
                  www.tuolumnepress.com
                  info@tuolumnepress.com
Visit our website for ordering information.

Cover Photos:

Front: "No Way" Ray Echols at Porcupine Creek campground, August 26, 2005, three days before reaching the US-Canadian border at the end of his PCT hike.

Back: Ray Echols at Thousand Island Lake with Mts. Ritter and Banner on the skyline, July 11, 2005.

for Buddy

Happy the man, and happy he alone,
He who can call today his own,
He who secure within can say,
"Tomorrow do thy worst, for I have liv'd today.
Be fair or foul, or rain or shine,
The joys I have possess'd in spite of fate are mine.
Not heav'n itself upon the past has pow'r
But what has been, has been, and I have had my hour."

Odes, Horace

———⟫●⟪———

**Endless days, alone.
Joyous, only earth and sky.
A thru-hiker's heart**

Mū Dō

Pacific Crest Trail
Locations mentioned in this narrative

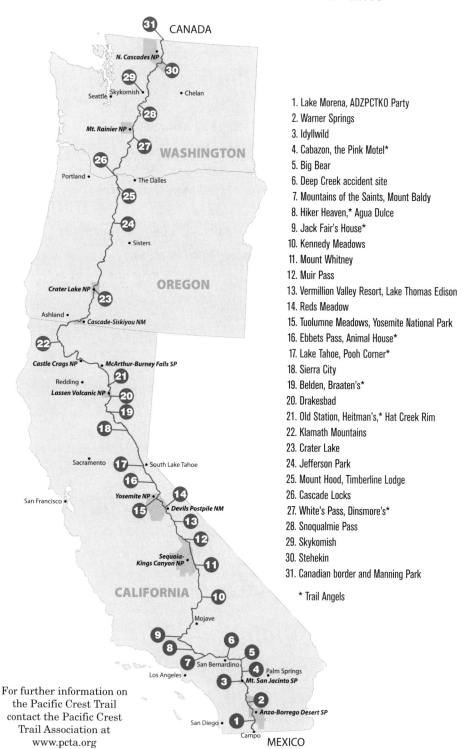

1. Lake Morena, ADZPCTKO Party
2. Warner Springs
3. Idyllwild
4. Cabazon, the Pink Motel*
5. Big Bear
6. Deep Creek accident site
7. Mountains of the Saints, Mount Baldy
8. Hiker Heaven,* Agua Dulce
9. Jack Fair's House*
10. Kennedy Meadows
11. Mount Whitney
12. Muir Pass
13. Vermillion Valley Resort, Lake Thomas Edison
14. Reds Meadow
15. Tuolumne Meadows, Yosemite National Park
16. Ebbets Pass, Animal House*
17. Lake Tahoe, Pooh Corner*
18. Sierra City
19. Belden, Braaten's*
20. Drakesbad
21. Old Station, Heitman's,* Hat Creek Rim
22. Klamath Mountains
23. Crater Lake
24. Jefferson Park
25. Mount Hood, Timberline Lodge
26. Cascade Locks
27. White's Pass, Dinsmore's*
28. Snoqualmie Pass
29. Skykomish
30. Stehekin
31. Canadian border and Manning Park

* Trail Angels

For further information on
the Pacific Crest Trail
contact the Pacific Crest
Trail Association at
www.pcta.org

CONTENTS

PREFACE

A tall man casts a large shadow and a smaller man's shadow is a diminished one, but a man like my friend No Way had such a smiling face that even a shadow would not hide it.

We come to this book to read the words written by No Way Ray. Come inside these pages with me and together we attempt to learn who this man was, and what his dreams were. We'll find what made this man stand out from others of his age and background. Let the memory of his shining face comfort you as you read these tales from the trail of his mind. He let his mind work wonders with the people and events he encountered every day.

Many of us who count ourselves his friends are long distance hikers, but few of us can put into words why we do it. It's hard to tell our family and friends at home not only why we hike, but what we saw and what we did day after day for half a year. No Way Ray can hold you spellbound with the reasons why he hiked. His reasons may not be the same as yours for going on a hike, for following your dream. Maybe it is impossible for you to articulate the reasons, but reading this book may help you feel why he and many others go on these long hikes.

No Way Ray was a teacher in many ways. Teachers appear in all walks of our lives and if we are smart enough, we find that we never stop learning from them. The wisdom of their words dwell with us for a lifetime. Perhaps we already have met a special teacher in our lives, someone who has now passed on. Yet his life's lessons are still with us. In the pages to follow you will meet such a man, a man who became my friend for life. It was not that he was smarter than the rest of us, but he had a way with words. You could not help but see the logic behind these words of clear and uncommon vision.

When we leave the nest of home and go out to hike in the wilderness, another family comes into our lives. This is a family of kindred souls whom we learn to love as much as the family we were born into. Some of us are blessed with these two families who understand the pull of the unknown horizon. When I met Ray at the ADZ[1] Kickoff for the first time, it was like meeting someone one saw in the mirror everyday of your life. A few days later, up the trail at Mount Laguna, we shared beans and hot dogs and wine, and then we were off and running as friends. We would see each other a few times a year at the Kickoff and again at Kennedy

---

1 ADZ, short for ADZPCTKO, the Annual Day Zero Pacific Crest Trail Kickoff Party, also known as the Kickoff.

Meadows. Ray was the host for my 60th birthday bash up there with over sixty other friends and hikers. It was there I met his wife Alice for the first time. After hearing about her over the years, I felt she too was already a friend. Sadly, my 61st birthday spent at Kennedy Meadows was also the day we held the hiker's memorial service to say goodbye to No Way Ray. I say sadly, but in hindsight, it was a good day, too. We were gathered to celebrate the memory of this man, this teacher who taught us all about getting along better in our hiking world, and who taught us about seeing the lighter side of life. Leave it to Ray to bring humor with his words of wisdom and keep us all at a saner level.

Ray was fortunate to not only love the Sierra Nevada but also lived in them, near Yosemite National Park. Show him a picture of a mountain top or tell a story about a place on the trail and Ray could tell you just where it was. He was a man at home on the trail and he belonged to it as if he owned it. He had long ago lost count of the trail miles, passes, and sunsets he'd seen in the mountains. But he was willing to share this love of the trail with anyone who he met, whether Ray was a hiker or helping as a trail angel himself.

How do you say goodbye to a man who belonged not only to his family, but to all of us who knew him from personal encounters on the trail? Many of us in middle age have had to say this final goodbye to loving family members as well as long time friends. Such a farewell is not easy and it is one loss we all have our own way of coping with. In May 2007, a year to the day after No Way's death, my friend Pinhead[2] and I went to the Deep Creek accident site to commemorate this event. Two days earlier, Stone Dancer[3] had also passed the spot where he died, as she hiked north on the PCT again. Certainly, it was hard for all of us to stop there and look over that rotten rocky cliff. We realized that the loss of a loved one leaves an empty hole inside that may never be filled. It is always okay to grieve for a loved one anywhere the memory of this person brings them to mind. There's a spot in the Grand Canyon where I spent time with Ray. Now when I pass that spot, I remember seeing him standing there waving at us.

When Ray passed away, messages arrived from friends and hikers everywhere. I could not help but be awed by the number of people who had never met him but felt compelled to say they will miss his wit and wisdom. They only knew him and his way of looking at the world from the hiker internet chat room, the "pct-l." Now, through this book, you too will meet a man who changed many lives.

---

2 Terry Thompson
3 Ray Echols' wife, Alice Tulloch

In February, a few months before No Way Ray died, he joined me on a short backpacking trip to the Grand Canyon. This was a special trip for me with some very special friends along. Billy Goat,[4] who hikes roughly 2,000 miles a year, was one of them. BG, as his friends call him, has the unusual habit of eating his morning meal still in his sleeping bag. Then he rolls up his gear in his pack before he even gets off the ground. He is always the early riser and gone in dawn's twilight, before most folks are up in the morning. Here are the six of us at the bottom of Grand Canyon and it's a zero day.[5] Ray looks over and sees Billy Goat still in his bag and not only snaps a picture of this, but does so by showing his watch with the time of 8:30 AM on it! Ray loved to tell this story about catching this irrepressible hiker slacking off!

At the 2006 Trail Fest event in Riverside, I met up with Ray and Alice. I had come directly from another hike in the Grand Canyon. I had made arrangements with them to get a ride home to my place in Pasadena. Later that afternoon, Ray and I retired downstairs to the elegant bar in the Mission Inn in Riverside. Ray's eyes lit up as he started to read off the names of their "top shelf" Scotch and Irish whiskeys. Here was a man who had a personal identity with these labels, and indeed had visited some of the places where they were made. Well, I am a scotch drinker myself and I was awed by his knowledge of the labels. Ray picked out a name for me and bought me a drink. I think it was in the neighborhood of $30 a shot. So here we are sitting down, gossiping and sipping fine liquor, when another good friend of mine, Paul, shows up. He sits down with us and tells the bartender his order and buys us a drink. The bartender leans over the bar and tells him how expensive our drinks are. Paul just looks at the bartender a moment and says, "Well, then bring each a double!" "Nice friends you have, Meadow Ed," Ray says.

Well, I would like to say here as I end this, to echo Ray's words, Yes, I do have nice friends.

Meadow Ed Faubert
Pasadena, California
December 2007

---

4 Billy Goat's real name was lost in some canyon long ago
5 Zero day = no miles hiked, a rest day

TRAIL GUIDE FOR THE READER

By Alice Tulloch

Although this book is based on the long, linear experience of hiking the 2,663-mile Pacific Crest Trail, this is not a linear narrative. While the feet are striding that distance, step by dusty step, one's mind is immersed in a much more fluid and turbulent environment. Thoughts flow, eddy, tumble and then race over the next cataract.

Many travel narratives give the reader a spacious overview of interesting places to visit. But the stories in your hand now dive deep into our interior. No Way Ray explores the landscapes of the mind and heart as he observes the world of the Pacific Crest Trail. This is not a story with a beginning, middle and end. Be prepared to bob along with an idea, leaping back and forth in time and place, to see the idea from many angles. As the editor, at certain points, I have inserted a signpost or two to keep you oriented to the progression of the physical trail. But I invite you to keep your attention on the ideas rather than the miles.

Ray Echols hiked the entire Pacific Crest Trail solo over 5 summers, repeating quite a bit of his favorite parts of the trail. For those keeping track, the chronology was:

2001   Mexican border to Agua Dulce, 454 miles

2002   Mill Creek Summit Ranger Station to Tuolumne Meadows, 523 miles

2003   Jack Fair's House[1] to I-80 Donner Summit, 640 miles

2004   Reds Meadow to Ashland, 820 miles

2005   Oregon and Washington, 943 miles

Adding in shakedown hikes and the 300 miles hiked in 2006 before his accident, his total PCT mileage was 3,705.

You will find mention of trail sections. Hikers refer to the parts of this long trail by means of the sections in the PCT Guidebooks (B. Schifrin and J. Schaffer, Wilderness Press, 3 volumes).

A thru-hiker is someone who hikes all 2,663 miles in one year. Each year had its distinctive events, lore and characters. But each year's herd of hikers plunged into the universal experience. They all faced the adventure of miles, snow, fires, storms, thirst, injuries, bugs, internal demons, strangers, new friends and incredible achievements. Ray's stories

---

1 Now known as Hikertown on Highway 138

are looking for the commonalities, among hikers and with our broader life experience as well.

One of those commonalities is our human aspiration to make something of our lives, to step out of the ordinary to see how far we can go. This book is incomplete. In the winters between hikes, Ray would write these stories in the evenings. He lost his life on the trail before all the stories were written down. The gaps point to the urgency of following your heart's compass in life. As a result of his death, I often ask myself "Just when was I going to get out there and do the most important thing?"

On May 15, 2006, No Way Ray was killed while thru-hiking the Pacific Crest Trail. He fell from the cliff where the trail edges high above Deep Creek, about trail mile 301, not far from Lake Arrowhead above San Bernardino. Three weeks earlier, Ray and I had started our life-long dream of hiking together for the whole summer, Mexico to Canada. We were finally free of careers, kids and car payments. He bubbled with excitement each day, delighted with the people and the places. That morning, he was hiking ahead of me and had gone around a corner, out of sight. The trail was very narrow, the tread was loose and rocky and we had seen rattlesnakes earlier. Suddenly, I heard the scrabble of rocks. When I raced around the corner, he was nowhere in sight. I will never know what caused his fall on that rotten rock wall.

The Pacific Crest Trail is a path along the highest rim of the Pacific edge of North America, from Mexico to Canada. It is 2,663 miles to challenge your strength, your mind and your spirit. A thru-hiker makes the journey all in one summer, four or five months of continuous walking. Most hikers make the trip northbound, as snows recede and the trail opens up after April. A few travel southbound beginning later in June from Manning Park in British Columbia. Many experts consider the Pacific Crest Trail more demanding and more life-changing than climbing Mount Everest. Approximately 300 people attempt to thru-hike each summer. Often only fifty complete the trip.

Ray began his hiking life in the mountains around the Los Angeles basin as a teenager fifty years ago. When he cut class from high school, it was to climb Mount Baldy or Mount Whitney. On our honeymoon, we climbed up to the Palisades Glacier. We took our children and grandchildren to the mountains and deserts. Every summer was the answer to the question of "Where are we hiking next?" He chose his career as a schoolteacher partly to have summers off for hiking. His hikes included Mount Whitney many times, the John Muir Trail several times, the whole PCT over three summers, numerous PCT Sections and other hikes in the Sierra Nevada, Grand Canyon, the Rockies, the Swiss Alps,

Scottish Highlands, the Karakorum Range in Pakistan and the Tien Shen Mountains in western China.

Ray had been a large format black and white photographer in college. I have selected a few of his 3,000 PCT photos for this volume. So many times, we'd be camped on the edge of nowhere, as the sunset and clouds painted the alpenglow. He'd snap off several dozen pictures to try to capture his feelings of exhilaration.

Ray claimed he was too shy to meet people, but the truth was that people always gravitated to him naturally. On the PCT in mid-April 2006, we had started south from Warner Springs to the Annual Zero Day PCT Kickoff Party at Lake Morena. I was anxious to make the miles and test my ability to keep on schedule. But Ray had hiked this trail before, so he wasn't caught up with the beginner's horse race. In fact, he was relaxed and loving it, meeting all the northbound early hikers. We took many a break to compare trail names, start dates, home state, water reports, trail news, and hitchhike plans to the Kickoff. The PCT attracts a diverse group of people, all ready for the challenge. While you might think of the typical hiker as young, tall, male, filthy and ragged (many are), there are not insignificant cohorts of strong women, empty-nesters, and super-seniors. A few amazing children. Professionals, vagabonds and professional vagabonds. The noteworthy and the self-effacing. The very fit and the soon-to-be-way-more-fit. Everyone's identity begins with the day they set foot on the trail.

All these new acquaintances were part of his constant interest in people. The tales he wrote are about the humanness of all the people he met on the trail and about his own failings, insights and successes. As you read, you will find out why, on the trail, he was called No Way Ray. He was no stranger to all terrains and all weather. Home was a backpack.

You will hear his voice. Hiking long distances gives you the time to explore all the mind's long trails as well. This path is not a simple one, but maps the many trails of a life. All the triumphs and disappointments of one's life so far are revisited, re-evaluated. The future shrinks to the next few days and the next resupply point. The mind becomes keenly focused, naturally relaxed, in the present. Allow your mind to be present in the words here. The trail of the mind follows where the heart leads. My hope is that you will set your foot today on the trail where your heart leads. It's only too late if you don't start now.

PROLOGUE

The man who goes alone can start today.
(*Walden*, Henry David Thoreau)

Shifting nervously in my seat, I look out the window as we drive through Campo in the early, pre-dawn hours. I am about to set out alone—into the wilderness. In my shirt pocket I see the small spiral notebook that I plan to use as a journal. So I take it out and on the bumpy dirt road leading to the border, write: "Arrived at the Mexican border at 5:30." Three days later, I am sitting on the porch of the Mt. Laguna store. It's nearing six in the evening. I've had three V8s and started on a beer. I glance at my journal. It says, "Arrived at the Mexican border at 5:30." About eighty miles further down the trail in Julian, I throw it in the trash. It still contains only those seven words.

By the time I make the infamous San Felipe traverse, I find that I begin to forget where I have been and how long it has been since I was somewhere. I repeatedly find myself patting the zippered back pocket on my shorts to make certain that my zip-loc hiker's wallet is still there. It is as though soon I will need to check my wallet to make certain who I am. If I lose it, I too will have disappeared.

So in Warner Springs, I buy another notebook. Three days later as the sun goes down, I am lying on the Desert Divide above Palm Springs watching a full moon rise, and trying to back date my journal and at least fill in the days and mileage. I work diligently at it until it is too dark to write. Even so, the days don't seem to add up quite right; I am missing a day somewhere. Days later, even though up to date, the journal still contains only minor information about mileage, people, places and such.

Then, four days after leaving Idyllwild and only a few hours short of Big Bear, I have an almost other-worldly encounter with a dayhiker, which gets me to thinking. There has, in fact, been a lot going on, more than just sights and people and miles. During the day, I begin to jot down thoughts and ideas, things that seem at once both mundane and celestial that are combining to make this journey unique and unrivaled among my experiences. As the days and weeks begin to flow into one another, they become punctuated by epiphany and serendipity.

My journey becomes highlighted by these experiences, both on and off the trail, for town stops become as magical as the Trail itself. And so this is not a journal exactly, although it talks of days and miles and people. It is not a guidebook, for that which guided me will surely not guide anyone else. Nor is it a formulary; all must find their own prescriptions and chant their own incantations. If you are looking for a history of the PCT, it is not here. What is here? Just a simple story of one thru-hiker.

And too, things do not always go as planned. As the saying goes, "The gods are never so amused as when we think we are in control of our destiny." And so this thru-hike, this trip of a lifetime, metamorphoses into something else; a trip of three years, punctuated by severe food poisoning, a broken bone, and other surprises, pleasant for the most part.

There are those who argue, with cause, that a thru-hike is not the same as a section hike, and I vouch this to be true in a number of ways. Still, a walk of a thousand miles is not a day hike. At the end of my second summer, hiking thirteen hundred miles, I come to understand the difference. And yet I have tried to make my journey as thru-like as possible. Each time I have taken up where I left off at exactly the same place, returning to the Trail on the same date I left. I have hiked the PCT in three sections. Still, there is disappointment at not completing that which I set out to do, and if conditions change, I may do it yet and am quietly hatching plans for the not too distant future. For though a section hiker I have become, within this graying crown, undimmed by fifty years of mountain travel, burns a passion for these wild lonely places, that grows only stronger with every mile I tread, and within this aging frame, beats ever stronger, a thru-hiker's heart.

IN THE BEGINNING

He who would travel happily must travel light.
(Antoine de Saint-Exupery)

Dark Thirty—four o'clock in the morning, April 27th—finds me in a car headed out from San Diego. A friend is driving me to the southern terminus of the 2,650-mile Pacific Crest Trail in Campo, California. We drive through the dark, talking apropos of nothing. Somewhere along the way is a leisurely breakfast that leaves me fidgeting nervously. I am anxious to get started, yet at the same time, afraid. About an hour out along Interstate 8 is Buckman Springs Road. We turn off and head down into the Campo Valley.

Although it is still nearly dark and I can see precious little, I know that the valley through which we are driving is roughly foot-shaped. The earliest inhabitants of this area, the Digueño Indians, called it *Milquatay*, a word that rhymes with both milk and tea, and translates as Big Foot after its shape. The valley was soon discovered by the White Man, with the usual consequences. And though it is said that these Indians of the southernmost coast and mountains of California put up a struggle greater than any of the dozens of California's other tribes, the end result was the same.

Those Indians not killed found themselves "pacified" and living, first in Mission compounds and later on reservations or rancherias. It's a common enough story, retold again and again westward across the continent, since 1492, when Columbus sailed the ocean blue. The Indians lived in societies that valued the common good more than individual interests. To quote an old Navajo saying, "A man cannot become rich who properly cares for his family." So they could not compete with, much less understand, a society whose chief weapon, as Kurt Vonnegut says, was the capacity to astonish. The Indians could not ken, until it was far too late, how heartless and greedy were the white men.

After the demise of the mission system, the Digueño continued to have occasional run-ins with the locals, most often concerning their use of cattle ranchers' stock for food, but by-and-large they coexisted. Early on, Mexicans, on their way through, gave it the name *Campo Valley*, a field or camp, finding it a good place to stay over.

About twenty minutes down the road is the small town of Campo, just a short mile from the border. In the pre-dawn hours it doesn't look like much, probably not much different than it looks during the day. We stop briefly at an old rock building, which turns out to be a museum. On the wall is a large rectangular bronze plaque portraying the old Campo Store and the "Famous Bandit Raid of December 5, 1875." We study it a minute.

The town of Campo was founded by the brothers Gaskill, who arrived in the spring of 1868 after several years of ranching ventures further north in the San Bernardino and San Jacinto area, the mountains of which I will pass through in the days to come. When they showed up, there were more than four hundred inhabitants in the valley. They purchased large tracts of land and established the town by building a store, blacksmith shop and a gristmill. The building in front of me is not the original, for that store sat astride Campo Creek where the bridge is today. A trap door in the floor allowed them to lower meat, eggs, and the like down into the creek—a kind of cooler.

On that fateful December day, a group of Mexican horse thieves stopped by to rob the Gaskills. Lumen Gaskill, firing from the store until he ran out of ammunition, dropped through the trap door and escaped by way of the creek. He made his way to another gun and more ammunition to continue the fight. His brother Silas, who was working at the blacksmith shop, grabbed his gun and joined the fray. Of the five would-be robbers, three were wounded in short order. The other two, abandoning their compadres, took off on their horses. The three wounded men were put into a shack near the store to be guarded by one of the townspeople, one Jimmy by name.

Word of this kind of excitement seemed to have traveled fast in those days, for by evening a group of cowboys came by. They had been driving a herd of cattle through the area, heard the news, and stopped in for a friendly drink. They brought out some whiskey, and in no time at all Jimmy was out cold. In the morning, the three prisoners were found hanging from a large oak tree nearby. It is said that the tree is still there today, standing as a branchless stump over by the lumber company. But in these twilight hours, like the past itself, all is obscured.

Trouble was not a stranger to the Campo area. Troubles with horse thieves, desperadoes, and Indians were reported as late as 1895. Today trouble of a perhaps less violent sort, but far more common than even in those wild days, is afoot. Border Patrol agents spend their nights chasing down illegal immigrants and herding them back across the border. An attempt to contravene drug smuggling also appears to be on their work orders. We pass by a border patrol station. In the parking lot are thirty or more vehicles—serious business, this border patrolling.

We arrive at the Mexican border at six o'clock. There is already a van here with a gaggle of people standing around. I wrestle my pack out of the truck and a lady yells out, "I know that pack, and I know those shoes!" I look at my not-so-white Kelty Cloud pack and my almost-new New Balance 801s. "You're falling water," she says. Thinking it to be a verb, I glance involuntarily at the front of my shorts to see if in my nervousness I've somehow wet myself. Seeing my confusion she says, "Fallingwater...Ron Moak?" Hearing the negative, she allows I will meet my twin twenty miles up the trail at Lake Morena, at the ADZPCTKO Party. ADZ stands for Annual Day Zero. It is a kick-off party for the year's crop of hopefuls, trail angels, previous PCT hikers, friends and lookers-on in general. Lost in my own world as usual, I had not even been aware that such a shindig existed and serendipitously arrived on the very weekend of its occurrence.

A few yards south of the monument lies the border, a twelve-foot high fence made of perforated steel plates. It stretches out across undulating chaparral-covered hills, to the horizon in both directions. A strip of land about thirty yards wide has been scraped nude along the fence. Oddly, a few hundred yards to the east, the fence disappears for about twenty yards where it runs into a pile of granite boulders. It appears as though it would be an easy scramble across the border at that point. I peek through some holes in the metal and see a chaparral bush that looks identical to the one on my side. It seems incongruous that the only difference between a supposed land of milk and honey and a land of struggle and want is this thin iron plate. I stick my finger through a hole. It doesn't feel any different over there.

I get my picture taken standing next to the official PCT monument and with a quick farewell take off down the trail. Within a few minutes, the group goes by laughing and chattering and moving with the speed available only to the young and the packless. Their gear stashed at Lake Morena, they will slack-pack[1] this twenty miles quickly and be drinking milkshakes by early afternoon. I, on the other hand, have all my gear because I think I will make it only to Hauser Creek on this first day, since I have never hiked more than fifteen or eighteen miles in a day, and that only after two or three weeks of on-the-trail conditioning. I watch the happy group disappear quickly down the trail, not without envy at their speed and camaraderie. In all my years of hiking and climbing, I have always traveled in a small group, usually two, infrequently three. I have virtually no solo wilderness travel. It's going to be a long lonely walk I think, little realizing just how wrong—and how right—I will turn out to be.

---

1 A term applied to hiking without a pack. Your gear is carried for you, generally by car, to your day's destination.

The trail wanders downhill toward Campo for about a mile, then angles west to cross Highway 94 and Campo Creek. It heads up the hill northward and in a half a mile or so, crosses an abandoned railway. The tracks are rusted. This is the old San Diego and Arizona Railway. It brought its first passenger to Campo from the east in 1916. By then the Gaskills were old men and gone, having retired to San Diego in 1902. Great plans were afoot as the railway construction continued east to San Diego. By 1932 the railway was finished, linking San Diego with the east by way of the Southern Pacific Railway through El Centro. Passengers continued to ride until 1951. The railway was used for freight, off and on, until finally abandoned in 1983.

There's loads of other history, like the story of army troops being stationed here. A huge army camp, Camp Lockett, was built on old Gaskill land. Part of the camp remains and is today operated by the City of San Diego for youth who can't seem to get along in polite society. And on it goes; there's history everywhere. I wonder who Hauser was, who got a broad, unimposing mountain (and a canyon and creek as well) named after himself, and who or what was Morena to deserve buttes and a community and a lake. Ah, but then there's talking... and there's walking.

I cross the tracks and head onto Hauser Mountain. The trail crawls in and out of a number of washes, finally passing through one with a beautiful rippling band of cool, cool water. The guidebook warns that it will be dry, but luck is with me this year. Although I have been on the trail little more than an hour, I stop to drink my fill and rest a wee. Gaining little elevation, the trail makes the first of its interminable traverses, but not before coming back to the railroad tracks, whose more direct route took perhaps one quarter of the distance to get here. Soon the trail begins a more earnest climb of Hauser Mountain. There has been a fire here at some time in the past, and the still nearly naked slopes are alive with beautiful chunks of massive quartz.

I've always had a thing for rocks. My home, both inside and out, is littered with rocks of all kinds, from small pocket sized beauties right on up to four hundred pound glacial boulders that I strained to roll into my pick-up bed. Once, on a trip home from the Highlands and Western Isles of Scotland, a customs agent, hefting my suitcase said, "What've you got in here, rocks?" Lo and behold, his probing fingers dislodged more than twenty pounds of Lewisian Gneiss and Torridon Sandstone, at 3.5 billion years old, some of the oldest exposed rocks in the world. And I hold a grudge against gravity and look to undermine its inexorability by carrying rocks from the low places to the high, namely, my home in the Sierra Nevada foothills. I have also occasionally been known to test it by kicking huge boulders down a mountainside. Most will click their tongue and shake their head at these admissions. After all, if everyone who came to the planet took a rock, or kicked one downhill... But the laughing ghost of Edward Abbey looks over my shoulder and nods in approval.

As I near the broad summit, a huge plume of smoke appears over the west shoulder of the mountain. With visions of a hike cut short by wildfire—or worse, being caught therein—I travel on. To my relief, the trail heads in a more easterly direction and the smoke plume abates. At last I come to a pipe gate followed by a rough jeep track that runs through a mountainside swale. On the other side is another pipe gate and there I run into Bob, a burly young Border Patrol agent. He is hiking uphill at a brisk pace. I stop to chat. I ask him what he is doing. He replies, "Just trying to keep ahead of runners." The runners are illegal aliens from Mexico, dashing across this desert land, headed for a better life in America. Bob says he is out checking seismic sensors. The Border Patrol plants them along trails and roads where they broadcast their messages back when traffic along those avenues create miniature earthquakes. I ask him how they manage along the PCT when so many hikers are treading the trail these several weeks of April and May. He says they are sensitive enough to differentiate cars from foot traffic, groups from singles, and running from walking. They pay special attention at night, the time when hikers are fast asleep and runners are running. I ask him about the gap in the iron curtain along the border. He replies that all during the day, the apparently empty miles of border are under constant surveillance, and that at night, thermal imaging devices are used. He is on a mission, so we don't talk long.

At long last the trail, which has been winding along the east side of the mountain, reaches the northeast ridge and Hauser Canyon bursts into view. Across the way, and about a mile and a half northwest are the Morena Buttes, a large granite outcrop near which the trail ascends. But it's still almost three and a half miles away by trail, traversing down and uselessly switchbacking across the face of the mountain to the creek, my supposed destination for the day.

Not far down the north side of Hauser Mountain a horse rider overtakes me. My hackles are instantly raised, for I am no lover of horses on the trail. After forty plus years of wandering every trail and pass, cross country route, and most of the peaks in the Sierra Nevada, I could rail about my dislike of horses in the mountains. I dislike everything about them, their smell, the mess they leave, the flies, they way they pound the trail to powder. I recall the three foot tall fire rings full of cigarette butts and tin cans at Puppet Lake, setting up a tent during a summer storm near Lake Ediza to find it shortly awash in a sea of horse manure, the attacks of flies in the Pioneer Basin, at Selden Pass, at Siberian Outpost and a hundred other places. I could go on and on. All evidences left by those who don't have to carry their own gear and those equines that carry it for them. And I guess I should confess to a slight sneaking envy. I hold strong in my mind the memory of ending a two week long trip in the High Sierra, when climbing up the five thousand vertical feet out of the South Fork of the Kings River, to be confronted with a pack train whose last three pack animals contained cases of beer.

And so my ire is roused, but I am polite, for I have learned in my old age that sometimes the courage of one's convictions is better coinage for the young, who know no better; the weak and powerless, who have nothing left to lose; and the rich and powerful, who rarely if ever lose and thus, have nothing to fear. And besides, as Joseph Conrad said, "There are times when a man must act as though life were equally sweet in any company." And so, I am polite. The horse rider is not only polite, she is a fine lady, and grudgingly I admit to myself that perhaps I should rethink some of my cherished prejudices. She is "Go Forth" and riding the PCT on her horse.

———>◦◦<———

Nearly two weeks into the future and more than a hundred miles down the trail, I am sitting in The Pink Motel with a frosty beer in hand and listening to the *1812 Overture* on a battery-operated radio. I watch the clouds scud across the ten thousand foot face of Mt. San Jacinto. I have just spent the morning stressing in Cabazon, trying to get my re-supply package from the post office and make it back to the trail. Just over a mile down across the desert, I can see the traffic, like lines of ants crawling silently along the Interstate. A mighty symphony of cannons and cathedral bells rings forth from the radio while the desert wind sings counterpoint.

On the table is a pile of computer printed papers from some horse riding discussion group. It's not something that interests me terribly, as you might guess, but I am lazing away the afternoon and so I idly glance at them anyway. They're all about some trail-ogre who is beating a horse to death on the PCT. In fact, it's Go Forth they're talking about. One message is about how she flogged her poor horse the whole twenty miles from the border to Lake Morena in one day.

———>◦◦<———

Along a stretch of dirt road, Go Forth and I walk the remaining miles to Hauser Creek. She is walking her horse because it has some foot problem or another. We make idle pleasant conversation. There are bright yellow signs in Spanish along the road. It says there is no drinking water, and *Don't expose your life to the elements*. And, *No vale la pena*, it's not worth it, although considering the effort and expense to which our government goes, it obviously is. A dirt road runs along the creek. We have been warned that this road is a major thoroughfare for people from Mexico trying to make the difficult run into the United States.

I have two opinions concerning the problem of illegal aliens coming into these United States and neither is friend to the other. To paraphrase Winston Churchill; he who is not a liberal when young has no heart, and he who is not a conservative when old has no brain. And so it is that in my oldening age, I have become more politically conservative and do admit to harboring some negative feelings towards illegal immigrants. On the other hand I am still plagued by a heart, and I think it not hard to understand the desire of a man to try to make a life worth living for himself and his loved ones. It is easy to see the degree of their desperation, evidenced by the conditions they are willing to chance in this hot waterless land. I will find out much later that more than four hundred will lose their lives along these thousand miles of desert border this year. It is said that campers in this canyon rarely get much sleep due to the voices and noise of people passing in the night. I hope it is an exaggeration, for I have planned to stealth camp somewhere nearby, off the trail.

I arrive at the so-called creek at one-thirty. My plan to spend the night here evaporates, just as has all the water. Several green, bubbly pools that look like they might at any moment gain a life of their own, and like some giant amoeba set off up the trail, pseudopodium by pseudopodium, are all that is left of the creek. This is just as well for I have traveled the almost fifteen miles much quicker than I anticipated. I have become a recent convert to ultralight backpacking and my customary forty or fifty pound pack now weighs but twenty, but I am out of water.

Go Forth is here, tending her horse, and has some extra water. I spend a leisurely hour for lunch and now with a liter of water set out to hike the last four and a half miles to Morena. Go Forth passes me shortly and goes on up the slopes of Morena Buttes. She stops often and arrives at the top only minutes ahead of me. She is talking to another horse rider, Crest Rider, and I pass them by, anxious to complete the four miles to the lake. Dog tired and more than a little dehydrated, I beat her to Morena by several minutes.

Now I don't know Go Forth, other than by those few minutes we shared along the trail, but my experience with how she treated her horse differs greatly from what I will read, beer in hand, at The Pink Motel. Perhaps she really is an ogre and all of the verbiage I will be reading is true, but I fancy myself a good judge of human character and am skeptical.

You already know my opinion of horses in the mountains, but to my certain knowledge, she "beat" her horse less than this old man "beat" himself on that first day out of the border.

⸺▸●◂⸺

Back in The Pink Motel, I leaf through the sheets. The one I read is one of the nicer ones of page upon page of expert testimony by people, full of self-righteous indignation, who may or perhaps not mean well but are not on the scene. The Army grunts who put it on the line every day and sleep eyes open in the jungle at night, have a name for these armchair experts who call the shots from the safety of the rear. They call them REMFs. The RE stands for Rear Echelon, but I can neither confirm nor deny the meaning of MF.

⸺▸●◂⸺

Arriving in Lake Morena just a bit after five o'clock, I stumble another long three-tenths of a mile to the Malt Shop and down a glass of water, a fresh banana shake and a large soda. I am exhausted yet exultant, for I have hiked the entire nineteen plus miles!

As I walk out of the malt shop to head for the park and the ADZ Party, a bus arrives. A backpacker with large pack and big smile steps off, gives me a big hug, and says, "It's good to see you again!" I'm still stunned from my ordeal on the trail so I stammer a few words, but I have no clue who he may be. Because of the long day I have forgotten the early morning Fallingwater episode. He mistakes me for the same wet personage. Before the next three days are over I will be mistaken for him no fewer than eight times. That night I meet Ron Moak, who *is* Fallingwater. From Oregon, he is, or was, the Webmaster for the Pacific Crest Trail Association's web site and designer of fine lightweight backpacking gear. He is already forewarned that his evil twin is roaming around. We eye each other, both thinking no doubt, "Nah, this guy looks older than me, and weighs a lot more." Sometime during the evening we get our picture taken together, saving the federal government the added expense of two post office flyers.

The barbecue, the show-and-tell, slide show and carousing-in-general last far into the night. We hikers are outdone only by the group of five hundred Girl Scouts camped across the wash, who are it seems, far more adept at carousing than we. I stumble to bed around midnight to discover I am adrift in a sea of snoring. Ultimately, my snoring joins the cacophony.

The next morning finds me having breakfast at the malt shop with most of the van-people who started out the morning before. I meet Ann from Seattle, who as Ian-The-Brit is wont to say has been "made redundant." Jobless, a casualty of downsizing, she is hiking to Canada.

Swiss Miss and Lutzia are two nurses from Zurich, Switzerland. Swiss is a veteran of the PCT and the Appalachian Trail, and a hiker with which few can hope to keep pace. They chatter in the Swiss version of German and laugh and laugh and laugh. Lutzia knows little English but Swiss translates for us all, and we laugh and laugh and laugh. Mad Monty is also from Seattle. Having hiked the PCT in 1977 he is the group's Patriarch of The Trail, even though much of the trail is different these twenty-five years later. Ian-The-Brit, by way of the Caribbean and New York State, is a physicist by training, who was also made redundant and retaliated by moving to the Caribbean for some years, later becoming a rock climber in New York. To support his habit he remanufactures and repairs antique clocks. Tony, also a Brit, is a retired ship's captain who is fresh from an African safari. Robin and Marcus, a young couple from the San Francisco Bay Area, the Two Daves, Singing Steve, and Jeff Z from Pennsylvania, who like Mad Monte, hiked the PCT in 1977. These are great people whom I will see on and off for weeks to come.

After breakfast, a number of people find rides up the trail, some as far as the twenty-two miles to Mt. Laguna, to slack-pack back to Morena, in time for the barbecue and equipment competitions to be held in the evening. By means of the PCTA's website, I have learned that the Forest Service is warning hikers not to camp in either Fred or Long Canyons, dirt road crossed canyons that occupy the next eighteen miles, because some hikers have been robbed by drug runners. Days before, I tried to track this down by making several calls to the Forest Service. I could find no one to verify the report. "It must be a PCTA deal," I was told. I try to imagine a drug runner, car filled with perhaps millions of dollars worth of something contraband, stopping along the way to relieve some poor hiker of his flimsy Zip-Loc-bag wallet filled with ones and fives. Taking time to rifle through a pack, he selects several bags of freeze-dried noodle-something and a couple of "luscious" Clif Bars to sustain him on the dangerous trip while his armed companions nod in approval at his choices.

Logic dictates that this drug running be a nighttime activity and I feel certain that if I stealth camp well off any road I will fare well. Yet, all alone, I am reticent to chance it. I begin to think I can't make the twenty plus miles and three thousand plus foot rise to the relative safety of Mt. Laguna in a single day, so at two-thirty in the afternoon, I leave and begin the six-mile walk to Boulder Oaks Campground. A public campground in the shadow of Interstate 8 must be safe, I think.

The trail skirts Morena Lake for a while before climbing over a granite ridge, which is weathered much like the rounded boulders of the Sierran Alabama Hills. In four miles, after traveling through, in some places, a chamise jungle, the trail tops the ridge and drops down into Cottonwood Creek. The valley is lush and quiet on this late April day. I make my way through willow and alder trees and cross the creek in a few swift steps. The trail meanders through oak-jeweled meadows and at last makes its way into the back of Boulder Oaks Campground.

I arrive late in the day to discover that the campground is closed, as is the nearby convenience store. Apparently, this is the choice place for the endangered Arroyo Toad to mate. An attempt to keep these toad orgies mannerly is evidenced by twelve inch-high toad-fences throughout the campground. A trailer housing the camp host is nearby. A couple of dogs are barking madly, but their tails are wagging, so I chance it. They are friendly. Putting on my most plaintive, tired-old-man face, I knock and ask the host if it is possible to spend the night here if I promise to carefully avoid all toad-like happenings. He agrees but asks that I go to the back of the campground so as not to be visible from the road, and to leave early, lest his boss arrive. Although tomorrow will be Sunday and I am highly skeptical that a Forest Service boss would be out and about in an official capacity, I readily agree.

A bit later two other hikers arrive. I meet Frank-From-Alaska, whom I will see off and on for many a long mile. A slight quiet man of sixty-three, he is carrying a pack that seems to weigh fully as much as his years. I struggle to lift it. This does not seem to slow him down considerably. A seasonal worker in the Alaskan oil fields, he has spent many years on the trail, hiking the Appalachian Trail twice, the Long Trail, bicycled across Australia, canoed down the Kobuk River of Alaska, and many other exploits, as I will learn in the weeks ahead. Paul, who at seventy-four is more ultralight orientated than Frank, comes in a bit later still. His sixteen years on me do not seem to slow him much either. He will suffer painful blister problems in a few days and disappear. I will last see him above Oriflamme Canyon, where he vows to rest a few days in Julian and be back on the trail. I hope he makes it.

The next morning I get an early start. Saying good-by to my new friends, I head for Mt. Laguna and its post office. Passing under Interstate 8, I see plenty of signs of passage by illegal aliens. There are several places where holes to facilitate travel have been cut in the chain-link fence bordering the freeway, but, just as in Hauser Canyon, there are no signs of life.

It's a long day, in and out of canyons where oak and cottonwood trees find enough water to thrive, and across hot, chaparral covered slopes. The ridges are fully-chaparraled, with huge waist-high thickets of chamise and manzanita. At least two species of ceanothus, one with blue flowers and one with white, bloom in profusion. Ultimately the trail passes above five thousand feet and chaparral vegetation gives way to Jeffrey pine forest, a welcome change. At long last I arrive at Burnt Rancheria Campground and find the water fountain is dry. It is only a bit over a mile to the picnic area and nearby Mt. Laguna store. A couple of dayhikers assure me the quickest way is to hike through the campground to the highway and thence to the store. Sadly, because it is late in the day and I am tired and thirsty, I take their advice...without looking at my map. This causes me to hike more than a mile extra, a couple of miles that will have to be retraced on the next day when I resume the trail. Not a lot of mileage in the grand scheme of things, but late in the day it seems daunting.

The store closes at four o'clock PM on this Sunday afternoon and I arrive late, with just minutes to spare. I buy two V8's and a beer, and sit down in front. A few miles earlier I was nearly run down by two mountain-bikers barreling down the PCT. They stopped and I said, "You probably don't realize that this is the Pacific Crest Trail and that it's illegal for bicycles to be on it." The lead rider shrugged and said, "Oh, it's OK. We're in pretty tight with the local ranger." I asked them to tell me their names, so I can tell the ranger they said "Hi." They silently declined and slammed on down the trail. Sitting on the porch, V8 in hand, I idly look for a ranger station; I see none.

Within minutes a van drives up bearing Hal and Meadow Ed, an infamous local hiker and trail angel. There are more than a dozen hikers gathered around the post office and store, and Hal and Ed gather up a van-full to take down the road to Laguna Campground, saying he'll return for me. By four-thirty, Hal returns and takes me and another hiker named Dave, a.k.a. Lightningbolt, back to the campground for dinner. Lightningbolt is a slender quiet man from Low Gap, North Carolina. He has a marvelous soft Appalachian accent and wears the perpetual hint-of-a-smile of someone who has just heard the most outrageous joke and is moments away from laughter. Asserting that he is no lover of hot dogs and is anxious to keep hiking, he joins the conversation at the campground for a while, until it is nearly dark, then shoulders his pack and disappears. I will see him no more, though his appropriate trail name will appear again and again in the hiker sign-in books up the trail as he steadily increases his distance from the slow and the old, of whom I am one. By the time I have hiked two hundred and fifty miles, he will be nearly a hundred miles ahead. It's good to be young. And so I spend the night at the campground with two other hikers, Ian and Ben.

So far the lonely trip I had anticipated has resulted in the meeting of fifteen or twenty hikers. I realize that this is just the beginning and as days stretch out so will my connections with these people. It is almost seven hundred miles to the Sierra, a great part of it desert or desert-like. Three days and less than fifty miles have passed. The reality of the journey has set in. I wonder how it will be.

ALONE IN A CROWD

The trip down from the Laguna Mountains is fairly uneventful. I drop Meadow Ed and Hal off at Pioneer Mail Trailhead and drive Hal's van back to the post office. Locking the van, I hide the key on a rear wheel, as pre-arranged. Yesterday at day's end there were more than a dozen hikers milling around. This morning all is quiet. It doesn't take long, however, for the rest of the crew to show up from wherever they spent the night. The post office finally opens. We retrieve our food parcels, sign the trail register, pack and repack our gear and prepare to head out.

It's quite a sight. Looking through the viewfinder of my camera, I count twelve people, their packs open and boxes of food strewn about the porch of the store, engaged in congenial pandemonium. Counting me, there are thirteen. The variety and quantity of food is amazing. One hiker has bags and bags of home dried vegetables and corn pasta. His next re-supply is three days or so, in Warner Springs. He seems to realize that he has enough food for a platoon and is discussing (with himself) the pros and cons of each bag and whether it goes or stays. Some are comparing contents and discussing favorites. Trading goes on. Others, with little muss or fuss, are methodically stowing the contents of their various boxes in their packs.

All this slow, friendly, casual activity belies the frantic work that goes into organizing all the food one will need for four or five months on the trail. Unless you've actually done it, the amount of work is difficult to comprehend. My food drier ran most of the winter. One chore was dehydrating homemade spaghetti sauce, one of my staples. I have found that if I put the dried sauce, which looks like fruit leather, into a zip lock bag with a cup of water, then stow it carefully in the cook pot in my pack, in two or three hours time, of its own accord, it will be sauce again. A cup of boiled water to which the noodles from a package of Ramen soup and the reconstituted sauce have been combined comprise, at least for now, about two out of seven of my meals.

On warm afternoons, if I arrive at camp early enough, simply setting the whole mess, noodles and sauce, in the sun for an hour warms it to a perfectly acceptable temperature, thus requiring no cooking at all.

Two more meals of the seven consist of dried chili, made with beans, tomatoes, onions, and corn, similarly soaked—though they take longer—and poured over a serving of instant mashed potatoes. At least that's the theory. In practice, it will come to pass that things work out differently. In the coming weeks, it will become my habit to have dinner in mid-afternoon and lunch at the end of a twelve to fourteen hour hiking day. For the remainder I have purchased a limited number of commercially prepared freeze-dried meals, of which half of one is sufficient for dinner.

For breakfast I have a sealed package of granola with some powdered milk added. As I tend to "rise and run," I rarely bother with anything requiring cooking. I do include a few packages, perhaps two out of seven, of Quaker's Minute Oats, spiced up with dried cranberries and pumpkin seeds. As the trip winds on, I will find that just before breaking camp in those early, pre-dawn hours, pouring water (hot water in the case of the oatmeal) into the bag and eating while still in the warm confines of my sleeping bag will become a comfortable ritual. After a month or more, this will become my least favorite food, and, at least for a while, Pop-Tarts will become the breakfast of choice.

Lunches are jerky, fruit and granola bars, candy bars, pop tarts, nuts, dried fruit, and the like. I take few of the "sports" bars, like Power Bars or Clif Bars. My experience is that their taste and rubber or sawdust-like textures ultimately relegate them to the bottom of the food bag and saved, until out of desperation they are grudgingly consumed, or more likely, carefully hidden for ground squirrels and other critters to find, sample, and likewise discard. I imagine that even those tireless, voracious scavengers, ants, would ultimately give up on them and search further afield. Moreover, comparing the contents and nutritional value of these bars against plain candy bars shows but little difference—a few grams of more complex carbohydrates, a few grams less sugar. But it's all personal. Ian-The-Brit will cheerfully consume two Clif Bars a day for lunch...for weeks and months. And, as chance will have it, two thousand miles up the trail, I will "re-discover" Clif Bars and find them to be among my favorites. As the saying goes, "Battlefield plans are perfect until the first shot is fired."

Ray Jardine, in his PCT Hiker's Handbook, suggests avoiding hard foods, like corn nuts, to minimize risk to teeth. It seems like good advice, and due to an unfortunate experience, I likewise shun fruit roll-ups—a treat for which I have some fondness—and any other unduly sticky fare. A few years ago, two days north of Tuolumne Meadows, headed south from Sonora Pass on the PCT, with fruit roll-up in one hand and a crown from one of my molars in the other, I learned a valuable lesson... enough said.

And, of course, my fare will be subject to random acquisitions in stores along the way. Being relatively undiscriminating in terms of cuisine, at some places I plan to simply buy enough of whatever is available to get me a day or three down the trail. The acme of this plan, to the amazement of several fellow travelers (and myself as well), will occur nearly three hundred and fifty miles into the trail, at Cajon Pass, where I will buy a dozen McDonald's cheeseburgers for the two-day trip to Wrightwood.

The hiker's winter entertainment and solace is organizing the next summer's food and gear. There are the boxes and boxes of supplies that fill a room and spill out into the hallway. Lists are checked and checked again, and again. Still, I make mistakes. Most often the mistakes are non-critical. In Lake Hughes I will find that I failed to include toilet paper, a problem easily remedied at Harley's Rock Inn. Others are more serious. In Mojave I will not find the guidebook pages for the next section in my re-supply box, and, even though I am able to copy the pages from another hiker, a critical missing page will cause me to miss McIver Spring. Perforce I will go long miles with little water. I will find in Lone Pine that I have sent too few Esbit tablets for my little stove to make it the seven days through the High Sierra. I will manage though by breaking them into pieces and using them to start small twigs in the stove's confines. Experience is a great teacher, though, and frantic calls home requesting a thorough check of the contents of subsequent boxes solves the problems.

Every box is labeled for post and ready to go. Since I live near Yosemite National Park and am driving to San Diego and the Trail's start, I actually hand-deliver all the parcels for the first 647 miles of the trail, from Campo to Walker Pass. You still have to pay the postage though... storage fees. My wife will mail the others as needed. My plan is to re-supply relatively often so that I can keep my pack weight down - a thing that an old, somewhat over-the-hill man feels is a key to success. It's a bit less than seventy miles to Warner Springs (the planning for which includes an overnight stop in Julian) and I am carrying only two breakfasts, four lunches, and three dinners. The remaining meals - breakfasts in Mt. Laguna, Julian, and Warner Springs, and a dinner in Julian and Warner Springs - are factored in.

———>⊃●⊂———

All around me people are talking and laughing and packing. Soon enough it's eleven o'clock, time to go. I make a quick pass through the store, buying a banana and a couple of candy bars. Outside, I eat the banana. Everyone but me heads north a quarter of a mile along the road to the trail. Bound and determined, at least for now, not to skip that mile or so of trail, I head the first mile south to Burnt Rancheria Campground and wander a mile through it back to the place on the trail where I left off yesterday.

Out of curiosity, I check the water fountain once more; it is still turned off. Heading north, I immediately ascend along the Desert View Trail, which is just that. Here, right along the crest, huge ridges run east, like fingers, off the Laguna Mountains. One ridge is large enough in its own right to be called a mountain range - the Sawtooth Mountains. These ridges produce a number of canyons dropping a vertical mile to the desert below. This, the first canyon, just north of the Sawtooth Mountains, is called The Potrero and runs all the way out, north and east, to Vallecito Valley and the Vallecito Mountains beyond. Far out into the desert I can see a dot of greenery and some buildings, which I take to be the Vallecito County Park, site of the Vallecito Station of Butterfield Overland Stage fame.

After dropping down to a picnic area, the trail turns back into the forest, a few hundred feet below the crest, along the western flanks of Mt. Laguna and Stephenson Peak. It crosses the paved road leading to the old, now abandoned, Mt. Laguna Air Force Station. This is the road that I should have come to yesterday, for a few short yards west lies the Sunrise Highway, which leads, in four tenths of a mile, back to the Mt. Laguna store and post office.

To say the air force station is abandoned is not truly correct, for today it houses an FAA radar site that is used for on-route flight safety and air traffic control. Starting in 1952 and continuing through the Cold War, it was a different story. It housed radar as part of the air-defense and long-range radar facilities that were designed to let us know that the end of the world was at hand, should a bomber attack, or a bit later on, a ballistic missile attack from the former Soviet Union be eminent.

After two days in the chaparral I feel lucky to be walking, for the moment at least, here in the shaded, mixed, oak and pine forest. But I know it won't last long. The Laguna Mountains, like many of the short north-south running ranges here in southern California are fault scarp mountains - miniature versions of the Sierra Nevada, and related to them in both rock and time. From the crest, the slopes fall precipitously to the east, but are broad and gentle on the west. On their western slopes, these mountains were once covered with coniferous forests all the way to their bottoms. Early in the last century the slopes of the Laguna Mountains were pillaged for lumber, principally for constructing the nearby, and now defunct, San Diego and Arizona Railway railroad. But here, in a narrow band along the summit, for some reason, they were saved. Conditions still allow tall Jeffrey Pines, interspersed with a number of large, deciduous black oaks, to thrive. Well... mostly to thrive. No small number of the pines are dead or dying. I recognize the drought induced, top-first death caused by the Western Pine Beetle and its relatives from experience in my own Sierra foothills home.

The trail continues its northward undulations. As it traverses the slopes of Mt. Stephenson, I can see the two, huge, puffball-shaped radar domes on its summit. Hidden on the northwest slopes of the mountain are the remains of the Cantonment Area, which housed the personnel. It had a headquarters building, well, mess hall, wastewater treatment plant, swimming pool, solar panel array, auto shop, helicopter pad, and, of course, barracks. All of which are mostly gone today, leaving only piles of rubble, holes in the ground, and assorted litter. While only a few hundred yards from the trail, the ruins are shielded from the hiker's view by the thick growth of pine trees.

All of this, of course, is useless knowledge. Many thru-hikers, perhaps most, pay little attention to this kind of trivia. I have heard many discussions about all the "extra" pages one is forced to deal with in the current trail guide, which contains—in addition to maps and trail mileages—photographs, and some small bits of information about side routes, re-supply towns, geology, biology, history, and the like. There is an abbreviated "data book" version available which lists little more than names and miles, for which many thru-hikers opt. Perhaps they believe, as it says in Ecclesiastes, that "He that increaseth knowledge increaseth sorrow," but I suspect the rigor of keeping on the trail and maintaining significant daily mileage, day after week after month has more to do with it. I, on the other hand, follow the words of the philosopher Bertrand Russell, who said, "There is much pleasure to be gained from useless knowledge," and, in fact, have made a lifetime and a profession of it. It also occurs to me that as the days pass and begin to flow into one another, I, too, may be less interested in all that surrounds me. I hope not.

Some years ago, my nearest neighbor (living half a mile away in the Sierra foothills) and I were in his jeep, driving slowly down a narrow, twisted and obscenely rough four-wheel track into the South Fork of the Merced River. I had not been on the road before, but had read a book about a famous gold mine that had once been the destination of the road. Several beers had tempered the roughness of the road and assuaged the fear of its narrow, outwardly tipping track. Near the bottom, the road is hacked through a cliff of marble. Uninvited, I began to tell him of the formation of marble, from the leftovers of ocean dwelling critters to sedimentation to compaction...and so on. In mid-metamorphosis he cut in with, "What are you, some sort of tour guide?" It caused me to wonder just what life would be like without wonder...how it would be to go through the world and never wonder about who traveled through it before you, or what miraculous processes created all the splendor in front of you. One part of me says, "How unrewarding, how boring." Another exclaims, "How Zen!" I walk on through the forest.

At the head of Storm Canyon, the trail comes quite close to and parallels the Sunrise Highway for a bit. Just above me I see a wooden platform cantilevered out over the canyon. Ascending up to it, I find it is a scenic viewpoint. Across the highway and up the hill is the Al Bahr Camp. I cannot tell if Al Bahr is a man's name for which the camp is called, or if it is an Arabic word chosen, for reasons no doubt mystic, by the Ancient Arabic Nobles of the Mystic Shrine - the Shriners. All I know for certain is that, on this late April day, it is bereft of Shriners and playing host to the handful of hikers who went north from the post office earlier in the day. I traipse across and say hello.

Sitting on the lawn are those same folks who swept by me four days and nearly fifty miles ago on that first morning out from the border—Mad Monty, Jeff Z, the Two Daves, Singing Steve, Ann, Marcus and Robin, Ian-The-Brit, Swiss Miss and Lutzia, Ben, and some others whom I don't know. Although friendly, they seem like a "group" and I an outsider, and so I sit a bit off to the side and have lunch.

After a little while, I notice that there are hose bibs on the side of the nearby buildings, so I walk over to see if they are on...they aren't. I go back, hoist my pack, say goodbye, and head back across the highway to the trail.

Not much further down the trail I come to the mysteriously named G.A.T.R. Road. I will find out much later that it is an acronym that stands for "Ground to Air Transmit and Receive site." A short distance up this road is the old site that housed the air station's radio equipment that had to be separated from main site to avoid interference from the radar. Here, a few tenths of a mile to the west, is a trailhead parking area boasting running water, so I make the trip, not knowing where my next water may be. I sit a few minutes at the faucet, "camelling up," as the phrase goes—drinking all I can hold, and more—and with full containers, head back to the trail. Within minutes, laughing and chattering, the group from Al Bahr flows by me and disappears.

As the afternoon wears on, I meander in and out of chaparral filled washes, ultimately coming west around a corner and back into the piney woods of the same Pioneer Mail Trailhead where I dropped of Meadow Ed and Hal only this morning. The group is all here. It is nearing five o'clock and due to the late start, I am only a bit more than twelve miles into the day. I stop a hundred yards from the parking lot. On a picnic table, I spread out my gear to air and dry from last night's dewy camp and walk over to the water.

To my dismay, but not surprise, for the guidebook advertises this horse trough, the water looks horrible. A circular concrete container, perhaps four feet in diameter and the same in height, is filled nearly to the brim with an ichorous yellow-brown fluid. The filling pipe, for reasons unknown, extends down into this well so far that I have nothing with which to capture the water before it hits the surface. A sign on the side proclaims the water unfit for consumption by all but horses, and though it goes unsaid, for thirsty thru-hikers. Putting faith in technology, I filter a few liters, trying not to imagine what marvelous, microscopic creatures sport and frolic in this primordial soup.

I idle away a few minutes reading a large three-sided sign, which states that the picnic area is dedicated the pioneers of the first transcontinental overland mail route, the Birchland Overland Mail Route, which went from Texas to San Diego. The actual site of the mail route is some distance north of here. It came in from the east, through Vallecito Valley, into the mouth of Rodriguez Canyon, hung a left at Oriflamme Canyon, then up and over the crest of the Laguna Mountains, and hence to San Diego. The route up Oriflamme Canyon was so rough that the mail and passengers had to be switched from coaches to mules, and so it was dubbed the "Jackass Mail."

The area into which I will be descending, in what remains of this day and tomorrow, passes through territory with loads of history attached to it. Known collectively as the Pioneer Corridor, it has served various groups by various names throughout California's history, and before. From bedrock mortars and pictographs left by the Indians in Smuggler Canyon near Vallecito, to Diaz in 1540, to Anza in 1774, to the Mexican Mail route of the 1820s, to the Mormon Battalion in 1846, to Kit Carson and Kearny's Army of the West in 1847, to the 49'ers who took the Southern Emigrant Trail to the gold fields, to the travelers along the Jackass Mail Route and the Butterfield Overland Mail Route, to the nameless, mysterious "Lady in White," who while on the way to meet her true love in the northern California goldfields in the late 1850s, died and was buried in an unmarked grave at Vallecito Station, to the southern sympathizers who came to San Diego (known as a hotbed of "Copperheads") during the Civil War, to the Julian gold rush of the 1870s, to even General George Patton, who traveled through here in 1942 on his way a little further to the east to train his troops for the invasion of North Africa. If the ghosts of all those who lived and traveled through here were to suddenly materialize, it would look like a Los Angeles freeway on Friday afternoon.

I head back to repack my gear and cook a hasty dinner. My plans include a hitch into the little mountain town of Julian tomorrow, so I need to travel several more miles today. The trail leaves the picnic area and starts up what appears to be a portion of a highway, although it is unpaved. At its head, it meets a paved road, then turns into a trail again, at the head of Cottonwood Canyon, and begins to work its way around Garnet Mountain.

The day is almost done, and I am almost done in. Although I had spent some good bit of time trying to condition myself before the trip, I still find the rigors of that first day of twenty-one miles, and yesterday's seventeen miles and nearly three thousand foot climb to have taken their toll on this sixty-year-old man. My feet, although not blistered, are feeling the stress. I am wearing New Balance 801 Trail Shoes in size 13EEEE, which are both two sizes longer and wider than my normal size. I wear only a single, short, lightweight liner sock. It sounds as though my feet would be floating and sliding in Bozo-the-Clown-sized shoes, but this seems to work for me, and I will suffer zero blisters...ever. And this is a revelation to me, for in a lifetime of hiking and climbing, always wearing monstrous leather boots, I had come to believe that blisters were simply a part of hiking.

One last time the group passes by. I begin to look for a place to be. The trail meets a jeep road above Oriflamme Canyon, and winds its way northward through the chaparral. Oriflamme Mountain is directly east of me. It's rather unimposing from this angle, just a slightly higher bump on a several thousand foot long ridge, and I am about level with its summit. It would have been a different story during the Jackass Mail days for the route came from the east, directly at it. From that angle it would present a two thousand foot wall, which had to be passed by on the north through Mason Valley and into Cottonwood Canyon, where it turned south into Oriflamme Canyon, which lies below me now—a full 180-degree traverse around the mountain. The Jackass Mail was never very successful, partially because its dynamic founder, James E. Birch, was drowned at sea while the first mail, which left San Antonio, Texas, in July 1857, was still enroute.

In September of the following year, the Butterfield Overland Stage Route began service. Covering much of the same ground, its destination was San Francisco, and so, instead of traveling the Jackass Mail's route around Oriflamme Mountain, after the Vallecito Station, it turned northeast into Box Canyon and made the trip all the way around Granite

Mountain and northwest, through Earthquake Valley and into Warner Springs, my destination three days hence.

The Jackass Mail continued to operate, more or less continuous with the Butterfield Overland Stage, each going to their separate destinations, until the beginning of the Civil War, which making a route through the South unfeasible, caused their demise in 1861.

I cross the jeep trail and trudge wearily uphill, to contour around the head of the canyon. My route winds in and out of sandy, chaparral-choked washes. In the third one, a tent sits down-wash a few yards. It's Paul, whom I met two nights ago in Boulder Oaks Campground. I take off my pack and go for a chat. He is examining his feet. I look; he has huge blisters on the pads and heels. At seventy-four, he is the oldest person I will meet on the entire trail. He says that he plans to make it to Julian, spend a few days recuperating, and be back on the trail. We discuss this for a few minutes, and I head back to my pack, having decided that this tiny sandy wash is my home too.

The sun is sinking low and since we are some distance east of and below the crest of the Laguna Mountains, it will soon be dark. Oriflamme Mountain truly is in flames as the last light of the sun flashes across its crest. It may not be much of a mountain, but its name—Oriflamme—is beautiful. Meaning "Golden Flame," it is supposedly named for the mysterious "Ghost Lights" or "Phantom Lights" observed on its eastern slopes many times over the years, although it has been argued that it was named for a steamer of the same name that plied the waters between San Francisco and San Diego in the late 1860s and through the Julian gold rush years of the 1870s.

In 1858, a stage driver for the Butterfield Overland Stage reported seeing the Ghost Lights. Others, soldiers, prospectors, travelers, reported seeing them in succeeding years. In 1892, one Charles Knowles and two fellow prospectors witnessed them. He described them as balls of fire that rose approximately a hundred feet into the air and then exploded. "Like fireworks," he said. It happened three times, and then stopped for a half an hour. Then, beginning again, the fireballs rose in an arc, rather than straight up, and returned to the ground without exploding.

It's all very mysterious stuff. A scientific explanation is that they may be bursts of static electricity caused by sand being blown forcefully against quartz outcrops. Others say they are the "money lights," seen most often in South America and associated with veins of gold. Considering all the gold found in the Julian gold rush, perhaps it's true. During Prohibition it was thought that they were signals from or to bootleggers, but of course the lights long pre-dated as well outlasted Prohibition.

The last light is fading from the mountain as I make camp. Then, another hiker shows up. It is Ian-The-Brit, whom I met two days ago, and with whom I camped last night, along with Hal and Meadow Ed and Ben. Ian agrees this looks like home. And so it is. I set up my tiny shelter in an area just barely big enough, while Ian finds another spot a few yards away. It's been a long, hard day, on this, my fourth night out. Seventeen miles traveled since eleven o'clock. Without much ado, I fall asleep only to awaken in the middle of the night with a monstrous cramp in my left hamstring. Striving not to yodel in pain, I sit up and stretch forward trying to touch my toes and stretch out the muscle. The cramp subsides. The stars are bright and hard in the desert sky. I look toward Oriflamme, hoping to see Ghost Lights of my own, but of course I'm on the wrong side of the mountain. No matter, it's a good night after all.

I am an early riser and waste little time in the morning before hitting the trail. As I leave, Paul and Ian are just rousing. My legs are very sore and tight this morning, and there is a pain, although it comes and goes, like a hot needle in my left thigh. I must be moving slowly because before long Ian catches up with me. Paul fails to appear, and I will never see him again. We travel along the undulating trail for a mile, through impenetrable chamise, punctuated occasionally by hilltops covered with bursts of manzanita, when suddenly we come upon a water cache. The trail, coming within yards of the Sunrise Highway, is littered with welcome water containers. This is the "Lucky 5" water cache. Many are empty, but many are not. The work of Meadow Ed, there are one gallon milk and water containers and not a few plastic 1.75 liter vodka and whiskey bottles containing water. We take only what seems fair, leaving plenty for those behind.

Water needs met, we travel on. Hiking rates being different for different people, over the next hours I begin to pull a ways out in front of Ian. Notwithstanding a jaunt up and around Chariot Mountain, I have been mostly descending ever since I left Mt. Laguna yesterday morning, and the temperature is climbing. Soon I will drop down into the Colorado Desert, the first true desert of the trail. I check my tiny thermometer. It reads 98°F at ten o'clock in the morning. This bodes ill for the day.

Finally, I am on the northwestern slopes of Granite Mountain. The view is fantastic. Across the valley are the infamous San Felipe Hills and Grapevine Mountain, where a shortage of water and an abundance of heat conspire to create a nearly twenty-four mile purgatory...so it is said. Perhaps a mile down and away, across the desert, I can plainly see Highway 78 heading into Julian, my destination for the day, but it's further still for the walking. A hodge-podge of desert dwellings speaks of private property, so the trail must traverse five miles and fully half way around the mountain, to reach a corridor of public land where the trail races another three miles straight out to the highway. Barrel cacti, cholla, and prickly pear dot the slopes. On this late April day many are in bloom, and their brilliant yellow and electric crimson flowers offer marvelous counterpoint to granite, sand, and sky.

A bit before the trail heads out into the flats, I come around a corner and find Monty and Anne sitting in a cool, shady cave created by an immense granite boulder a dozen feet above the trail. This is the only shade for hours circling Granite Mountain. They are taking a break and waiting out a bit of the heat of the day. Although the granite of these southern California mountains is supposedly part of the same great orogenic movement that gave birth to the Sierra, it is certainly different. There is none of the salt-and-pepper look of the great Sierra peaks, or the fine, white crystalline granite of the Yosemite area for this rock. It is coarsely crystalline rather than fine, and is filled with large black shining clumps of plate-like mica.

I sit and have a snack and chat for a spell, but soon move on, down towards the highway. It's getting on in the day, and I still have to catch a ride into Julian - my first hitch of the trip. Out in the flats there are strawberry hedgehog cacti everywhere, little clusters of spiny barrels, each topped with a crimson bloom. Inside, a spray of yellow stamens greets whatever pollinator happens along. The trail meets the highway and parallels it for a mile before crossing over to the creek at the "scissors." This is the S2 or Imperial Highway, today a connector going from nowhere to nowhere, but once an integral part of the great Butterfield Overland Mail Route.

Now, I drag out my Tyvek ground cloth. Folded to fit into the pack, it opens to reveal a number of large rectangles. On one of them I have written with a large felt tip marker, "PCT Hiker, Julian Please." Other squares contain other messages designed in the dead of winter to cover all contingencies between Campo and Sonora Pass - hopefully. Rather than follow the trail a mile along the fence, I crawl under the wire fence and get to the road immediately, ready to flag a ride. In the fifteen or twenty minutes it takes me to walk the distance to the crossing, not a single car passes. I reach the crossroads, where S2 intersects Highway 78 on its journey from the ocean side of Oceanside, through the coastal mountains and into the desert, ending on the Arizona border at Blythe. A "major" road, think I, but standing next to the monument to the Great Southern Overland Stage Route of 1848, few cars pass and none stop.

Within an hour, Monty and Anne arrive. I think it will be impossible to get a ride now, being a threesome, but I am wrong. Having charming feminine company, a "ride bride," makes getting the ride a snap, if not a terribly comfortable one. And, one thru-hiker whose group of four or five guys was picked up by a little old lady, reported that, when asked why she wasn't afraid to pick up a group, stated that mass killers and sundry wierdos generally travel alone, which only makes it harder for only slightly-weird solitary hikers, such as myself, to secure a ride. A small pick-up slows and stops. We pile in back amidst toolboxes and hoses and buckets of whatever for the uncomfortable half hour ride to Julian.

In Julian we head for the Julian Lodge, advertised as a bed and breakfast and costing a mere one hundred dollars a night. Much of the whole clan that I have seen on and off since the border is there. Others arrive as the afternoon wears on. Five of us check into one room, which boasts two full-sized beds. We head out to the Rongbranch Inn, whose claim to fame is the best pie in Julian, for dinner and an evening of cold beers and conversation. Julian, sporting that happy combination of heat and frost that apples require, is a great southern California tourist town, boasting gold mines and apple pie. Every restaurant, and there are many, advertise their pie as "the best in town," and probably it is.

That night I stake out a place on the floor, for I tend to toss and turn and change positions frequently during the night. I am lying comfortably on the floor, half-interestedly listening to the conversations, when I begin to smell a distinctly aromatic, not terribly pleasant smell. I open my eyes and see a pair of bare feet about two yards away. I try to ignore the aroma and eventually fall asleep to dream of French monks kneading and kneading curds with their feet to make that questionable delicacy, Limburger cheese.

By 10 AM we are all breakfasted, apple-pied, and loaded up with extra water for the traverse of the San Felipe Hills. Walking east out of town, six or eight of us stop at the post office. Some are trying to get rides from post office patrons. I head to the driveway and hold out my "PCT Hiker, To Trail Please" sign. Swiss Miss and Lutzia join me. Not having learned my lesson from yesterday, I think a threesome will never get a ride. Five minutes later, a guy in a pickup with a camper shell pulls over and asks me where we are going. I tell him, but he allows that he is headed down the other fork in the road, to Lake Henshaw, for a bike ride. Not wanting to get hung up in town forever, and knowing I must make the nearly nine mile climb up the San Felipe Mountains today, I offer him twenty dollars to take us. Without much hesitation for a guy who was intent on bicycling, he readily agrees. Swiss and Lutzia pile in the back, along with Jeff Z and their gear and try to sandwich themselves amidst a couple of bicycles. They sit uncomfortably in back while I sit up front, uncomfortably making small talk, a skill of which I have but little, until we reach Scissors Crossing.

We pile out and head for the bridge, to hide out in its shady underneath and wait for Monty, Anne, Tony, Ian, Tony and several others to make it out of town. It is about eleven o'clock and the temperature is already in the high nineties. The creek, such as it is, is only a few feet wide and runs listlessly. Willows choke the creek, but here the east wall of the overpass offers a sandy "beach" and shelter from the sun. The wall is entirely covered with black and red gangster painting, most of which is apparently coded for initiates. Over all this, in brilliant lime, are a swastika, an iron cross, a three foot tall "SS" and the words "White Power." It seems really odd to find this kind of stuff so deep into nowhere.

Lutzia has carried a watermelon all the way from town with her and we share that while waiting. More than an hour passes and no one else shows up. I begin to feel nervous, since it is eight and a half long miles up to the first decent camping spot, the "sandy wash" described in the guidebook. At one o'clock I announce that I am going to head out. They allow as how they will stay a bit longer. I mount up and head out to the road, S2, which heads up San Felipe Canyon, over Teofulio Summit. This is the lowest crossing of the Peninsular Ranges between San Gorgonio Pass, fifty miles north in Riverside County, and San Matias Pass, two hundred miles south in Baja California, and hence, the route of the Butterfield Overland stagecoach. It is the route ultimately to Warner Springs, my destination. I walk up the road awhile, looking for the trail. After a half mile, I stop and look around. I can see the trail several hundred feet above me; I have gone the wrong way. I head back down the road toward the junction. Finally, I can see the trail no more than a couple of hundred feet above, still heading down and east. I walk out into the desert, up a wash to its head, and finally scramble up thirty or so feet to the trail. Finally I am on the trail, during the hottest part of a triple digit day.

It is not an unpleasant trail, this, the first true desert the trail passes through. The plants are sparse, with plenty of rocky ground between them, not crowded together, in whatever passes for "cheek to jowl" in the plant world, as is the chaparral. Yucca, barrel cacti, prickly pear, cholla, and all manner of wildflowers are in bloom. The numerous ocotillo are striking with their myriad tiny green leaves bursting out of what appear to be eight-foot-long dead sticks. The tops are crowned with brilliant sprays of red flowers. And there are Desert Agave here, too.

Related, of all things, to the daffodil, and famous for their use in the making of tequila, they stand out like huge, solitary stalks of asparagus. They are monocarpic, which is a fancy way of saying that they bloom once and die. Some are in bloom, and one is close to the trail. Its spray of light yellow flowers stands out against the deep blue sky, and I can smell it from yards away. The smell is sweet and so strong that it would not surprise me to see birds and insects lying drunk about its base.

Once the trail makes an adequate switchback up and around Grapevine Mountain, it begins the long traverse northwest along the San Felipe Hills. The ridge is deeply cut by steep canyons, and the trail winds in and out of every one of them. This would not be so bad if you could not see the trail for miles ahead, taunting you with "so near and yet so far."

To make matters worse my pack, which has weighed less than twenty pounds so far, now weighs a good bit more than thirty with the extra water I am carrying. I have mistakenly thought that my Platypus containers hold 1.5 liters, when in reality they hold 2.5 liters. So far, I have used only one along with my one-liter water bottle. Now they are both filled and, in addition in Julian I purchased a gallon bottle of water and added it to my pack. I think I have roughly eight liters, sixteen pounds. But I really have two liters, four pounds, of water more than that. Because my pack has been generally less than twenty pounds total, I have not been using the HDPE plastic frame sheet or aluminum stays or any waist belt at all. The thirty-eight pound pack digs mercilessly into my shoulders all the long afternoon. Fortunately the pain in my legs, so pronounced two days ago and yesterday morning, has faded away, although I fully expect to be reminded tomorrow.

The temperature, which had risen to 104°F, has begun to drop as I gain altitude and the day lengthens. About ten miles southeast Granite Mountain dominates the skyline. The sun-fried air is dancing across the desert below. Earthquake Valley looks for all the world as if it is under a gentle seismic siege as the air through which I view it buzzes and dances in the heat. It is so hot that the air appears faintly smoky, as if the whole world was just moments from bursting into flame. Of course I know it's just haze, but the image is strong, nonetheless.

To many, these temperatures seem devastating. During the long winter before this trip I read dozens of online journals and learned of people becoming dehydrated, dismayed, discouraged, disorientated, disabled, and, in general, discombobulated in these desert climes. I suffer no such symptoms...well, perhaps the "dismayed." This is my home turf, for I grew up in southern California, and the desert has long been my playground. I wear a legionnaire's style hat with plenty of side and neck cover. Over the top I have laboriously taped silvery Mylar to reflect the heat...causing some to question whether I am trying to keep the flying saucers from beaming subtle orders directly into my brain. By the time I leave Big Bear, I will have lost the hat which, being well enough known, will chase me up the trail until I finally outpace it at Wrightwood. Although I wear shorts, my torso is covered with a white (well, it started out white) long sleeve Supplex nylon shirt. This keeps moisture in and slows the loss of water (i.e., sweat) through evaporation. And after all, if you have enough water, it's only heat, and as the Zen saying goes, "...when it's hot, be hot."

At long last I near the crest, stepping my way through metal gates, and in a half a mile, walk on down into the "sandy wash" described as the first likely spot to camp. And so it is. Within an hour the rest of the group arrives. It turns out that they left at three o'clock and took only three hours to travel the same distance it took me nearly two hours longer. Ah well...

The "sandy wash" is a lovely campsite, being nearly level and having many open spaces in the chaparral and juniper. My only complaint is the number of shallow "cat holes," bearing toilet paper streamers to announce their presence, and announcing themselves far too near the trail-side camp sites. In this spacious draw, with its soft soil, there is no excuse.

Once again, the others all plant themselves in a close group a dozen yards away. These folks seem to be traveling in a fairly cohesive group, and when I see them, they are walking together and talking. I had thought that most hikers, even those in groups, would spend much of the day alone, their conversations limited to rest stops and gatherings at water holes, and nightly camps, like that before me now. As time passes and the pack spreads out, doubtlessly this will become more and more true. So far, though the number of hikers seems large, I have had relatively little contact and conversation with others. Yet on this, the sixth night, I have yet to spend a night alone. Surprisingly enough, the aloneness during the day has not really bothered me...yet.

There is much commotion as camps are made and dinners cooked. Daylight does not linger long in desert country, and so it is here. A wind comes up, feeling deliciously cool. My small tent flaps noisily. Some find this a bother and have trouble finding rest. Earplugs are common. To me, it is music, akin to the sound of rain on a metal roof, a sound that calls to mind a rural Oklahoma childhood, tucked in and warm, in a bed having been duly inspected for scorpions and centipedes by my mother. The stars twinkle and dance in the hard night air, and my tent-flapping lullaby sings me to sleep.

In the morning I am on my early way. For about half of the fifteen-plus miles to the next water at Barrel Springs, the trail continues its way along the crest of the San Felipe Hills. Then, near the northern end of the range, it heads across and down and around the northeastern slopes. Here in the many shaded gullies through which the trail winds, I run into my first poison oak. In some places its growth is so lush that you have to consciously avoid brushing through it. I, bearing genetic proof against it through my distant Mongol ancestors, am neither allergic nor much worried. I wonder about the others. At some point I cross a sandy flat, inadequately, but nonetheless protected by a scrub oak. In the shade are Marcus and Robin, a couple from the San Francisco Bay Area, only a few hours from my Sierra foothills home. They are spread out in casual array, having what appears to be a picnic. It's a wondrous sight in this waterless land. They offer me a chocolate covered blueberry. Ordinarily, I am no great lover of chocolate, but I gratefully accept this rare treat, chat a minute or three and move on.

Finally the trail winds, after numberless twists and turns, down into Montezuma Valley and stops at Barrel Spring, a four by eight foot concrete trough full of deliciously cold water. Well, cold compared to the heat of the day. Here, at just past the one hundred-mile mark on the trail, a grove of oak trees provide a cool, shady rest site. A number of hikers are spread out. A couple of hikers are sitting several feet up the hillside. I ask them if they saw all the poison oak along the trail. They reply in the affirmative. I tell them that there is no point, then, in me warning them that they are, at this moment, cozied up to a particularly malevolent looking patch right behind them. They look startled, but say nothing, as they inch their way down slope and away from the evil herb. All around are growing patches of lush miner's lettuce, a tasty, succulent plant on which I munch like a grazing cow.

Not one to overstay my time, I saddle up and head out across Montezuma Valley Road and soon pass into a beautiful grassland in the drainage of Buena Vista Creek. There are long reaches of California poppies, as well as lupines and other wildflowers. This is one of the distinct plant communities, the Valley Grassland, which is seen in only a few places along the entire Trail. There are numbers of cows grazing. But John Muir's assessment of sheep, that "they can hardly be called an animal for an entire flock is required to make one foolish animal" seems likewise appropriate to cattle. As I approach, they look at me in surprise, and bolt, wild-eyed, as if I were an emissary from McDonald's here to apprise them of their fate.

At still-flowing San Ysidro Creek, I overtake Frank-from-Alaska and stop to water up. I set my pack on the sandy banks and notice a tick walking across its white surface. A hasty examination of gear and body finds no others. In fact, it will turn out to be the only tick I see on the entire trail.

The trail climbs over a ridge and into Cañada Verde - the Green Ravine. In about a mile or two, we come to a stream. Across the stream and up the hillside a few feet is a fine sandy flat, one of the few spots mercifully bereft of the innumerable cow pies that clog the landscape. Within two hours, the entire area is taken up with hikers, laughing and chatting and preparing dinner. The sun goes down on a twenty-two mile day and just a few miles short of Warner Springs. I plan to be there for breakfast the next day. Listening to the several conversations going on around me as "hiker midnight" (9:00 PM) approaches, I fall asleep.

I pack quietly and leave before dawn. The rest of the hikers are just beginning to stir. Traveling the four or so miles to the second crossing of the highway, I arrive at Warner Springs well before seven o'clock, on this fourth day of May. The Golf Grill is open, so I order coffee and wait. Within thirty minutes the rest of the crew arrives and we all order huge breakfasts. The post office doesn't open until nine o'clock, so we take our time.

Ultimately, we head to the post office to retrieve our re-supply parcels. A group of us gathers in the parking lot behind the post office. Mad Monty, Jeff Z and some others are leaving here for Los Angeles and back to their lives in that Other World. Singing Steve unpacks his parcel; it is a backpacking guitar that he plans to carry along with him. We take pictures of everyone, and loading into a car, they drive off. Lutzia and Swiss Miss are going on to San Gorgonio Pass before they head out. Ian-The-Brit is headed to Tuolumne Meadows in Yosemite before he heads back to New York State. Only Marcus and Robin, Anne, Tony, Singing Steve, and I have plans of continuing on to Canada. Four of us have decided to take the rest of the day off, so we head over to the Warner Springs Ranch to get rooms. Ian and I wind up sharing a room. We both harbor a fondness for the Highlands of Scotland and the Hebrides, me from two trips there, and he from college days in Edinburgh, where he majored in hiking and rock climbing...and, incidentally, physics. I have eight ounces of a fine old single-malt scotch in my re-supply, which is an instant hit.

We check into one of the two hundred fifty small bungalows, getting one - with neither refrigerator nor air conditioner, for a mere thirty-eight dollars each. Later in the afternoon we while away the hours in the Butterfield Cantina, followed by dinner in the beautiful-but-expensive Anza Dining Room.

The following morning Ian and I, deciding to travel together for a time, are on the trail early. We stock up on water, for in theory, it is nearly twenty-three miles through the hot chaparral to the next certain water at Tule Springs. One last breakfast at the Golf Grill, and we are on the trail. Agua Caliente Creek is flowing, and we ford it several times during the next six or seven miles. A recent convert to hiking poles, I am still working through the logistics of using a pole to scratch the back of my leg while walking, and so I manage to trip myself a couple of times to Ian's great amusement.

Coming up out of the creek and onto the ridges, the trail ultimately rises up enough for Coulter pines to make a stand. In another nine miles, we cross Chihuahua Valley Road. Across the road in the lee of some chamise plants are a dozen or more gallon water jugs. I trot across to check them out. Unfortunately all are empty. So we are faced with the short walk of three tenths of a mile to a private residence, which in theory allows hikers to fill their water containers. We walk past the large tank and down to the house. A dog is barking vigorously, so we stand there a few minutes hoping to be noticed. No one appears to be home, so we walk back to the tank, which has a large gate valve near the bottom. We drink our fill and with full containers, head back to the trail and up.

The trail winds almost due north, along the flanks of Bucksnort Mountain to a northeasterly descending ridge, then southwest to the slopes of Combs Peak, where a nearly-flat ridge-top about 600 feet below the summit offers up a camping spot among the pines. It is nearly sunset. The view to the north is striking. About fifteen miles away and a bit to the east is Santa Rosa Mountain, where as a kid, I drove to search on its slopes for crystals of red garnet and pale green sphene. More northerly, and perhaps twice the distance, I can see my destinations for the coming days, the snowy San Jacinto Mountains, and just peeking over the western-most ridge is Mt. San Gorgonio, the highest mountain in southern California and more than a week away.

The day has been hot and tiring. I set up camp quickly and eat my dinner, an MRE, cold out of the bag. The MRE, a Meal Ready to Eat, is considered fit fare for our fighting men. In addition to beef stew, it contains a shortbread cookie, crackers and cheese, a raspberry fruit pastry and spiced cider drink. Weighing in at over a pound, it is far too heavy for the 800 calories it contains and renders up as much as a quarter of its weight in trash. Be that as I may, I eat it cold, right out of the bag...a veritable feast.

To the east, a soon-to-be full moon is already a ways up into the sky. A deliciously cool breeze begins to blow. The Anza Valley, below and to the west is already in shadow; only the mountains are still in light. Widely scattered lights sparkle here and there throughout the valley.

As the evening settles in, perhaps eight o'clock, two hikers approach. They find a place to be and quietly prepare dinner. One pulls out a cell phone and in no time is talking to a mother, on an entirely different planet, somewhere beyond this lonely vista. From the downy confines of my bag, I watch the evening progress.

The next day can be described briefly, an all-day hike in hot, nearly waterless chaparral. My journal says only "Hot!!" and "interminable chaparral." Not far into the morning we pass a sign indicating we are once more in the Anza-Borrego Desert State Park. After about eight miles, we get water at Tule Canyon Spring. A short side-trip down a dirt road brings one to this charming little spring. Another seven miles and we arrive at a surprise, a wooden structure housing gallons and gallons of water. It is the water stash, built and stocked by the folks at the Camp Anza Hiker's Oasis. Ian and I decide to push on rather than visit this highly recommended stop because we both re-supplied only two days ago and have adequate supplies to get to Idyllwild. The next time I come this way again, I would certainly make the detour.

We begin to see houses, some not too far off the trail. Reaching them from the trail however, would be a nightmare, for the chamise, about eight feet tall here, is so thick that passage would be nearly impossible. We are trapped in a tunnel of chaparral. Finally, the trail circles around the slopes of Table Mountain, and winding through granite boulder-choked ravines, up Lookout Mountain. At last, twenty-three miles into this hot, protracted day, we arrive at a sandy wash on the shoulder of Lookout Mountain. I don't even remember making camp or dinner. It's early to bed while the moon rides high in the sky all night.

The next morning I am on a mission. Leaving camp before six o'clock, I walk the six miles to Highway 74, the Pines to Palms Highway. A fence with a gate lines the highway. Under a bush are several containers of water and a bag of oranges. A trail angel has fluttered by here! I have only a mile to go to the restaurant, so I leave the water, but cannot resist an orange.

My birthplace was Orange, California, in Orange County, at St. Joseph's Hospital. My grandmother lived at the end of a short road, Mountain View Drive, that was bounded by infinite orange groves, or so it seemed to a nine year old. I grew up playing hide-and-seek, climbing and free ranging in those orange groves. Today nothing of that small

Tustin street exists, nor does a single orange tree. That's progress...I guess; but I have never lost my passion for oranges, and so I snag one and lope on down the road.

I arrive at the junction of Highways 74 and 371—Paradise Corner—at eight-thirty in the morning. Unfortunately, on this Monday morning, although its sign announces breakfast, lunch and dinner, the restaurant is closed; it will open at eleven o'clock. Ian arrives minutes later and we consult, deciding to wait. After all, it's only two and a half hours!

Several cars make futile stops during the wait, hoping to find breakfast. At 10:30 a man arrives and goes in. Minutes later, he comes out and says we can come inside and wait until service is ready. We drink coffee and water and wait. Eventually, after a huge burger and fries and a strawberry shake, I am ready to hit the trail.

At one o'clock, we leave, hike back to the trail and start up through the sandy, granite-bouldered foothills of the San Jacinto Mountains. By day's end we are a bit over twelve miles further and 2100 feet higher. All things considered, not a bad day, nearly eighteen trail miles, plus two to the restaurant and back, with four hour hiatus.

Evening finds us on the narrow ridge of the Desert Divide, just a few hundred yards beyond the summit of Palm View Peak, flanked on the west by a line of wind-twisted trees. And truly, it is aptly named. To the east lies the Colorado Desert, from this distance appearing stark and barren, while to the west are trees and ranches and signs that life has found an easier grip on the land.

The sun goes down and a glorious full moon rises in the east. The wind howls across the ridge and drops down into the desert below. Snug in my bag and protected by the trees, I gaze at the Christmas tree-like lights of the thirty-mile long stretch of civilization that runs south from Palm Springs to Thermal, dancing and twinkling in the heated air. More than six thousand feet below me, and perhaps fifteen miles away, I can see the lights of individual cars as they make their lonely way to who-knows-where. Twenty-five miles to the south, the Salton Sea glows dimly as if illumed from within by some ghostly source. Although I know Ian has set up camp only a hundred yards down the way, it seems to me that on this, my eleventh night on the trail, I am truly alone and far from civilization. Though I am not Catholic, nor particularly religious, and I know not under the protection of which of the seventy recognized Saint Josephs I reside (and in whose hospital I was born), I trust it is Joseph the Betrothed, guardian against hesitation and doubt.

The following morning brings me at last, well and truly into the mountains, but not immediately, for there is a more than one thousand foot descent to Fobes Saddle that must be accomplished. That being said and done, Ian and I are taking an early morning rest at the saddle. We are trying to decide the correct direction, for the trail has a fork here, one moving slightly west and around the peak above us, the other traveling what looks like a more northeasterly direction. Just about having decided that the western trail is the correct one, we hear a shout and see three figures coming along that trail toward us. In a few minutes Swiss Miss, Lutzia, and Singing Steve arrive. We wonder why they are coming back on the trail. As it turns out, the west-bearing trail leads down to Fobes Ranch. Yesterday at just about this time, they made the very mistake we were just about to make, and wound up walking down towards Fobes Ranch. By the time the mistake was caught they decided to continue on, down several miles to Highway 74, where they hitched a ride north to Mountain Center and thence up into Idyllwild, spending the night at the Tahquitz Inn, the local hiker hangout. They got a ride back this morning, and plan to slack pack the 10.7 miles along the trail to Saddle Junction and the 4.7 miles down to town, and be back in time for pizza. We sit in the bright early-morning sun and chat awhile. They take off and soon disappear.

Now the trail heads earnestly uphill...and down. Along this ten mile ridge from the head of Penrod Canyon where the trail hits the Desert Divide to the shoulder of Red Tahquitz, there are eight peaks (as well as three minor, unnamed summits), each higher in elevation than the one preceding it. Yesterday we passed Lion Peak, Pyramid Peak, and Palm View Peak. Now we begin a period of rather serious climbing. First comes Spitler Peak, on whose slopes begins the signs of the Palm Canyon fire of 1980 which burned nearly thirty thousand acres. The vegetation of the chaparral, which thrives, and in fact depends, on fire has made a bountiful comeback lo these twenty-one years later, but the charred sticks that were once fir and pine trees will be in evidence most of the day. Next comes Apache Peak, Anstell Rock, South Peak, and finally in the late afternoon, the east ridge of Red Tahquitz Peak, over which the trail ultimately winds.

During the long winter before my journey began I spent hours and days on the internet, seeking out the history of the areas through which I was to travel. It was time well spent and provided many an entertaining evening, as well as food for thought on the trail. But of course, where there is gold, there is always history. Here, where there were no riches for the taking, there was little history for the finding. Most of my requirements are focused on just physically moving along the trail, and so my mind takes on a "mind" of its own and forages far and wide.

A succession of thoughts begins roll through my mind. The first, oddly enough, are scenes from movies I have seen. I make mental notes, only to forget, of course, that I want to see this or that one again. Next, logically enough, are books I have read. I consider a number of them...ones I remind myself that I greatly like but have not read in some time. After awhile I think of one of my favorites, Kurt Vonnegut's *Slaughterhouse Five*. I think about how the hero has come "unstuck" in time and travels back and forth seamlessly from present to future to past. Then it is as though I come unstuck. I begin to think of the past. Events of years ago begin to parade themselves through my mind. I think about people whom I have known and lost track of over the years, about events and places that are lost in time. I hear a snatch of an old Beatles song, *In My Life*:

There are places I'll remember
All my life, though some have changed.
Some forever not for better
Some have gone and some remain...

And I say hear, because oddly enough, that is exactly what happens, as though I carried a recording with me.

There are fantasies, what ifs, and alternate realities. I relive conversations, some of them years old. And incidents, some in which I reacted with brilliance, some with utter stupidity. Because my life has not necessarily been one of unmitigated bliss, I think much of the hard times and the losses and the pain...things that happened, things I could have done differently, things of great regret. Thoughts of the future, of tomorrow and next year parade by—things I have yet to do and want to, or perhaps need to do, or maybe won't have time to do, and ultimately come thoughts of death, for it looms much closer than it once did.

I remember my paternal grandmother who went to the hospital for minor surgery and never returned. I think about a book she gave me for Christmas in 1949. I was seven years old. It had an inscription, "To my little Buddy, love, Grandmother." It was one of the few possessions I had saved for years and years...that had survived the 1960s with me, only to be destroyed when all was lost to fire in 1977. I remember her as a tireless woman who spent her days washing and ironing, keeping a house, growing a garden, raising chickens and rabbits, who made her own soap, yet still took time nearly every day to bake some delectable pie or cobbler or cake. I loved her dearly. She was always singing while she worked... and she sang all day. She made time to take in a foster child, and cook dinner for those less fortunate souls whom she frequently dragged home from church on a Sunday afternoon. Her memory spanned the time from the end of the Wild West to space travel. She remembered riding in a covered wagon when her family moved from Texas to Oklahoma, and crossing a storm-swollen river. She remembered the pain at the loss of her youngest brother, who died of the flu when he was only two years old. And as she lay dying in a hospital, Sputnik worked its tireless way across the night sky. She was truly the religious one of the family.

Her husband, my grandfather, was a carpenter and a preacher—a man of fire and brimstone and eternal damnation. And he had a wandering eye. Although, as a child, I spent much time with my grandmother, I don't remember him being around very much. Later, I came to think of him as an Elmer Gantry-esque character with a whiskey bottle in one hand and a Bible in the other. A holy man, though not always practicing and preaching the same thing, he seemed a character who came home once in a while to beget one of his eight sons and two daughters, only to disappear again when it was time to do some "ministering." Only in the last few years have I learned that my juvenile visions were both right and wrong.

And so, even though I was steeped in Christianity as a child, and almost forcibly "saved" when barely a teen, I neither expect nor much desire the eternal bliss of the Christian heaven, nor do I worry about Beelzebub, the Prince of Hell, or Satan, the Prince of Death. I am not much frightened by death and I have fairly well come to terms with the thought of non-existence. Early on I came to believe that living this life as if it were a dream from which one would awaken in heaven was not enough. This is the world we are in…this is where people ache and yearn and bleed, where children starve and monsters (in human bodies) truly do roam the nights, and where men will kill in the name of their God and think it a righteous deed. This is the world where something must be done, where we must live, not by faith alone, but by good deeds. And if I am wrong, surely my punishment will lie at the gates of Dante's Hell among the virtuous pagans, afflicted but by melancholy and desire without hope, not eight circles down in Malebolge, suffering the grievous agony of flames and boiling pitch and leaden mantels with the hypocrites and simonists that fill this world.

It is a curious process, this "mind storm" that so often occurs during long solitary days, and those who have experienced it will, I think, readily understand. For my mind takes not a path, like the one on which I tread, going from A to B, but, as images and thoughts parade through my mind, like balloons floating in lazy circles on a summer's breeze, it grasps and fondles them, extracts a flavor, experimentally rolls it across the palate of my life, and moves on. Nor is it a singular, continuous process, but more like a "television program," broken on occasion by "commercial messages" from the world at large—a jet high above making its lonely way through infinite blue; the buzz of a rattlesnake, disturbed from its own unfathomable contemplations in nearby brush; a throb of pain in one shoulder or the other caused by the shifting of the pack; the sun, glinting on hard crystals in nearby rocks; the beauty of a single wildflower, or the far-away call of a solitary Mountain Chickadee; a stab of pain in the left foot; a sudden need for a drink of water.

It occurs to me that this seemingly unavoidable thought process is not one which many people like nor can long endure. I believe age to be a factor, and those younger, I think, tolerate it less than those older. Many simply refuse to travel alone, sometimes citing safety as their reason, but I am suspicious. I have also heard this long distance hiking described in many journals as at some point ultimate boredom, but again I am suspicious. Perhaps, somewhere along the trail, I will come to think likewise, but I doubt it.

This marvelous, achingly beautiful world is all there is. This is where my heart goes; this is why, as an old man, that many are the things that bring me close to tears...and not because life is sad, but because it is so perfect, and we are not allotted enough time to fully apprehend...to fully appreciate. In a letter to Jeanne Carr, his friend and mentor, John Muir, when he was only twenty-six echoed these thoughts. Unable to decide what to do in life, he said, "...and then, a lifetime is so little a time that we die ere we get ready to live...but could we live but a million of years...then perhaps we might, with at least some show of reason, 'shuffle off this mortal coil' and look back upon our star with something of satisfaction." He understood and made his choices early; far too many live and toil most of a lifetime before they see.

Five hundred miles up the trail I will meet Bryan, a young naval engineer recently returned to civilian life. He too is traveling alone. We discuss this a few minutes, and I say, "Well, there's certainly plenty of time to listen to the voices in your head." To which, he replies, "That's why I carry a radio, so I don't have to listen to them." And so, many do carry some form of electronic distraction. I have none, but I understand, and may too before this journey ends, come to long for the "silence" of a radio. As Charles Caleb Colton, that British purveyor of aphorisms, said so long ago: "There are many who had rather meet their bitterest enemy in the field, than meet their own hearts in their closet." It takes long years before many can wrestle with their demons and hope, with luck, to win two out of three falls.

The trail, which has been running pretty much due north for the last two days, now makes a sharp jog to the west. Skirting the summit of Red Tahquitz on its eastern side, it mounts over a northeastern ridge and turns due west. Slowly shedding elevation, it makes its way down a mile into the creek that flows down from the slopes of Tahquitz Peak and waters the Little Tahquitz Valley. I pause here to camel up and fill my water bottles.

Moving on, I follow the trail as it ascends the five hundred foot wall that makes up the north ridge of Tahquitz Peak. The trail runs just a few yards below a saddle, and I pause to walk up and check it out. It is getting late in the day and I am confused, for though I am beat down, the mileage covered seems minor. I shed my pack and take a break, pulling out the guidebook to illuminate me. I camped last night about two miles before Fobes Saddle. I begin to add mileages. Those two miles and the remainder, from Fobes to here make just less than twelve miles! I am only about a mile from Saddle Junction. That means I am only 3.5 miles from pavement - a distance I could still easily make today, since it is only a bit after five o'clock, but I am still surprised at having walked so short a distance.

The guide book shows only a 2,500 foot difference between here and where I started this morning, but this tells little of the true story, and closer inspection reveals that there has been almost 6,500 feet of ups and downs today, 4,000 feet up and 2,500 feet down. I tell myself this is the reason for such short mileage. While I am pondering these facts and trying to decide whether it is worth the dash down the mountain to arrive exhausted and after dark and wondering where to go for the night, Ian arrives. He allows as how he too is worn down by the day. We decide to spend the night here and make the short trip down to Idyllwild early in the morning. And so we do.

Since I will be in town almost immediately in the morning, I decide to sleep in. But the following morning, I awaken automatically and am on the trail by the usual six o'clock. The mile to Saddle Junction and the 2.5 miles down to Humber Park pass quickly. Well before eight o'clock Ian and I are standing in the parking lot and wishing someone would give us a ride the two remaining miles to Idyllwild. There's not much activity this early in the morning so we start walking down the road. Within five minutes a faded orange pickup truck stops and forces us to accept a ride. It turns out to be less by luck than design. The driver is Barbara Sargent, who along with her husband Bob, is owner and proprietor of the Tahquitz Inn, Thru-hiker Central. She had driven by on the way up to deliver some hikers to the trailhead. Minutes later we are checked in and headed for breakfast, and what a breakfast! Jan's "World Famous" Red Kettle Restaurant justly announces itself. It becomes the standard against which all subsequent town breakfasts are measured. For example: Jan's...10,

Reds Meadow...2, Copper Kettle in Chester...8, Timberline Lodge breakfast buffet...13!

The morning passes quickly, the time being spent locating the post office, retrieving my re-supply box, shopping for a few needed items, and stumbling up and down the aisles of the supermarket. Two in the afternoon finds me sitting in a dark corner of JoAnn's Bar and Grill, enjoying a wee dram while watching the everyday drama of life in Idyllwild swirl mysteriously about me.

Back at the motel I put several inches of warm water in the tub, add my clothes and some detergent, and do the Hiker Trash Wine-Stomp Clothes-Wash Dance. I can't remember if I even asked if there was a laundromat at the Inn, though I must have, mustn't I? With clothes hanging everywhere to dry, I go out and join the barbeque. The Inn has provided tables and BBQs and a hiker barrel for our enjoyment, and so with fifteen or more hikers sitting around drinking wine and cold beer and waxing philosophic, we cook dinner and relax. It's a fine time. I stumble to bed just after midnight, terribly late for one used to going to bed with the sun, and sleep fitfully, visited by fantastic dreams, as I will come to find common on nights off the trail when sleeping in beds too soft and bounded by walls and ceiling and civilization.

The next day it's up and do it all again...breakfast that is. Then there's the sorting of food, the trip to the nearby lumberyard for Tyvek ground cloth for a couple of other hikers, brunch, lunch and afternoon beers. In the Good Times Pub and Grill, touting itself as home of the "best burgers on the hill," we meet a couple of hikers just arriving. BJ is from Latvia...well, not really. He's actually from Texas, but lives in Lativa with his wife, who is an attorney for the State Department. His last trip was a 12,000-mile bicycle ride with his wife from Point Barrow, Alaska to Tierra del Fuego, at the end of South America. A hundred miles up the trail I will travel with him for a few days and hear more of his trip. Chris (later to become Knight Rider) is from Gold Bar, Washington, not so far from the very end of the Pacific Crest Trail. He and BJ are both ex-Marines, so they talk MOS and DEROS and other things for which I have no decoder ring. Their talk turns to firearms, and Chris says the first thing his friends asked him when he announced his hike was "What are you packin'?" This translates as "what gun are you carrying?" Ian says, "If there were fewer guns in America, perhaps the police would chase after criminals and catch them, rather than shoot them." Without missing a beat, Chris responds, "If the Brits would quit getting rid of all theirs, maybe countless American lives won't be lost when we have to save their asses again like we did in the Second World War." In the close confines of the Good Times Pub and

Grill, a dozen heads turn our way and an awkward, palpable silence descends. But, moments later, Ian, always the gentlemen, raises his beer, smiles and says, "touché," and the conversation turns away from the things which divide to that which bind us all together, The Trail.

By four o'clock, Ian and I are ready to get a ride back to the trail rather than spend another night in town, so we pack our gear. Bob takes us back in the old Chevy truck, and we head up Devil's Slide. It's good to get into a trail town and dine and carouse; it's better yet to leave and be on the Trail again.

A TALE OF FOUR TOWNS

The mass of ordinary men lead lives of quiet desperation.
(Walden, Henry David Thoreau*)*

I can't say with any certainty that the reasons for, or the degree of desperation of which Thoreau wrote more than one hundred fifty years ago have changed, but it's clear that James Thurber was right when he said, "Nowadays, most men live lives of noisy desperation." It is no longer all that quiet. I'm sitting in the bar of JoAn's Restaurant, Idyllwild. It's mid-afternoon. From invisible speakers, music with a catchy, driving beat floats through the background. Monotonously repetitive, the lyrics speak of pain and anger, the end results of this not-so-quiet desperation. This would normally jangle on my nerve ends like an ancient oriental water torture, but sitting here in the quiet recesses of JoAn's I take notice without emotion.

At the bar sit three men in working clothes. They discuss their week in the common language of those who have wedded themselves to lives of voluntary servitude in pursuit of...what? I did the same myself for forty long years and still cannot answer the question. The word *responsibility* floats through my consciousness, but it carries the nagging tone of a mother lecturing her teenage son, so I let it float on by. Their conversation is desultory and mostly negative, centering on the ridiculous situations of the workweek. It's Thursday afternoon and time, evidently, to unwind. Underpaid and overworked, ill-appreciated, wrongfully blamed and misjudged, both commanded and served by inferiors, and trapped in the amber of what Thoreau called the "spending of the best part of one's life earning money in order to enjoy a questionable liberty during the least valuable part of it," they represent us all. Their language is not coinage solely for those with blue collars, for I have heard the same words from engineers, teachers, attorneys, and others.

These are the ordinary conversations of disenchantment with life by ordinary people. I understand the words and know what they mean, but the reality of which they speak is so far removed from that which I have been living these past days on the trail that I may as well be an Alien from some star-distant civilization, here to study the creatures of Earth, having learned flawless English, garnered entirely and painfully from recordings of television talk shows. The words have meaning, but fresh from the trail, I lack a frame of reference to which they can be attached. I get a feeling that nothing is quite real and for a few moments I experience the curious sensation of being just slightly outside myself—about eighteen inches up and a couple of feet to the right—and looking over my own shoulder. I am acutely aware of my bodily boundaries, and suddenly feel warm and secure in my lack of comprehension of the events transpiring around me. Perhaps the warm glow comes, too, from a body cranked up by more than two hundred miles on the trail, metabolizing a wee dram of fine scotch at warp speed.

Idyllwild, the scene of rustic simplicity implied in its name, *idyll*, is apropos and also a play on the word *idle*. Perhaps it's a little early in the season, but on this fine May day there doesn't seem to be much going on, which is fine with me. Long ago in another lifetime, I used to come here to practice the art of climbing on the great faces of Tahquitz Rock. The locals called it *Ta-keets* in those days. Hiking down into town from the parking lot at Humber Park this morning, at length I am picked up by a lady in an old pick-up who drops me off at the local hiker hangout, calling it the *Ta-quits* Inn. Coming into town it appears that other than the pronunciation of the name of its local landmark, little has changed in the forty years since I was last here.

It's a compact little town with a well-stocked grocery store, restaurants, bars, the essential pizza parlor, library with internet connection, and sports shop with a good selection of hiker gear, everything the traveler on foot needs, all found with three or four or five blocks in any direction. Less idyllic is the handful of cutesy tourist stores, Cabin Fever, for the video game junkie, Wylld Fibers and Weavery, Florist in the Forest, the Wilkum Inn, the Idyllwild Cat House...no, it's a pet shop, A Light in the Forest (candle shop), and not to forget the Idyllwild Jerky Shop, where the dried muscles of four different beasts are available in five different flavors. I give the stores with the names Out There and Sacred Spaces a wide berth, unwilling to discover just what ludicrous merchandise lines their shelves. Clearly the names and kinds of stores must have, to my way of thinking, devolved along with the wares, although I have no memories of these from long ago. These tourist stores look fresh and shiny, but are surrounded by plenty of shops with a more worn and seedy look. There are a number of less-than-sparkling stores, staffed by indifferent workers, selling tawdry merchandise at inflated prices, and not a few stores are empty, telling tales of better times.

Sitting on a shoulder of the great granite pluton of the San Jacinto Mountains, Idyllwild is surrounded by the water-starved lands of southern California. To the south is the Anza-Borrego Desert, a portion of the vast Sonora Desert through which I have just traveled. East, one runs into the Colorado Desert, another part of the Sonora Desert and the driest desert in America, containing the Imperial Valley and Palm Springs with its thousand and one golf courses—a desert made green by gulping every last drop of water from the Colorado River. A little north of that in the Mojave Desert lies Joshua Tree National Monument, a higher and colder desert and thus able to support great "forests" of the giant tree-like members of the Lily family, whose name it bears.

Mormons crossing the California deserts so named the plant because they fancied that the angular branches looked like the outstretched arms of Joshua leading them out of the wilderness and back to Salt Lake City, to where they had been recalled...at least that's how one story goes. Directly north is the section of the Colorado Desert through which hikers must make their way across the wind-blown steppes of San Gorgonio Pass and thence up Mission Creek to gain the next island oasis, the San Bernardino Mountains. West are the artificial oases of the Great Los Angeles basin, touched by fewer than twenty inches of rain a year and technically in the chaparral, but certainly desert-like, sustaining its millions on water hijacked from wherever the taking of it was least opposed.

Adrift in this waterless sea, Idyllwild nestles just above the snow line and dense, beautiful stands of Jeffrey and lodgepole pines are the order of the day. But water seems to be the great limiting factor here too. Riding down into town we passed a fire station. Although it's early in May, a sign in front proclaimed stage-two water restrictions in place, whatever those are. But after all is said and done, Idyllwild is more idyllic than not, and hiker-friendly to boot.

Sitting in the cool darkness, I realize that I love coming into town from the trail. It is an experience that brings to mind what the traveling Sacred Dance shows of Gurdjieff in the early part of this century must have been like. To see a dancer suddenly streak across the stage, and with an inhuman yell, throw himself through the air, land sitting in an empty seat twelve rows deep in the audience, and begin talking to the person next to him as if nothing was out of the ordinary—that person in the audience could have been no more surprised than I am sitting in a restaurant or bar in those first marvelous hours off the trail.

There is a stunning surprise that accompanies the radical violation of our expectations. We work and live from day to day, operating on a set of stereotypes and expectations that really are rarely violated. We see what we expect to see and we hear what we expect to hear. What we know we understand, and we feel comfortable and are lulled with that understanding. When those expectations are dramatically violated, it causes an effect that is reminiscent of old cartoons—where eyes and ears and tongue and teeth and lips and jaw all fly in different directions, to come reeling home with an audible thud.

Coming off the trail after days of solitude and inner dialogue is like that, albeit in a slightly different way. Time on the trail so focuses and condenses life, so reduces and distances one from the distractions of society in general and "normal" social interactions, in particular, so narrows one's expectations, that every town-event in those first hours seems a violation. I feel the thud of all my parts flying back together and euphorically stagger around like a punch-drunk boxer. Nothing makes sense and truly, ignorance *is* bliss.

Some days before, I made an early morning lunge down the trail to Warner Springs Resort and arrived at the restaurant at the country club for a six-thirty breakfast. Warner Springs is barely a town at all, boasting only a post office and gas station-mini mart with extremely limited supplies. In 1844, John Warner acquired the land and built accommodations on the more than two and a half thousand-acre site in the foothills of the Palomar Mountains. It became a stop for the historic Butterfield Overland Stage. From desperadoes to Ulysses Grant and Kit Carson, Warner's became a haven for people on their way to fame and fortune in California.

It became a private resort about forty years ago and other desperadoes, actors from Hollywood searching for a different fame and a bigger fortune, made it one of their favorite haunts. Situated at about three thousand feet in elevation and roughly halfway between Los Angeles and San Diego, and boasting hot springs, spas, golf course, tennis courts, damnable horse stables, three restaurants and a bar, *and* air conditioning, it is a popular place. Later in the day, I hid out in a non-air conditioned room for only thirty-eight dollars (my half) and tried to run the hot water tank dry. It is one of the handful of spots of "civilization" along the whole of the PCT that is an easy walk from the trail.

I sat there in the Golf Grill drinking coffee, waiting for some other hikers to show up. All about were people, mostly men, dressed in costume and carrying the accoutrements of their present trade, golf. Humans apparently more successful, or at least more affluent no doubt than the working stiffs of JoAn's in Idyllwild. Perhaps money assuages desperation, or at least better equips one to deal with it, for there among the recreators Thoreau's quiet desperation was still quiet. Their laughter and careless talk assailed me from all sides. I'd walked just over a hundred miles to get here and listened to men discuss the merits of walking the course today, which is 3.9 miles (if you are a good player) or 3 miles (if you're a duffer), according to the brochure on the table in front of me. Just how the distance could be longer for better players was a mystery to me. This was less than the distance I had walked this morning for the cup of coffee I held in my hand. Like the Alien I am, I felt smug and briefly savored the feeling of superiority I got as they opted for one of the little golf carts lining the drive, and the fifty-six dollar price tag that went along with it.

At a nearby table four men discussed the previous day's game in terms of birdies and eagles and bogies and strokes and pars and slices and who knows what all. One, dressed in the outrageous tartan of Clan MacGarish, spoke of a "good lie" as if it was something of which to be proud. Soon Swiss Miss and Lutzia, Anne, Ian- and Tony-The-Brits, Mad Monty and The Two Daves, Singing Steve, Jeff Z, and Marcus and Robin arrived. We all sat in one corner of the room, ordered huge breakfasts, and laughed too loudly at apparently meaningless jokes that only Aliens would understand.

Nearly three hundred miles into the trail and six days in the future from Warner Springs, Big Bear City has a different flavor. After a long day, which ends frustratingly with more than an hour's attempt to hitch a ride from Highway 18 at Baldwin Lake, I stumble into the post office to retrieve my food box. My camera, which I had assured myself I would not want, is now waiting for me too. A couple of hikers ask me if I have been to the fire station yet. I answer in the negative and head for Moreno's restaurant and bar, a few hundred yards down the main street, for cold liquids. I am there for no more than fifteen minutes when Ian shows up. I throw a friendly curse at him, for once again he has managed to hitch the ride in minutes that invariably takes me a lifetime. We sit a bit and then head for the fire station.

Two blocks from the post office, the fire station has made itself a haven[1] for those having survived their trek across the Colorado Desert from the bottom of San Jacinto in Snow Creek Canyon to near the head of Mission Creek Canyon. A small lawn-covered courtyard, surrounded by a wooden fence, contains several hikers, some familiar, some not, who have strewn out their gear in an attempt to regroup. Inside is a thirty-gallon plastic trash barrel crammed with food and equipment, the hiker box. It's filled with stuff previous hikers thought they would surely need, now abandoned to other hikers who will surely think they need it too. Under zip-locks of the ubiquitous corn pasta, a jar of peanut butter, and a couple boxes of macaroni and cheese, is a bottle of white wine, which I

1 Sometime during the 2001 hiking year the fire station will have some kind of problem and sadly, their hospitality is no longer available.

immediately appropriate. Outside I display my treasure to an interested group. Some allow as how a nice cold beer would be desirable too, but they don't think we should or maybe cannot drink on the grounds. I am much more of an experimentalist than a theoretician, so I walk inside in search of someone of authority. Finding that one, whose name, rank, and serial number should most likely remain anonymous, I ascertain that this activity would be okay, if it is a quiet activity with no fuss, no muss, and no empties. I part with his warning: "This conversation never took place." We desert-thirsty travelers are only too happy to comply. It's near dark and after long showers and a fine dinner at Moreno's we sit in the cool of the evening and solve the problems of the Trail and the Universe.

The next morning finds a large group of hikers occupying much of one corner of Thelma's. After a huge breakfast, including the glass of freshly squeezed orange juice, free to all hikers, I head out on the day's errands. Although Big Bear is friendly and knowledgeable about Pacific Crest Trail hikers—there are banners all over town welcoming PCT hikers—it was certainly not laid out with walkers in mind. The town is spread out along several miles of road. Ian and I hike down the road a ways. Spying a Motel 6, we stop by and check in. We have decided to stay another night, and a shower, bed, and laundry facilities sounds like just the ticket. I need groceries, socks and shower/camp shoes, all to be had if one is persistent.

Conveniently, there is a bus system running throughout the area, but every stop requires an hour before the next bus comes along, so obtaining a few items in a strange town winds up taking all of the morning and some of the afternoon hours. Still feeling dazed and euphoric from the trail, I stumble down the aisles of the Stater Brothers Market. The shelves radiate colors not seen for days while on the trail—innumerable fine hues, indescribable in colorless words. The fruits and vegetables seem to glow with an inner light. Everything looks so good that I am filled with indecision. Although there are numerous shoppers, it is oddly quiet. Conversations are muted and indistinct, as though heard through ears stuffed with cotton. I feel as though I am making rapid changes in altitude and frequently try to clear my ears. I wind up buying an avocado, a tomato, a sweet onion, some good Swiss cheese, and sour French bread. These I have to carry for three more hours while I locate socks, get a haircut and beard trim, and buy those shower sandals, whose two-inch-thick soles were apparently designed by some platform-shoe-wearing 70s disco singer. Waiting out the final hour for the bus in a small pizza parlor, I laboriously, to the amusement of the pizza workers, who no doubt nudge each other, wink, and point to their heads when I am not looking, pare at least an inch of sole from the sandals with my tiny knife blade. Gotta keep that pack light!

Back in the motel at last, I take another shower and make luscious sandwiches. I turn the TV on but leave the volume down. It is far more entertaining to make up the conversations rather than listen to them. Dinner at Moreno's is another Alien Affair, and at the nearby bar sit clones from Idyllwild telling similar tales of woe in the same voices of outrage and sorrow. That night I sleep restlessly on a bed too soft, in a room whose walls loom menacingly over me in my dreams.

———⟶⟩●⟨———

"There is no time for hesitating, pain is here, and pain is waiting, primed to do its educating..." Back at JoAn's in Idyllwild the music tinkles through the glasses and escapes an open window. Clearly the people around me are still primed for learning. In the far corner the television is on, but mercifully the volume isn't. On the screen the host is interacting with several people who suddenly jump up and start hitting each other. Large goons appear from off-camera to make certain no one suffers grievous injury. The camera pans the audience, showing a crowd of elated voyeurs, all signs of people trying to put together a meaningful life by watching television shows featuring those who apparently have no life at all, and certainly no dignity. Ah well ...if there is solace to be found in knowing that there are those whose lives are more pathetic than our own, so be it. For surely we all deserve better than we get, deserve a fairy tale in a world sadly bereft of happily-ever-afters.

———⟶⟩●⟨———

From Idyllwild I will hike more than twenty-eight miles in a long, long day, my greatest distance in a single day—ever. It takes as much light as there is on that May day, from not long after sunrise until well after dark, fourteen grueling hours, to drop back into the desert. As it gets darker and darker I can no longer see the trail distinctly. Visions of running right over the top of a rattlesnake float through my mind. Just a mile or so before the water fountain at Snow Canyon Road, the trail comes around the front of a ridge. I can see civilization, the houses and lights of the little Snow Creek community, just below. I figure if a rattlesnake does get me, I can make it there. So ...on I charge.

Finally, in near darkness, I come to the water fountain. After drinking and drinking, I unroll my gear and plop down in what I hope is an inconspicuous place only yards from the fountain and its miraculous water. Camping here is illegal and I am paranoid, but too exhausted to care. The next day is Saturday and I must retrieve my food parcel from the Cabazon Post Office. If it is open at all, certainly it will close early, and so

I'm on the trail by five AM, sore from the day before, and walk the four miles to the frontage road near Interstate 10. Paradoxically, my early start has almost made certain that I will not get a ride into town, and so I don't. I walk another very long four and a half miles into Cabazon, the entire distance into a twenty-knot wind. I arrive tired and wind-dazed around nine AM and find the post office will not be open until ten o'clock.

The town of Cabazon, a step up from Warner Springs (though not a huge one), is a bit more than two hundred miles into the trail. It lies but a little east of the Los Angeles Basin, that foul lair of the great beast of the Hobbit, fearsome Smaug, on the northernmost extension of the Colorado Desert. It is a quarter of an hour west of the golf course-clad kingdom of Palm Springs. In the shadow of the ten thousand foot scarp of Mount San Jacinto, Cabazon sits quietly astride the San Andreas Fault like a rider astride a bull in those few still moments before the gate flies open and hell is loosed. It's nearly lost in the sand and chaparral, the failed housing developments, the cacophony of ceaseless traffic on the Interstate and the myriad glinting blades of wind farm generators. Its main street, aptly named Main Street, is perhaps three blocks long with one cross street. Of a dozen or so buildings, only three—the post office, a bar, and a convenience store—show signs of habitation. I doubt if one in a hundred people flying down the eight-lane interstate that crowds close to Main Street notice the town, for on the north side of the freeway, strategically placed to divert one's attention, are huge concrete dinosaurs, standing hard in the lee of a mile-long factory outlet mall.

The two life-sized dinosaurs are Cabazon's claim to fame, if any such fame may be claimed. Sitting along a short stretch of the old and once famous Route 66, next to the Wheel Inn, and made famous by Pee Wee Herman and his Big Adventure, is an Apatosaurus, once known as Brontosaurus, and a Tyrannosaurus rex. Although they lived perhaps as much as seventy million years apart, one a plant-eater and the other a fearsome carnivore, they reside here in quiet harmony. One Claude Bell, who ran the restaurant for many years, constructed them. Dinny, the Apatosaurus, took eleven years to build. The T-rex was nearing completion when Claude died in 1989. He had envisioned other denizens of his concrete menagerie, all projects left undone by his demise.

Garishly-painted and clashing outrageously with their desert surroundings, the stores with their dinosaur shoppers, look so out of place that the Alien feeling crashes over me like a tsunami, leaving me curiously afloat in a sea of incongruity.

On the corner of Main and the only cross street in town, both sitting and standing, are close to a dozen louche characters, including a couple of women, unselfconsciously drinking liquor out of paper bags at nine in the morning and watching my every move. If these are not the people Jack London called "The People of the Abyss, who eke out an wretched existence on the garbage dumps of civilization," they certainly have caught the occasional whiff of garbage, as I have a few times in my life.

I go into the convenience store and come out with two bottles of V8; they watch. I make a couple of calls from the corner pay phone; they discuss. A pick-up truck stops in front of the bar. Unlocking the door, the driver goes inside only to emerge moments later. He introduces himself as Don, owner of the Village Pub, and asks me if I am a PCT Hiker. Discovering I am, he produces a business card on which he writes "good for one free drink." I ask him what time the bar opens. He allows that it will open at eleven, only a couple of hours from now, leaving just time for breakfast and sorting through my food parcel.

The corner-dwellers watch and discuss. It reminds me of Mack and The Boys from John Steinbeck's *Cannery Row*, those mostly-idle empty-lot-dwelling boys who note, with both passion and disinterest at the same time, the passing of every soul. They spend long hours discussing conversations they cannot hear and the lives of people they do not know, often with sagacity and insight that seem inconsistent with their station in life. I imagine the conversation at the corner.

"Look at that old man with a white pack!!"

"Who do you think he is?"

"He looks like a loony to me!"

"His hat is covered with aluminum foil."

"It's to keep the CIA from reading his thoughts!"

"He is a loony!!"

"Where do you suppose he comes from?"

"Maybe he's still fighting the war, be careful!!"

"Look, he's making a phone call!"

"What's that he's drinking?"

"Look, Don is giving him something!"

"It's money, he's giving him money!!"

"He doesn't give us money!!"

"No... it can't be money!!!!"

As I head for the post office I picture them making up detailed stories concerning my life and times, stories most likely more exciting than I could boast. Coming back with my food package, I say hello to them and stop briefly for a chat. They are flabbergasted that someone would choose to walk so far, for fun. This is a detail of which I have had to remind myself more than once since Campo. The hat reflects the heat from the sun. No, it was not money that Don gave to me; it was a card for one free drink. One tells me there was another hiker here just minutes ago. From the description I know that Ian-The-Brit must be nearby. I say good-by and head out for breakfast. Later I learn that Ian, who, although at daybreak was a good three hours behind me, was once again smiled upon by the Hitch-hiking Gods and arrived in town before I did! I silently curse him—again—as I will the several times I suffer grievous injustice in this dueling hitchhiker saga...me standing ride-less for hours and him cheerfully accepting rides within minutes of making that same road. Like ships on the ocean, we pass through our private fogs without seeing each other.

Carrying my parcel I walk the half-mile across the freeway to the Wheel Inn, dinosaur central. Under the smile of old T-rex I order bacon and eggs and pancakes and two glasses of orange juice. After breakfast I go out and sit next to the trash dumpster at the gas station sorting through my parcel. I wonder why much of its contents look far less edible than it did when I mailed it weeks ago. I choose enough to get me through the two and a half days to Big Bear and regretfully toss the rest into the dumpster, not knowing that I could have put it into the hiker box at the Pink Motel later on in the day... primarily because I didn't know the Pink Motel even existed.

Eventually I arrive back at the Village Pub for my free drink. It turns out they have only beer, which is fine. I have one, and Tina, the manager, promptly refills my glass. I feel the need to get on down the road, since, though I have a nagging suspicion, I don't know how long it will take to get a ride—if I get a ride. Clouds have started to cover Mt. San Jacinto, and rain is in the air.

Outside the wind has picked up to a steady thirty knots. Don arrives back, and he and Tina discuss the disastrous events of the night before. It seems as though they hire some of the Cabazon Boys to clean each night. They pay them with minimum wages and free beers. Last night they arrived early and took their beers before work. Unfortunately and probably neither for the first nor last time, they became garrulous and got into a fistfight with some of the customers. Don and Tina discuss whether to fire the Boys or not. Don allows that as employees, they need to be held to a higher standard and should be fired. Tina pushes for continued employment but no free beers for two weeks. Ultimately she wins out and Don leaves for parts unknown. The whole scene is so Steinbeckesque that goose bumps stand up on my arms and I glance behind me, expecting to see his smiling ghost at my shoulder.

I start to pay for the second beer and she says, "You get one hour of free drinks." I look at the card and sure enough it says, "On the House, 1 hour free drinking." Good old Don. Unfortunately (or fortunately, more likely) I feel the need to be on the trail. Tina gives me a couple of cans of V8 and a small bottle of water for my pack. She scratches out the "1 hour drinking" on the card and writes, "Good for 5 drinks." "In case you come back," she says. I thank her and head for the on-ramp.

An hour later, having taken refuge a couple times behind some inadequately dense chaparral to take scanty protection from a few minutes of driving rain here and there, I walk back to the bar. No one has heeded my needs or my "PCT Hiker, To Trail Please" sign. So close to Palm Springs it is mostly tourist traffic, and the occupants of the cars stare at the outlandish looking hitchhiker and at the same time try to avoid eye contact. One car with two younger men actually comes right at me before honking, extending the universal middle finger greeting and veering up the on-ramp. I laugh and wave at them.

Inside the cool dark lair, I order one of my five remaining freebies and listen to Tina argue with her chunky twelve-year-old daughter who apparently has been sleeping in the car this whole morning. She is waiting for someone, an aunt I think, to pick her up for a trip to the movies. She's bored so she punishes everyone by repeatedly walking into the bar, a place she cannot legally be, just to make her mother yell at her and send her back out. In a while her ride arrives and much to the relief of all she disappears. Now able to think about other things, Tina takes pity on me and talks one of the customers into driving me back to the trail.[2] I pass under the interstate amid piles of trash, abandoned furniture and walls coated with gang-sprayed slogans. Before long the roar of the traffic is muted and begins to sound like rushing water; the tribulations of civilization likewise fade. Still taking refuge from the rain under my ground sheet a time or two, I head up the trail.

———⟫●⟪———

But three days earlier, I'm still in JoAn's in Idyllwild. The locals are still discussing Life, the Universe and Everything, when a woman arrives. Clearly known to the group she is rough in dress and speech and tells a story of having just this day completed a forced move. She's certain some of the so-called friends who helped her move have ripped her off, of something, she knows not what. It's just another day in the life.

---

2 Two years later, I will return to Don's bearing my "Good for five free drinks" chit, only to discover that the Village Pub has burned down and nothing remains but blackened ground and a memory.

The emotions broadcast by the radio, television and these late afternoon denizens, loneliness, pain, anger, frustration, outrage, despair, fear, boredom, becoming as palpable as waves breaking on some alien shore, wash over and through me. Although I am usually well protected by a durable windbreaker of prickly cynicism, days ago I have mailed it home, along with my rain gear, as unnecessary weight. I burst quietly into tears and turn quickly away, embarrassed and afraid someone will notice.

I love all of these people whom I have never met and will never see again. I love them for their ridiculous ideas and their outrageous notions that life owes them something, and their casual attitudes toward the sometimes seemingly insurmountable odds of existence, and for their unsupportable faith that free will is alive and well in the Universe, and for their futile attempts to create a life, somehow noble and worthwhile, from the shards of an existence slowly ground finer and finer by the mill of time, and for their unalloyed yet unfounded optimism that it has to get better...doesn't it?

Earlier in the afternoon several of us hikers made a trip from the motel to the local lumberyard. We had heard that they sell Tyvek[3] by the foot there and a couple of hikers, liking the feel and weight of my ground sheet, allowed as how they wanted one. Four of us walked the few blocks. Only two wanted the material so one of the hikers, who is my age plus a bit, and I stood in the shade and made idle conversation. I asked him if he was married and he replied with evident sadness in his voice that he had never been. Wistfully echoing the Talmud, he added that a man is not complete until he has married and had children. I reminded him of the saying of the poet William Butler Yeats: "I have known more men destroyed by the desire to have wife and child and to keep them in comfort than I have seen destroyed by drink and harlots." We both laughed but I could tell he remained unconvinced. I see the same looks of yearning, of life-unfulfilled, in the faces of these denizens of JoAn's that I saw on his.

Seemingly adrift in a sea of chaos, their words bespeak a bleaker side of humanity, but in my vulnerable state I see all that is noble in mankind. Charles Dickens said, "Who can tell how scenes of peace and quietude sink into minds of painworn dwellers in close and noisy places and carry their own freshness, deep into their jaded hearts." And so it is...who can tell? I wish I could drag them with me across snowy Fuller Ridge and down into the desert tomorrow, to see the multiple blues of the sky; the fours and fives and sixes of petaled flowers so dear to Nature; the cracks and angles of banded and crystalline rocks; the scaly back of

---

3 An almost waterproof material used as a vapor barrier in home construction.

rattlesnake or horned toad, nearly invisible in patterned sand; to hear the timbre and cadence of a single three-noted Mountain Chickadee that seems to follow you untold miles across the lonely skyline; or smell the blooming agave, as if knowing it blooms but once then dies, smells all the sweeter.

That night I sleep in a real bed at the Tahquitz Inn. This is a marvelous place that caters to PCT hikers and offers deals on rooms, rides to and from the trailhead and to town, space to cook meals, and in general hang out. After a huge, boisterous barbeque with a dozen hikers and a sit and chat in the hot tub, I make my way to bed. Falling asleep at last, I have incredible, kaleidoscopic, fantastic, color-filled dreams, dreams of heroic undertakings, both successful and unsuccessful, dreams of flying alone through the infinite blue, of walking and walking...and walking.

⟶►●◄⟵

I hear a song, complete with music and lyrics, and awaken with a start. It is just before two in the morning. Getting up for a drink of water, stumbling through the darkened motel room, I remember a bit of the dream-song and sleepily make a couple of notes. In the morning, my notebook says,

> Tell me again I'm not alone on this ocean.
> Tell me it's someone else, not me.
> Tell me again how this can happen,
> If not the low purpose of Heaven, working free.

I stare at the words for a moment; these are the words of all of us, alone in a crowd, fighting the inexorable tide of time and circumstance, still striving, like Papillion the Frenchman who escaped from Devil's Island, alone on the ocean on his raft of coconuts, sustained only by the power of his will, shouting to the sky, "It's me...I'm still here, you bastards...I'm still here!!!"

But I see things differently in the first, bright light of morning. The line between ignorance and stupidity, exuberance and arrogance, between integrity and intransigence, and pride and hubris, between courage and stubbornness, and bravery and bravado, between acceptance and resignation are sharp this morning, not blurred and indistinct as they were yesterday. What then seemed fraught with nobility and meaning and insight, today seems more than a little corny, plebian thoughts rendered noble by endorphins and alcohol and sensory overload. Suddenly the pleasures of town seem thin and sere. I put the notebook away and hastily load my pack. I've been in town long enough.

But getting out of a resupply town like Idyllwild is often more difficult than getting in. What with breakfast to be had...and lunch, it takes the better part of the day. Finally, late in the afternoon, getting a ride back to the trailhead, I shoulder my pack and head up the trail. The next morning finds me headed out from Saddle Junction. I am walking again and thankful to be back on the trail, because here life is so marvelously simple. I have re-entered the true stores named Sacred Spaces and Out There that I so assiduously avoided in town, and what I have found is much to my liking. It's just me and the trail, one step at a time. If the human spirit is truly to thrive, it is here in these light-filled, wild places that the miracle will occur, not in the dark recesses of the minds and bars of the Idyllwilds of this land.

Thoughts of town recede like balloons drifting away into the morning sky. By noon I have covered more than a dozen miles. Tomorrow I have to make that rendezvous with the Cabazon Post Office, still more than twenty-five miles distant. The trail stretches out invitingly before me. Unconsciously, my speed increases.

TWICE ABOVE THE PINK MOTEL

Outside, the wind is howling across the San Gorgonio Pass and through the eaves of the Pink Motel. Yesterday I didn't know this place existed. Today, I am sitting comfortably at the kitchen table, cold beer in hand, and enjoying the view out across the desert to the ten thousand foot precipice that is Mount San Jacinto. Clouds scud across its sheer face—now covering it in fleecy gray, now exposing it so that its wet granite glows in the afternoon sunlight. The highest slopes are speckled white, where snow has just been dusted.

Down a mile across the desert crawls Interstate 10—a multi-lane concrete behemoth that in the 1960s and '70s, mostly devoured the old romantic Route 66—known alternately as The Main Street of America, The Will Rogers Highway, or The Mother Road—running from the city of Santa Monica, on the Pacific Ocean, through the deserts of the southwest to Oklahoma City, St. Louis and then north to Chicago. America's first interstate highway, it was 2,448 miles long, just short of the length of the PCT, and, like the PCT, it was often re-routed and realigned. John Steinbeck, in *The Grapes of Wrath*, called it the Road of Escape, where "refugees from dust and shrinking land...from the twisting winds that howl up out of Texas, from the floods that bring no richness to the land and steal what little is there" would find their way towards the Promised Land of California...they thought. Tom Joad and his family, along with nearly two hundred thousand real migrants (some of my ancestors among them), driven from their land by the Depression and drought, desperately piled their hopes and dreams, along with their families and what few possessions they could manage, into dilapidated cars with paper thin tires, and made their way along its checkered concrete surface ...across the very slopes below me.

But now, like fiery pismires with news of some distant picnic, the lines of traffic stream back and forth, soundlessly from this distance. Normally, I suspect, it would be audible from here, a droning sound akin to rushing water, or a tamboura, resonating with the sound of Om. "Many an irksome noise, so a long way off, is heard as music," is the way Thoreau put it, but the wind is howling across the San Gorgonio gap and rattling through the windows and eaves, and that is the music I hear.

It's a Saturday afternoon on this, my seventeenth day on the trail. Two days ago I was in Idyllwild. On the morning of the second day there, feeling the need to be walking once again, I hastened to depart. What has transpired since then? Things being what they are, what with the siren-song of restaurants and pubs ringing in my ears, it was well into the afternoon before I tore myself away. Ian and I caught a ride to Humber Park and the Devil's Slide Trail. We were on the trail and made the two and a half miles from Humber Park up to Saddle Junction well before dark. At the top we met Swiss Miss and Lutzia. They were waiting for Singing Steve, who forgot his hat in the pizza parlor back in town. He had hiked down to get it...and a pizza as well! Camping is purportedly not allowed at the saddle, so we left them and pushed back into the trees a quarter of a mile to find a stealth site for the night.

Next morning, back at the trail we found Swiss and Lutzia and Steve having cold pizza for breakfast. They offered some; I politely declined. It's me for the trail, and I needs must burn up the miles. Tomorrow would be Saturday and I had to get to the Cabazon Post Office, or I would be stuck in town until Monday morning. At least that's what I thought. With only two and a half days from Cabazon to Big Bear, it would not be unthinkable, really not even difficult, to procure adequate stores in town to make the journey. But this early into the trail, at only my third mail drop, I am still shackled by my preconceived notions of what it will take to make the long journey north.

I figured to make the 28.2 miles to the fountain at Snow Creek, and then into town early the next morning. The fact that I had never hiked that many miles in a day, or even near to that many, was worrisome. Nonetheless, off I went. The trail followed the saddle due north, climbing nearly a thousand feet in less than two miles to where it hit San Jacinto's south descending ridge, then turned due west to traverse, ultimately, nearly 180° around the mountain, hitting at last the dreaded northwest ridge.

That venerable traveler, Juan Bautista de Anza, who passed through the area in 1774, purportedly named Mt. San Jacinto, although the name did not appear in writing until much later. Before him, the indigenous people called it Ayakaitch, meaning *smooth cliffs*. But Anza named it for Saint Hyacinth, on whose day he arrived. Saint Hyacinth was a saint that some say left footprints on the Dnieper River, over which he walked carrying a statue of the Virgin Mary, as the Mongols sacked Kiev in 1240. The mountain beneath my feet was part of an enormous Spanish land grant from the 1820s, Rancho San Jacinto.

Mt. San Jacinto itself is a huge massif more than a mile square in size and spawns six other named peaks on the five ridges that descend from its summit. On the north side of the mountain, these form four immense canyons that comprise the watershed for Snow Canyon, whose water fountain was my goal on that day.

Rounding west of San Jacinto through piney slopes, I reached the North Fork of the San Jacinto River. At the "river," which was just a small burbling stream, I camelled up[1] and filled all of my water containers. This was the last water for twenty-two miles, until the fountain at Snow Creek. Within a couple of miles, I hit the torturous two-mile section of trail that wound in and out of rocky towers and over long patches of icy snow, the ill-reputed Fuller Ridge.

It was only ten in the morning and the snow still relatively solid. Although the going was treacherous, it was not terribly difficult. Only care was demanded. Numbers of hikers had already been through, so footprints, many of them postholes, marked the path. I use hiking poles, which served me well here. The only problem was, that thinking more ultralight than practical, I had left off the basket ends to save weight! Now, in the first snow, I found the poles constantly plunging through the crust and burying themselves a foot or more into the snow below. This caused me to slip, and on more than one occasion, take a slide on the icy crust. Fortunately, no damage either to the poles or to myself occurred. It was an error that I would remedy by having the baskets mailed to Wrightwood, two weeks up the trail.

Ian had forged on ahead here, and I finally caught up with him twelve miles into the day, at Fuller Ridge Trailhead Remote Campsite. At last, making it through the snow and ice, the trail dropped a thousand feet to the very end of Fuller Ridge, serviced by Black Mountain Road. It was not yet twelve o'clock. We took a lunch break in the pine-coated campground, but I was anxious to move on, for 16.2 miles remained to be traveled that day.

The trail went in and out of the trees, crossed the road, and began the trip down...and down...and DOWN. The view, nearly 7,000 feet down into the wind-swept pass of San Gorgonio, was fantastic. Mt. San Gorgonio, the highest peak south of the Sierra, loomed on the horizon more than fifteen miles distant. Its summit, the high point on the Ten Thousand Foot Ridge, was covered with snow and shone whitely in the afternoon sun. I promised myself to come back here one day—by car of course.

The next eight hours went by in something of a blur. The most memorable experience would wind up being a near disastrous encounter with a sizeable rattlesnake. During the course of the afternoon, I began to pull far ahead of Ian. He was carrying food to get him to Big Bear, so he felt no great need to race headlong down the mountain. In the late afternoon, charging around a bend in the trail, I was confronted by a coiled

---

1 A term describing the drinking of vast amounts of water in a relatively short period of time in the often futile attempt to stave off dehydration.

and furiously rattling snake no more than three feet ahead. Backpedaling frantically, I calmed myself and tossed a couple of rocks in his direction. No luck. He wasn't budging. Finally, I extended one of my hiking poles to its maximum length, a length that seemed frightfully inadequate, and managed, after a couple of tense tries, to give the recalcitrant reptile a relatively gentle flying lesson down the hillside.

Striding on, I now saw ropy coils of reptile in every shadow and around every curve…in my mind. I actually made the acquaintance of four more rattlesnakes in the next several miles, though all were well off the trail, thus presenting no serious threat.

Ultimately the trail jiggled and twisted its way down to a tremendous, long switchback just above Snow Creek. Here I found Robin and Marcus spread out in regal picnic. They had come upon the only open, sandy, level spot on this entire boulder strewn section of the trail, and there they were camped. It was nearing dark and the offer of a chocolate covered blueberry nearly halted me in mid-stride. I had been out of water for a couple of hours, but Snow Creek was just below. I couldn't afford to stop then, so I thanked them and moved on.

At long last I stumbled exhaustedly into the flat area of Snow Canyon and came upon the most beautiful sight imaginable: a three foot tall concrete monument, whose sight thrilled me as would no pyramid nor sphinx to a desert traveler—a drinking fountain that pours out unlimited quantities of icy water. Snow Canyon is not only a water source for Palm Springs, it is alleged to be a game refuge, so camping is not allowed. But it was dark, and I could go no farther. Feeling more than a little paranoid, I unpacked my ground pad and sleeping bag. Tomorrow I needed to get into town early in case the post office was not open all day, so I set my alarm for four AM and fell—nay, plummeted—into a deep sleep.

The next morning found me watered up and on the trail in the dark. The eastern horizon brightened rapidly as I headed for civilization. Feeling sore and stiff, I hobbled a good long while until my muscles grudgingly warmed up. In about three and a half miles, the trail reached the tunnel under the I-10 freeway, and I was faced with a decision. I climbed up out of the creek to Railroad Avenue, which runs along the south side of the interstate. And here were the choices to be made. The first was to hitchhike west along Railroad Avenue the four and a half miles to Cabazon. The second choice was to head east a little to the Verbenia overpass of I-10 and attempt to hitch down and onto the freeway and into town from there.

At the beginning of the hike, on my way to the border, I drove through the little town of West Palm Springs Village, and it appeared more ghost town than not. The area was full of once-paved roads, outlining and partitioning what was meant to have been a community. The roads were in need of repair and few, very few, of them boasted houses. (I know you're asking, since I drove through this area, why don't I know what hours the post office is open, or, for that matter, why didn't I call from Idyllwild? My answer…uh…I don't know.) And so I chose Railroad Avenue as the route most likely to get me a ride. Wrong!!

At nine o'clock, I stumbled into Cabazon. In the four and a half miles, exactly three cars went by me towards town, and zero stopped. I guessed all those wind generators were doing their job, for the wind had been blowing hard and steady, right into my face. My adventures in Cabazon have been previously chronicled, so I'll not repeat them here. By the time I got back to the interstate underpass, it was nearly two o'clock. Rain had squalled several times already, and so with food retrieved from the post office, I hurried north. It hit twice more in the next mile, so I pulled out my Tyvek ground cloth, wrapped it around me, and hunkered down to garner what scant protection a feathery creosote bush had to offer. At last, I came to a 4"x4" post bearing a PCT emblem, the usual marker out here in the desert. Attached to it, enclosed in plastic, was a notice that the Pink Motel was just ahead. I wondered what that was all about. As I moved north, I began to see a hillside above, covered with something…everything. Eventually there was a gate. Stepping through, on the other side was a short piece of telephone pole stuck into the ground, sporting a sign that said *Welcom [sic] PCT Hikers*. In another forty yards was a chain link fence. There was a box, which looked like PCT register, and another sign that said, *No Trespassing*. It proclaimed The Pink Motel.

Torn over the conflicting signs of *Welcome* and *No Trespassing*, I stood for a minute or two in indecision, then headed on up towards the house. This place was fantastic. It is one of those not-so-rare desert curiosities, the…I don't know what to call it. In front of the fence was a wrecked BMW automobile, doors open. Next to it a motor boat, sans motor, and two huge commercial air conditioning units. Inside the fence lay a phantasmagoria. The driveway led up and around the left side of the hill, perhaps two hundred yards to the house. This road was lined with a collection of VW Bugs, perhaps eight or nine, and kitchen appliances, including a number of stoves, washing machines, driers, and water heaters. There were automobiles, too numerous to count. A large floating gold dredge sat next to perhaps two hundred bags of concrete stacked in a neat cube. There were pipes, both metal and plastic, of all sizes and lengths; great lengths of steel cable; rows of tires and piles of hubcaps, and not a few doors and hoods. There were delivery trucks and construction job shacks, a number of trailers, more commercial air conditioning units, and a couple of hot tubs. Great piles of chain link fence gates and poles lay next to a pile of truck parts. And there were more boats. The house itself was surrounded by at least six vehicles.

Working my way through the labyrinth, at last I approached the house. Looking for a door, I went around back. I saw water barrels piled around near the door. As I went up the steps, the door opened a crack, and a hand bearing a frosty beer emerged, followed by the smiling face of Ian-The-Brit. I don't know why I insist on calling him that since it's been twenty years or more since he left England. He lives in upstate New York. I guess Ian-The-Brit just rolls off the tongue more pleasantly than Ian-The-New-Yorker. And at any rate, he still wears his accent and has the cheery disposition and droll wit that is a British hallmark, but that one hardly expects of a New Yorker. And to all my New York friends, I mean that in the nicest possible way.

And so here I am sitting in the Pink Motel, which is in fact pink. It is an old stucco building with a rock chimney on its eastern wall. Along the south, facing Mt. San Jacinto, is a wooden awning. Attached to its west wall are parts of two mobile homes. The two mobile home parts make up a kitchen and living room, replete with couches, sink (no running water), wood burning and propane kitchen stoves, refrigerator (also propane powered), kitchen table, and several chairs. The Pink portion of the motel consists of a number of couches, a table, a hiker's sign-in book, and a library.

Out the kitchen window, the face of Mt. San Jacinto presents a formidable appearance. Ice cold beer in hand, I sit amidst the clutter of the kitchen table and watch clouds scud across its ten thousand foot north face—one of the grandest fault scarps in existence.

In 1891 C. Hart Merriam proposed his famous Life Zones: the Lower Sonoran, Upper Sonoran, Transition, Canadian, Hudsonian, and Boreal. He did his research in the San Francisco Mountains of Arizona, and thus failed to take into account the far greater complexity that life shows in other places, particularly California, which boasts greater diversity than perhaps anywhere else in the United States, if not the world. Today his zones have been modernized, that is to say made more complex, and are called *plant communities*. The numbers of these communities vary somewhat, from one expert to another, but at least sixteen of the twenty-nine listed by Munz and Keck, the definitive California flora, are traveled through on the PCT and are listed in the Guidebook.

Merriam should have traveled here, for I am looking out the window at perhaps the most stirring illustration of his thesis in existence. Across the broad flat sweep of San Gorgonio Pass, the north face of Mt. San Jacinto rises more than 9,500 feet, from Snow Creek to the summit, in just 4.5 miles. Its eastern slope, rising above Palm Springs, is even steeper, rising 8,000 vertical feet in only three linear miles. It is said that traveling a thousand feet upward is roughly the same as traveling 600 miles north, in terms of biotic communities. Within this three miles one passes through every life zone, ecologically the same thing as making a nearly 5,000-mile journey to the north.

Ian and I while away the afternoon. There is one other hiker here, whose name may have been Jake. I am here for more than two hours before he wanders in. He has been sleeping next door in the pink portion of the motel. Four days ago, coming into Warner Springs and exhibiting some symptoms of hypothermia, he elected to get a ride here and await the arrival of his travel companions. He tells his story, makes something to drink, and wanders back to the couch on which he has been potato-ing these past days.

Late in the afternoon, Don Middleton, owner, proprietor and trail angel extraordinaire, drives up. He is checking the stores, replenishing the beer and soft drinks, and can't stay long. We chat briefly. I ask him about the gold dredge, since I live in California gold country, have done some small bit of gold hunting , and felt the thrill of the flash in the pan. He flashes a ring adorned with a an ounce-sized, lumpy nugget and tells how he tows his dredge up to Alaska every year to search for gold. I wish he had time to stay, since I would love to hear more of his story, but it's hello and goodbye and off in a cloud of dust.[2]

The day is ending and the last light flashes across the rocky towers of San Jacinto. The clouds of the afternoon have disappeared, but the wind, if anything, is stronger. We head over to the house. Choosing one of the couches, I crawl into my bag only to be entertained for hours, and thus kept from sleep, by the sounds of multiple mice racing about for reasons, no doubt, perfectly sensible to them. I would much prefer to be sleeping outside, and had considered it earlier, but I doubt I could set up my tent in the Force 7 winds racing across the sands. Ultimately sleep claims me, and with it come dreams of Mouse Olympics, replete with cheering crowds and tiny gold medals shining in the dark. The gleam of gold fades and turns into a flashlight. Jake is wandering about. I fall back to sleep, only to awaken as customary, at five AM. I try to ignore my uninvited wake-up

2 In 2004, Don Middleton will announce that the Pink Motel is no more. The property, and its myriad treasures, have been sold.

call, but an old man's bladder being what it is, old, defies ignore-ance. Duty called and answered, I try to go back to sleep and manage to pretend for another hour or so.

After a leisurely breakfast, including a cup of coffee, a rare treat on the trail, Ian and I are walking by seven o'clock, a relatively late start. The trail heads north, then east, crossing a couple of roads and finally winds north up barren Gold Canyon. This truly is the desert and plant life is sparse. Walking through a windmill serenade, we reach the steep but low pass between Gold and Teutang Canyons. Descending and climbing a couple of more times, the trail, ten miles into the day, at last reaches Whitewater River.

Even though my thermometer reads 106° F, it feels deliciously cool sitting here soaking my feet in the rushing waters of the Whitewater River. Nearly fifteen miles to the south, peeking over a ridge, the snowy summit of Mt. San Jacinto dominates the skyline. Squinting in the harsh sunlight, I look around. The hills on both sides of the river are nearly devoid of vegetation. If I look carefully, I can see a few creosote bushes, their feathery, light gray-green foliage blending well into the gray-brown hillsides. Here and there a mesquite has managed to scrabble its way into the rocky soil. There seem to be more cacti than anything else, mostly beavertail and silvery cholla. Here in the riverbed, scraggly willow and a few junipers stand out as bright spots of green in an otherwise drab landscape.[3] Not that I am complaining, but this running stream of beautiful water looks totally out of place. On this 13th day of May, there is still plenty of water. Not only that, the fact that just downstream, less than two miles away, is the Whitewater Trout Farm, an endeavor that would seem to require water the year round, speaks of just that, year-round water. Here, where I am sitting, the river runs through several channels, each only a few feet wide, but the riverbed itself is more than 300 yards wide. A look at the map shows that it continues north and west at the same width for more than a mile and a half. Southward, with the exception of a narrows between cliffs, it runs at the same width for more than seven miles, emptying into the flats of San Gorgonio Pass. Two questions arise. The first: Just where does this water come from? Another glance at the map answers for that. The headwaters of the Whitewater River have their source on the southern and western slopes of Mt. San Gorgonio, at 11,502 feet tall, the tallest mountain in southern California, and several other nearby peaks. Mission Creek, toward which I am heading, finds its water from an area much lower in elevation and smaller

---

3 The following year much of this area will be scorched by a fire, started by a thru-hiker whose alcohol stove proved unmanageable in the winds that torture this land.

in size. The second thing is of course, the size of this riverbed. It is filled with a jumble of rounded boulders of granite, marble and other darker materials. In between the boulders, white sand viciously reflects back the sunlight. Clearly, at some other time, a lot water came down this way. It would have been quite a sight…water nearly a quarter of a mile across, pouring down from the mountains, tumbling boulders weighing hundreds of pounds as if they were ping pong balls. Of course there probably weren't too many people around to watch it, for these mountains were the site of the lowest latitude glaciation in the United States and all of this took place ten to twelve thousand years ago. Nonetheless, it is an eerie feeling to be placidly sitting in what was once a cataractous hell.

This stop is so pleasant it winds up taking two and a half hours out of the middle of the day, something I won't normally do. Finally, the moving sun reminds me that I'd better move on. There is no trail across the riverbed and so I lose my way briefly. Crossing where I can, I find my way to a small side canyon where the trail emerges and climbs above the river. More and more of San Jacinto becomes visible to the south. The trail reaches a saddle and drops down into the dry West Fork of Mission Creek, then climbs again to make its way to the hopefully wet East Fork. And it is. I meet up with Ian and we descend down to the dirt road. Following it north a short ways to where it ends, we decide to call it a day. Near a decently running stream, this short, seventeen-mile day comes pleasantly to an end.

The next day, day nineteen, turns out to be, far and away, the most difficult day on the Trail so far. In fact, it will turn out to be the most difficult day until, more than three hundred fifty miles up the trail, I cross the Tehachapi Mountains from Cottonwood Creek in the Mojave Desert to the town of Mojave in one long day. It's a combination of factors. The first is the heat, for the trail winds up through canyon walls that rise fully a thousand feet on either side and trap and reflect the stifling desert heat. The second, and more important, is the fact that the 18.8-mile day entails a climb of more than 5,400 feet, descending but 680 feet, to wind up at Coon Creek Jumpoff Group Camp. The jumpoffs are steep canyons that run down from the east-west ridge of mountains, forcing the PCT to wind its way north, then considerably west to eventually find its way to the top. To make matters confusing, the trail ascends the East Fork Mission Creek until it reaches the junction of the North and South Forks of the East Fork. I guess that alone is explanation enough of the tortured geography through which I am traveling. But most of all this has been a day of listening to the voices and wrestling with the demons, and they have won. This long, torturous, plodding day has proved a field day for a mind whose body, with other, far more serious concerns, has told it to "take a hike." For the first time, but not the last no doubt, I wish for a small radio. Perhaps in Big Bear.

Be that as it may, eventually Ian and I find ourselves on top of the ridge, near a dirt road at Mission Creek Trail Camp. While we are sitting in the shade, Chris walks up. He was last seen three days ago in Idyllwild. He is wearing naught but tight fitting, black spandex shorts. Ian asks him if that's what he normally wears back home in Washington State. He laughs and says the boys at home would "stump bust" him if they caught him so attired. He explains the term and we laugh, but decorum requires that I do not repeat his words. He passes on; we sit on. Then Frank from Alaska, also last seen in Idyllwild, plods in. We walk on together. A little over three miles later, he takes off to water up and spend the night at Hart Bar Creek, a half-mile off the trail. Ian and I continue on.

Another four miles brings me to Coon Creek Jumpoff Group Camp, where I plan to lodge for the evening. This picturesque site looks down on the desert community of Morongo Valley, more than 5,000 feet below, and is served with a well graded road from Hart Bar State Park, just a few miles to the west. Feeling like I am camping rather publicly, I move off a bit into the shelter of some trees, where I am not likely to get run over in the middle of the night, or discovered, for that matter. Call it paranoia if you will, but twenty years of martial arts training and ten years of firearms competition has caused me live comfortably in *condition yellow*, where the unexpected is always expected.

Perhaps a half hour behind me, Ian shows up. To my consternation, he sets his tent up forty yards away, right in the middle of an area that has clearly been used as a road. I say nothing. And wouldn't you know it, not long before dark a truck drives up some few hundred yards away, right at the jumpoff. We hear laughing and talking. Then gunfire erupts. Ian says goodnight, ducks into his tent, and with a zip, is safely inside. I am reminded of the old movie starring Charles Bronson, *Death Wish*. In it, he says to his son-in-law: "What do you call people, who, when faced with a condition of fear do nothing about it? They just run and hide." To which his son-in-law replies, "Civilized?" And I hope if Ian should ever chance to read this he will take no offense, for truly, I mean none. Knowing from afternoon conversations back in the Good Times Pub and Grill in Idyllwild that he is no lover of guns, I do not truly know if he was afraid, and in truth, he *is* far more civilized than am I. But, unwilling to ignore this potential problem, I put on my shoes and walk slowly through the trees towards the truck. There are three men with 22-caliber rifles, plinking and drinking. I hallo to them from a goodly distance. They reply in friendly fashion so I saunter on over, looking to yogi a beer. Ah, but no yogiing is necessary for they offer them up immediately upon discovering a madman in their midst, as anyone walking 2,650 miles of their own free will surely must be. I spend a quick half hour, consuming three beers and potato chips, and talking guns, before returning quietly to my tent. Shortly thereafter the truck drives off.

The next morning finds us up early and at it. Lowdown hiker trash that I am, I say nothing about the previous evening's beer to Ian. It is 19.3 miles to Highway 18 near Baldwin Lake and town is calling. The trail quickly ascends north across a ridge that separates Coon Creek from Cienega Seca Creek. Climbing six hundred feet over the ridge, the trail drops immediately back down and into the beginnings of civilization. We begin to cross trails and jeep tracks, and then an intersection of two large, well graded dirt roads. While we are standing there looking to see where the trail goes, a car drives up and stops. The driver, a lady, asks if we'd like a ride into Big Bear. We've come only three and a half miles, so as tempting as it is, we opt to walk the remaining sixteen miles to Highway 18.

Regretfully, we head up and across another ridge, where, near another dirt road rounding a shoulder, I am shocked into motionlessness by the sight of an African lion. Fortunately it is in a stout wire enclosure. There are other cages, and keeping it company I also see a bear and a white tiger. Lions and tigers and bears...oh shit! Hackneyed, I know, but it's more than a little surreal. The bear does what all bears do when caged. It paces back and forth and back and forth. It turns out that this is a place that houses and trains animals used in films by Hollywood, only a few hours away. Be that as it may, I hate to see animals caged, for I know it makes them crazy. My proof is the bear, which continues its ten or fifteen foot walk, back and forth, back and forth. I never go to zoos for it saddens me to see animals imprisoned for our entertainment, for no crime other than being animals. And yet I am also thankful for the stout fences, only yards away.

Eventually the trail drops down into Arrastre Creek and its Trail Camp. This is a secluded camp with picnic tables and piped water from Deer Springs. At just under ten miles into the day, it seems a fine place for lunch and a break. On one of the tables is a note, warning that just last night hikers here lost their food to a marauding bear. I sit on the table for a while, thinking this bear is certainly more lucky than his imprisoned brother, just six miles back. Hopefully by tonight I will be in Big Bear and doing a little marauding of my own.

After a half hour I am ready, but Ian allows as how he wants to take a longer break. So I hoist my pack and head out. The trail continues on down Arrastre Creek a bit, then climbs up and out of the trees and into the high desert of what, a few miles up the trail, will be Nelson Ridge. Here it touches the edges of the YMCA's Camp Oakes near the rifle range. There is no gunfire this morning, for on this May day, the camp is not yet opened for business.

The day drags on as the trail winds along the ridge top, often giving tantalizing views of civilization off to the west that appear no closer as I continue ever northward. Not many miles before the highway, I run into a dayhiker… almost literally. Lost in reverie, I notice him only when he begins talking to me. After a brief encounter, more of which is to be said later, I trudge wearily towards civilization. At long last Highway 18 comes into view. I stop short of the crossing, rest a while to re-accustom myself to things moving far more rapidly than my two mile-an-hour pace, retrieve my ground cloth, refold it to show the PCT Hiker Big Bear Please legend, and try to make myself look like someone whom it would be safe to pick up. Town awaits.

HIKING IN THE ZONE[1]

Ears hear and eyes see...what then does mind do?
(Zen saying)

"Did you know there are rare and endangered wildflowers around here?" With a feeling that must be familiar to a heavenly bunji jumper falling through endless blue on infinite rubber bands, to be jerked skyward at the last possible instant with both extreme violence and great tenderness at the same time, only in reverse, I lurch to a halt, stand erect, and look dazedly about, not certain where I am. I have been hiking in *The Zone.*

I use the term with hesitation, for commercial interests have worked hard to convince us all that wearing a certain essence, drinking the right alcoholic soda pop, driving the correct pick-up or SUV, or just putting on the right sport shoe will automatically transport one to this plane, but for lack of a better word, so be it. Nor do I know if other hikers experience that which I call *The Zone*, but I feel certain they must, in some form or another. I haven't really asked because I'm afraid that I may get the same look I got once from a half dozen men with pistols in their hands, when at a shooting range I exclaimed, "Hey, this is really Zen!"

When I first start walking my mind is full of thoughts. I think about how this or that muscle hurts, how heavy the pack is, how steep the hill is, how far is it to water, where will I have lunch, how many miles do I have to go today, and just where is that toilet paper—you know the stuff. After awhile, I get the rhythm and my mind starts to float; thoughts without order or relevance come and go...movies I've seen and would like to see again...books I've read and want to read again...poetry I've read or written...people I know...people on the trail...old friends that have come and gone...places I've been...songs play...scenes from movies roll...conversations are repeated...things I wish I had done or hadn't...or said...or didn't...matters philosophic...the Meaning of Life, both Monty Python's and my own. I compose letters that should have been mailed years ago, or perhaps tomorrow. I wrote *this*.

Eventually one has thought and delved and pried into every cranny of one's brain, laid bare the details of their life, reveled in every strength, and without ruth, exposed every weakness. I call it "wrestling with the demons." Because I tend to melancholia, once in a while I run some negative tape loops too. As Nietzsche said, "The worst enemy you can encounter will always be you, yourself; you lie in wait for yourself in

1 Previously published in the Pacific Crest Trail Communicator, May-June 2003, vol. 15, no. 2

caves and woods," and in deserts too. And so, the shattered marriage of a man—boy really—far too young and inexperienced and selfish to succeed upon a path partly chosen, partly forced upon him, and the subsequent difficulties of a single father adequately raising two young children, is a common enough theme. This was all nearly forty years ago and one would think I would have long since come to terms with it...and, of course, I have. But the mind has little sense of time and no sense of shame. Left to its own devices, it will dredge up events of yesterday and yesteryear, parading them, will ye, nil ye, through one's consciousness with equal cheerfulness—be they from times of joy or sorrow, strife or tranquility, drudgery or ease, poverty or plenty.

It's all just the usual tape loops and reruns of a mind without a task. There's no rhyme or reason or order or degree of importance—the loops just run. At last, they become as small balloons floating by. The thoughts are there and I notice them, but pay no attention. I notice the trail but it seems far away and unimportant. Sometimes those hiking behind me notice that at some point my pace changes appreciably and I tend to disappear down the trail. I'm in *The Zone*.

Perhaps my brain is just shutting down from hypoxia caused by the overuse of big muscles by an old man, but I think I have entered the meditative state that practitioners of Zen call *mushin*—no mind, *munin*—no thought. It lasts as long as it lasts, and some time later I awaken and time has passed, often hours. Although I have been walking for an extended period I am not tired. My heart, unmindful of the exertion, is beating regularly and without undue haste. I feel relaxed and at peace with the world.

But on this day, even though it is early, the shadows seem long and somehow foreboding. I stumble on a rock and hear something crash in the chaparral. I am afraid and cold at the same time and goose bumps pop up wherever they can. I wonder where I am. In moments those feelings fade, and although I feel at peace, I am aware of pain in my toes and shoulder.

"Did you know there are rare and endangered wildflowers around here?" My hiking poles clatter to the ground. Standing, totally unannounced, not ten feet in front of me is a hiker. His appearance is so incongruous with the gray-green chaparral that he appears to glow. Unlike me, who is dressed in a sweat stained T-shirt only partially hidden by my grime-jeweled, long-sleeved white shirt, he is dressed in green wool-looking forester's trousers, impeccably creased and held up by a thin leather belt with a shining brass buckle. His brown long-sleeved shirt is similarly creased and is partially covered by a vest. He wears a light brown fedora hat with a brown leather band and small brass buckle that matches his belt. Leather boots and a small daypack complete the ensemble. With finely chiseled features and a neatly trimmed beard, he looks like the smiling ghost of John Muir come to visit me, but only after jostling in line with the ghost of Hemingway for stylish safari clothing at the local Abercrombie and Fitch. I could not be more surprised if he had been a tall, silver-skinned alien with soft sad-luminous eyes standing next to a Greyhound bus saying, "I am here to take you to Heaven's Gate beyond Halley's Comet. Do you have your quarters ready?" My hands reach involuntarily towards my pockets. With effort, I stop them.

The last two days have been grueling. I have not seen or talked to a single person since earlier in the morning, so I struggle to find words. I am stunned by his sudden appearance, so I attempt to say that, but instead of stunned, I croak, "I'm stoned." The smile fades a bit and emotions subtly flicker quickly across his face like some claymation cartoon...surprise...alarm...fear? "This isn't starting out very well," I think. I try again. Perhaps a little joke would be in order. I clasp my hands together Buddhist fashion and, bowing a warrior's bow, low enough to show respect but keeping eye contact lest he attack, say, "Master, have you come to instruct me?" More flickering...yup, it's fear alright. This really isn't going well. Smile turning to a slightly perplexed frown, he says, "No, I'm just taking a day hike." I struggle and take a deep breath. My ears pop, and everything snaps into focus. I say, "I'm sorry, I was light years away and you startled me. Did you say something about flowers?"

The smile comes back. He explains to me that there are two species of rare and endangered wild flowers that grow only in this area and that I will see them along the trail for the next few miles. He tells me the names, scientific, so I ask for common names, which also sound like scientific names, so I promptly forget them. There are the white ones, which are a few inches high and grow in carpets, and the purple ones, a little taller, also growing in carpets—or is it the other way around?

He says, "I don't know if you know much about the natural history around here," and I become wary. He may be a Tengu, one of those crafty warrior-demons who inhabit the mountains. Their main joy in life is tricking and bedeviling passers-by. However, they may, if one appears worthy and it pleases them, choose to impart great knowledge or power. Using a technique that Carlos Casteñada learned from the Yaqui sorcerer, Don Juan, I turn my head a little to the side, squint slightly, and glance quickly and repeatedly at him out of the corner of my eyes. I expect to see his true form—red, bird-like face, long nose and wings—but no, the smiling, fashionably clad specter of John Muir remains unchanged. No matter, I know his true nature now. "I don't know if you know much about the natural history of this area." This is the test.

I begin to point to things. I'm standing on rocks of beautifully-banded gneiss, probably Pre-Cambrian (good thing I read the Guidebook). Finely-grained quartzites, formed from ancient sands, perhaps once lying on a sunny beach, also lie on the hillside. Nearby are clumps of mountain mahogany and juniper trees. Some species of paintbrush, one of my favorite sun-loving wildflowers, makes bright red exclamation points here and there on the otherwise drab slopes. I use the genus name for it, *Castilleja*. At my use of a scientific name, his smile broadens. I point out and name a half dozen other things before I run out. Becoming nervous, I add *Musca domestica*, the scientific name of the common housefly, which, unfortunately, I have been unable to forget since high school Biology. The smile turns quizzically up at its ends. I stop and smile back. Have I passed the test? So then, where is my Knowledge, my Power? I wait expectantly for what seems like an eternity, but is probably more on the order of two or three seconds, grab my poles from the ground, scrabble up the trail a hundred yards, sit down and lie back heavily.

He's still standing in the trail, staring back at me. I look around and see that I'm lying in a sea of small white flowers a few inches tall and purple flowers a little bit taller, all rare and endangered. Oh my God!!! With a move that would garner a passing thumbs-up from Baryshnikov, I leap to my feet and stare in horror at my pack-deformed silhouette outlined in flattened flowers. Feeling like Dickens' Oliver Twist, standing "alone in the midst of wickedness and guilt," I look from the ground back down the trail at the Tengu. He has started walking down the trail, away from me. I'm saved!

Woefully aware of every little pain, from toes jamming into the ends of my shoes, to that railroad spike someone is trying to drive under my left shoulder blade, I stumble the last four miles to the highway in just over two hours. Traveling west, then north around that last bump on Nelson Ridge before the trail hits the highway, I groan under my pack, which weighs well under twenty pounds at this point. It feels so heavy that I am certain that Sisyphus—that Greek hero, who for his sins was sentenced to an eternity of futile and hopeless labor by pushing an enormous rock to the top of a mountain, only to have it roll back to the bottom—being forced to shoulder it, would simply sit down in the trail and weep.

At long last the trail swings around the front of the knoll and starts its final descent. Not far away I can see the highway. A car comes around the corner. It's speed is terrifying; its noise hideous and discordant.

I involuntarily close my eyes, feeling certain it will crash right in front of me. It doesn't. Nor does the next, or the next. I decide to rest a minute to try to re-accustom myself to clamor of civilization. I remove my pack and sit down, my sundry pains dimming. Three days have elapsed since I left the Pink Motel, two days in the desert, plus this weird, surreal afternoon. It's all just a little too much.

After fifteen minutes I'm relaxed and anxious to make town. I shoulder my pack and quickly reach the highway. It's a Tuesday afternoon, just before three o'clock, and the traffic coming up the Johnston Grade from Lucerne Valley, down in the desert north of the San Bernardino Mountains and nearly a mile lower, is fairly steady, but no one stops. I wonder what's wrong with everybody! Why don't they pick me up?

As the cars pass me by, many of the drivers make a series of frantic gestures which include waving, pointing to the left or right, shrugging, and the universal symbol that something is shorter than it should be, finger and thumb parallel and an inch or so apart, other fingers in a fist...all signs that they're only going a short distance in some direction other than I want to go (no matter what that direction may be), and they hope I understand that they'd love to pick me up if circumstances were somehow different than they are. One gives me the thumbs-up, way-to-go gesture. I suppress the urge to give him a different single digit gesture which indicates a different way for him to go.

I have been holding out my folded-up Tyvek ground sheet. On one square I've written *PCT Hiker, Big Bear, Please!!!* in large, friendly letters. After nearly an hour and a half, I am just about ready to turn to the square that contains the words *To Town Or Else!!* and stand in the middle of the oncoming lane, when a pickup, delivering auto parts stops to give me a lift.

Only a bit more than four hours after the encounter with the Tengu, I am sitting at the bar in Moreno's, Big Bear City. I've finished two glasses of water, my first beer, and am halfway through the second. I begin to eye the dusty bottle of single-malt scotch, high on the shelf and well to the side. Behind the bar runs the usual mirror. I look at myself and in the gloom see a stranger. Staring back is a grizzle-bearded, scraggly-haired old man, eyes spinning like pinwheels—still throwing off the occasional colorful spark like a shorted out Christmas tree. My green tee shirt has jagged white lines of salt perspiration radiating out from the neck and armpits, a chromatogram of the last four days. On the bar is my white foreign-legion style hat over which I have taped mylar to reflect the sun, causing Ian-The-Brit to call me the "Silver Bullet," since, to his desert-crazed eyes, my head apparently looks like a can of beer.

Ignoring the eyes and dismissing the shirt, I say to myself, "No wonder I can't get a ride. I gotta get my hair cut tomorrow." I turn to Ian, sitting next to me, who although he was well behind me on the trail, got a ride before he could unshoulder his pack and cross the highway, thus arriving only minutes behind. I casually say, "So, Ian, did the guy on the trail tell you about the rare and endangered wildflowers?" "What guy?" he says, "I didn't see anybody." I look back to the mirror. "Bartender, I think I'll have a wee dram of that scotch now."

THE MOUNTAINS OF THE SAINTS

Solvitur Ambulando (walking solves all things)
(St.Augustine)

It's been a long, hot couple of days. From Big Bear three of us, Ian and I and another whose name I forget, and who was slack-packing the slightly less than nine miles from Baldwin Lake to Van Dusen Canyon Road and back to Big Bear, share expenses and take a taxi back to where the trail crosses Highway 18 at Baldwin Lake. After spending a frustrating hour and a half trying to get the same ride in two days before, I consider it the best five bucks I've spent on the trail yet.

Our packless companion soon leaves Ian and me in the dust, literally. The trail climbs west and up around the northern slopes of Gold Mountain and we're back into the San Bernardino Mountains, named after Saint Bernardine of Sienna, as was the Mission, the county, and its major city. This saint was a popular guy, who seems most noteworthy as a giver of good sermons, but also gave away his not inconsiderable fortune to the poor and worked in a hospital during Plague years.

Soon enough the trail climbs over the north ridge and heads south and west. I can see down into Holcomb Valley and Arrastre Flats. By the time we reach Caribou Creek in Van Dusen Canyon, it's break time. Watering up and resting a bit, we then travel west, circling above the valley to its head. Here we cross Holcomb Valley Road in Polique Canyon and stop for lunch.

Holcomb Valley was the site of the largest and richest gold strike in southern California. William F. Holcomb had come from Indiana to find gold in northern California. Since he got there rather late, that didn't work out, so he moved to Los Angeles. Hearing that gold had been found in the San Bernardino Mountains, he arrived at Starvation Flats in 1859. Today the parking lot of Stater Brothers Market, where I shopped just two days ago, covers the flats, which were so named because the pickings were pretty slim. Miners could scarcely brag about the $5.00 in gold they were taking out after a long hard day. Holcomb decided he could make more money by hunting bear to feed the miners. Grizzly bears were numerous in those days...hence the name Big Bear Valley. Climbing up Polique Canyon, at whose head Ian and I now rest, he crossed and climbed to the top of the ridge just above. From there, he spotted the valley which now carries his name, about two miles to the north.

The next day, wounding a large bear, he and his Indian companion tracked it into the valley, and by chance, passed a quartz outcropping in which the gold sparkled invitingly. The rush was on. By July 1860, there were five hundred prospectors in the valley. Within two months, that number doubled. Billy Holcomb joined forces with a friend and formed the Colwell Company, a group of ten men, who in the summer of 1860, with just picks and shovels, took out three pounds of gold each day. At today's prices, that would be more than $12,000.

Three towns sprang up in the valley, with Belleville being the largest. It was named after Belle Van Dusen, the first child born there, and daughter of Jed Van Dusen, a blacksmith and also the man who built the road to Holcomb Valley, next to which we are sitting. The town was the center of much entertainment, boasting stores, saloons, and houses of ill repute, whose repute in those days was not so ill. It was one of the most violent places to be found in all of California gold rush history. In two years, fifty murders occurred. There were dozens of hangings, and the *hanging tree*, a huge pine, reputedly still stands today. For a brief time Belleville, boasting a population of more than 10,000, was second only to Los Angeles in population in southern California, and would have become the county seat in 1860 had not an entire precinct of Holcomb Valley votes been mysteriously lost. As it was, the election was lost by only two votes.

There were two other gold rushes in the same area, but harsh winters with deep snow, lack of summer water, and the inability of the miners to find the Mother Lode caused all to disappear in only a few short years.

We begin to walk on, skirting Bertha Peak on its north side, then crossing over the south side of Bertha Ridge where Big Bear Lake comes into view, with the summit of Mt. San Gorgonio shining whitely above it.

As the afternoon wears on Ian falls behind, and near the end of the day, I arrive at Little Bear Springs Trail Camp, 19.6 miles from where I started. Both Frank and BJ, whom I haven't seen since Idyllwild six days ago, are here. I set up camp not too far from a small, quietly flowing creek. The piped water makes re-hydrating a pleasant task after the long, hot day. I keep expecting Ian but, as the late afternoon glides into evening, he fails to show. Finally, when it is nearly dark, he limps into camp. He is suffering from a knee problem. He quickly sets up camp and disappears into his tent.

This morning finds his problem none the better, so he announces he is going to stay here for the day. It occurs to me that I could hang out here today, and had I known how upsetting it would be to him to be left behind, no doubt I would have remained, but I feel an unaccountably strong urge to leave, and attributing it the fact that I was in Big Bear just this morning and took a zero day yesterday, I stow my gear and head out, fully expecting him to catch up somewhere along the trail, at Lake Silverwood or Wrightwood, or at Hiker Heaven in Agua Dulce perhaps. The Fates often dictate other than we expect, and so it will turn out that I will not see him again until Tuolumne Meadows, nearly 650 miles up the trail.

This day, the twenty-second of my journey, turns out to be long, hot and strange. Within minutes of leaving the trail camp, I come to Holcomb Creek and begin to follow it down and west. Within an hour or so, BJ catches up with me and we travel along the creek for some miles. He has an odd hiking style, his hiking poles flailing and scrabbling on the trail, but his speed is no laughing matter. In the long term I could not keep up with him, no matter what. After about six miles or so the trail descends down into the creek bed, crossing and re-crossing the creek several times. It crosses a final time to the south side, where a small, steep draw descends down into the creek and makes a sharp cut back towards the east and up. BJ begins to pull out in front and rapidly disappears. I wonder why the trail is headed this way, but don't bother to check the map. Within a few hundred yards I pull up. The trail doesn't seem to be cutting back as it should. I look up the draw, hoping to see the trail higher up, or better yet, BJ bustling along. No luck. I wait for perhaps five minutes before I decide to go back down the trail to the creek. When I get to the draw, across it and plainly visible is a sign, and the trail heading west down the creek. I wait ten minutes for BJ to show up, but he doesn't, and so I head on down Holcomb Creek.

The trail follows Holcomb Creek for some distance, then climbs up and over a ridge, down into the Deep Creek drainage, where it comes to a wooden bridge crossing the creek. I stop for an hour for lunch and a foot soak in the cool waters. At last I saddle up and move out. The trail crosses the bridge and heads due north, well above Deep Creek. A few hundred yards up the trail I look back and see BJ just approaching the bridge. Within twenty minutes he overtakes me and tells me his bizarre tale.

So intent on hiking was he that he failed to notice he had reversed directions and was hiking back the same way he had come. After some three miles, he came around a corner and ran headlong into Frank. Almost in unison they asked each other why they were going the wrong direction. It must have been a hilarious scene, for Frank had a difficult time convincing BJ that he was wrong. Faced with the fact that it was far more logical that he was going the wrong way than it was that Frank had somehow managed, without detection, to pass both BJ and me, and then become confused and now be going back the wrong way, he ultimately gave in. I believe it had a profound, if temporary, effect on his confidence, for we hiked together (at a speed considerably slower than his normal) for the next three days until I left the trail for Wrightwood, and he traveled on, not to be seen again.

The end of the day finds all three of us at Deep Creek Hot Springs. There are a number of people around, there being a relatively short trail into the hot springs from a dirt road to the north. There are several hot pools, variously populated with people, all sans clothes. I, being somewhat old fashioned, wind up alone in a small side pool on the river's edge wearing my hiking shorts. The afternoon wears on. A sign proclaims that no camping is allowed, but a young couple sets up camp and starts a big campfire within spitting distance of the sign. Hiking a quarter of a mile upstream, we find a place to stealth camp that we figure is safe, especially with those two decoys bobbing in the water near their campfire.

By noon the next day, BJ and I are sitting outside the Summit Valley Country Store. A mile off the trail, it is worth the trip, especially when I will find out how the day ends at Silverwood Lake. A wall is covered with Polaroid pictures of hikers and their packs and their pack weights. We have our packs weighed (being nearly foodless, mine weighs 10 lbs. 8 oz.), our pictures taken, and listen to the storeowner's soliloquy about tourists, taxes, the United States government, and a number of topics whose thrust I lose as my mind begins to wander. He speaks of selling the store and moving on. There are many shelves lacking contents. This lack, especially in the beer department whose stores are of special interest to me right now and the owner's loquaciousness makes me think perhaps he personally has been involved in some serious inventory depletion, and that this store is not long for the world anyway. As it turns out, a year later I will drive by and see that it has, indeed, closed its doors.

We move on, and in four more miles come to our first view of Silverwood Lake. The trail comes upon a small inlet, and there, just getting shoes-up, are Robin and Marcus. Some people in a boat have shared the cove and their ice chest with them. We make our way the remaining miles to Silverwood Lake Campground.

To make life easy and my pack light, I have carried from Big Bear only enough food, two and a half days worth, to get to Silverwood Lake where I plan to re-supply my pack at the store and my body at the restaurant, as advertised in the PCT guidebook. We complete the mileage, for me just under twenty-two total miles, to the entrance to Silverwood Lake State Park. Then, with the threat of rain in the air, I grudgingly walk the 1.7 miles to the vaunted store and restaurant. The store turns out to be a trailer stationed in the parking lot. Its supplies are poor to miserable. It's less than fifteen miles to Cajon Pass, a half a day's march, so I buy a few meager supplies to get me there. Worse, the restaurant is nonexistent, having been replaced by one of those little mobile hot dog stands that are towed behind a car, to be set up at will where business can thrive. Woefully eating hot dogs and seeking protection from the rain under the roof of the bathrooms, we wait out the storm and head back to spend the night near the park entrance.

It's been a long, nearly twenty-five mile day and I am beat. That night I hear Robin and Marcus arguing about something. I think back, for I have seen them abrade each other a couple of other times. Several of us spent the night in the *sandy wash* at the top of the San Felipe traverse. The next day I left early, but nearly everyone passed me by during the morning on the fifteen-mile sprint to Barrel Springs. Not too long before the springs, I passed Robin and Marcus again, while they were spread out along the trail. Not long after I pulled into the springs, they arrived. They sat down together, he resting a foot on hers. She pushed it away, murmuring some inaudible complaint. Some days later, in Big Bear, Marcus got his camera at the post office. It was a huge Nikon with monster lens, weighing pounds and pounds. She gave him some guff about it. And so again, here at Lake Silverwood there seems to be some friction, angry, undecipherable words murmured back and forth from a few yards away.

I do not know their history, only that they hiked a lot together to get in shape for the trip. I wonder if they will make it. The trail, it will turn out, is a marvelous place to learn about yourself...and others. All pretenses are stripped away. All games exposed for their shallowness. All habits, be they good or bad, are paraded forth, try as you might to closet them. All quirks of personality become as visible as taco sauce on your shirt-front. All selfishness glows like a halo around the sun. All self-consciousness is left at the cat-hole. Two people in these circumstances for four or five months, will come to know each other well, perhaps too well. And different hiking speeds cause one to always be going slower than is wanted, or the other to be hiking faster than is comfortable. Some like to sleep late and hike long, others leave early. One may wish to hike throughout the day, the other take significant rest periods. And food! The topic of greatest interest to thru-hikers could not help but ultimately be a source of conflict. A look at trail journals on the internet will confirm that duos have more than just the trail with which to contend. In fact, many who start together wind up finishing apart.

The next morning I leave early; they are just breaking camp. As I get ready to leave I walk over to say good-by. I say, "By the time you get to Canada, you will know each other so well that you will either never speak to each other again, or never be apart. I hope it is the latter." I wish them well and head on up the trail.

The trip to Cajon Pass is short and fairly uneventful. Robin and Marcus pass by early on, and in a bit we run into Frank, who did not stop in at Silverwood. The herd begins to thin, with Robin and Marcus somewhere ahead and Frank and BJ somewhere behind. The trail runs along a ridge above Little Horsethief Canyon whose claim to fame is it being the route by which in 1819, one Captain Gabriel Moraga chased a band of Indians, whom he suspected as being horse thieves.

By the time ten miles have passed, I once again come upon Robin and Marcus. I first met them way back at Lake Morena and have seen them from time to time, and camped a few nights with them along the way. I accuse them of being members of the Yamabushi Tengu, the slayers of vanity, mountain goblins who gain joy from bedeviling all those who come into their domain. These shape-shifters, capable of instantaneous travel, appear behind me, only to sweep joyously past and disappear down the trail, laughing and chattering. Uphill, downhill, it is no matter. They walk as if both they and their packs weigh little or nothing. It's good to be young. Sometime later I will catch up with them. They are invariably sitting on the side of the trail, talking and laughing, surrounded by a picnic, looking refreshed, and you'd swear, wearing clothes different than the ones they were dressed in earlier. Which is just how they look now. We chat a few minutes, and then I move on.

Not long after that, the trail winds along a cliff of beautifully eroded badlands. Below and only a few miles away, I can see the curves of the Interstate dotted with streams of vehicles. The trail winds down a ridge. At one point, I come to a sharp switchback. As I swing around it, something just next to my shoe catches my attention and I leap forward in Olympic long jump fashion. A five-foot rattlesnake stretches out full length inside the switchback, tail touching the top, head (and fangs) just inches from the lower...and my left foot. It doesn't move, so from a goodly distance, I take out my camera and make a couple of photographs. By the time I am a few hundred yards further, I see Robin and Marcus coming over the top. I yell and pantomime to him that there is a snake near the trail.

As we went into Silverwood Lake yesterday, I was fourth in line on the trail. Just as we came into some tallish grass, I heard a rattle next to my feet, and while in mid-air saw a small rattlesnake stretched out full-length only inches off the trail. Marcus commented that he had not yet seen one and wanted the experience...and a photograph as well. So my yell back today served double purpose.

This was my third close encounter with a rattlesnake. By the time I was six days out of Campo, traversing up and across Grapevine Mountain, I had formulated *The Plan*. I had not seen any snakes, but others had and the wisdom was that the trip across Grapevine Mountain and the San Felipe Hills was through prime snake country. I decided that I would scan the trail forward twenty or thirty yards, or as far as possible in that range, then sweep side-to-side right in front of me until I reach that point, and then begin again. This, I reasoned, should allow me ample warning. The first indication that this strategy was flawed was the striped racer that I nearly stepped on. No more than two feet long and hardly bigger in diameter than my small finger, it lived up to its name and disappeared in moments. A couple of hours later I experienced déjà vu when the story was re-enacted, that time with a beautiful rosy boa. Nearly three feet long, rose color overlain by silvery scales, and a rounded tail that looked more like a head than a tail, I nearly stepped on it too. So much for *The Plan*. It will turn out that I will have close encounters with six rattlesnakes on the trail (all in California), only one of which will be truly scary, and none will I see with any advance warning.

Robin and Marcus catch up with me at huge, buzzing Pole Transmission Pylon #63, under which we travel, less than two miles from civilization. He never saw the snake, alas. We come to a dry wash in Crowder Canyon where the direction of travel is not immediately evident. Marcus heads right, I head left. In a few dozen steps, I find the trail. Robin and I wait a few minutes for Marcus to return from his errant path. He arrives, and again, remembering my thoughts of yesterday, I listen to the friction between them. We walk along, through the narrow, watery canyon of Crowder Creek and hit pavement. A half-mile up the road, the arches of McDonald's gleam in the late morning sun. We make the dash and find a corner table full of thru-hikers. It's just lunchtime and the store is filled with boisterous travelers. The bedlam hits me hard, so I leave and go to the gasoline station next door. It has a great convenience store. I walk along the rows for a while and settle on three V8s. Back in McDonald's, I drink those and find I am so full that only french fries seem desirable.

After the group does some serious gorging, we all go outside to the lawn in front of the gas station. There we spread out our gear and relax while it airs, chatting away a quick couple of hours. While we are idling away the time, Frank arrives, has lunch, fills his canteens, and spreads out on the grass with the rest of us. He is an amazing man, quiet and unpretentious. I have camped with him several times since meeting him at Boulder Oaks Campground, just north of Lake Morena. Every time he has opened a can of tuna to put into his dinner. His pack seems to me to be large and heavy, but he shoulders it, seemingly tirelessly, for long days and makes fully as much mileage as do I. Maybe his quietness is due to exhaustion. I smile to myself; after all, he is older than me, if only by a few years.

My supply strategy from Big Bear to Wrightwood has been to buy food at the two places in between where the trail brushes civilization, Silverwood Lake, whose sad story I just told, and here at Cajon. I walk back to the mini-mart at the gas station. They have an amazing selection. Surely it will be easy to stock up for the thirty or so miles to my mail drop in Wrightwood. That being said, I spend only a few minutes in the store. It is crowded and noisy and there are too many choices. I feel both claustrophobic and ochlophobic at once, big words meaning closed in and crowded. So I bolt.

Back on the grass, we loiter a while longer and I wonder what to do about food. Finally, to everyone's amazement and amusement, myself as well, I buy a dozen cheeseburgers at McDonald's. I know, I know...but sometimes things that would seem sheer lunacy under ordinary circumstances, appear perfectly logical on the trail. I attribute my behavior to a natural panic caused by the crowds of weekend travelers flocking like seagulls on a city dump. And besides, I figure anything so full of sawdust and preservatives as these beauties couldn't possibly go bad in two days. And so that is what I will eat, two for dinner this night camped in the sand, watching the stars and listening to the occasional auto travel down Lone Pine Canyon, two each for breakfast, lunch, and dinner the next day, and two the final morning, watching the sun break out on the summit of Mount Baldy. I know, you're wondering what happened to the other two. They vanished before I left McD's parking lot.

Robin and Marcus have a re-supply package at the Motel 6 across the freeway, so they say good-by and head out. I will find out later that they wind up waiting two more days for it to show up. I will not see them again, but will receive an e-mail in late September announcing their completion of the trail. Frank packs up his gear and departs. Finally BJ and I saddle up and head under the freeway, through the creek, across the railways and around the humped outcrops of Mormon Rocks, around the shoulder of Ralston Peak, and another five miles to a sandy wash, where my second two cheeseburgers, still warm, make a fine evening meal.

The trip up to Guffy Campground from last night's campsite—in a small sandy wash in Lone Pine Canyon, hard up against the edge of Swarthout Canyon Road, astride the San Andreas Fault—and up into the San Gabriel Mountains at last, is a relatively short day as mileage goes.

It's only sixteen and a half miles, but the altitude gained is a bit more than a vertical mile; that's enough. BJ disappears up the trail

The spring, the first water since McDonald's at Cajon Pass, that the guide book says trekkers often complain about being difficult to find, turns out to be a lark. On the side of the trail is a piece of paper with an arrow pointing north, saying water. It is a note from BJ, a hello and a good-bye. I will not see him again as his speed will allow him to make it all the way to Agua Dulce before re-supplying, so he does not plan a stop at Wrightwood. I pass on by and come immediately to Guffy CG, a pleasant, secluded spot, replete with fire pits, full of the usual unburnable refuse of thoughtless car campers, and sturdy, wooden picnic tables. I set my pack aside and lie down on the clean, hard, flat table, purely for the novelty of clean and flat. Hard surfaces being a common enough characteristic of trail life.

It is late afternoon. I know that it is only eight more miles to Angeles Crest Highway and that I could make it this afternoon, but I am in no hurry. Tomorrow will do. A bit later Frank shows up. We sit a spell then head back for water. Turning left at the sign, we follow a clearly defined trail steeply down the eastern ridge of Flume Canyon and onto a scree slope. By the time the trail peters out, the remains of some wooden structure and an oasis of green in the middle of the slope is clearly visible. I guess it would be harder to find without the sign and the greenery.

A couple of hours earlier, I passed by the Acorn Canyon trail down to Wrightwood. The little community looked so invitingly close that it was hard to pass it by for the longer, but to me, more logical choice of walking the eight miles to the Angeles Crest Highway and hitchhiking into town. That means I would not have to hike the three and a half miles and two thousand vertical feet back up to the trail when I leave Wrightwood. As I walked up to the trail intersection, I saw a man seated on the side of the trail. His dog was running nearby. He turned out to be the owner of Mile High Pizza in Wrightwood, just below. I stopped to talk awhile. He said that just this afternoon he had seen a bighorn sheep, something he has never experienced, although he had spent many years hiking around here with just that goal. The Sheep Mountain Wilderness Area lies in the canyons south of here, between Blue Ridge, on which I was standing, and Mt. San Antonio. He pointed to a large talus slope nearby and says it walked right across in front of him. He was ecstatic! We talked a little longer; I told him of my plans to hitch a ride from the Angeles Crest Highway. He told me to get in touch with him at the pizza parlor if I need a ride or some help. I thanked him and moved on. Tomorrow I will have reason to wonder why he didn't give me just a bit more information, but all that is in the future and, hence, unknown.

Back at Guffy Campground it's still early, so Frank and I laze away the afternoon in idle conversation and dozing. As evening approaches, I begin to think about setting up for the night. Earlier, I found a spot way out on the south edge of the ridge, a couple of hundred yards from the campground itself. Across the canyon is a pretty good view of the north slopes of Mt. San Antonio, Old Baldy, the highest peak in the San Gabriel Mountains, riding out and above the nearly 9,500 foot summit of Pine Mountain. I enjoy the luxury of the table a bit longer, having dinner there, moving at last out onto the ridge, and set up camp. I sit in front of my little tent looking across the canyon. As the sun sinks lower and lower, Baldy's summit begins to take on a familiar rosy hue, alpenglow, no doubt intensified by the sun sinking through the dense, hydrocarbonated air of nearby Los Angeles.

A host of memories, dredged up from more than forty years ago, surface and ripple through my mind, for it was there on Baldy, that as a nerdy high school sophomore, I introduced myself to the mountains. It is the first mountain I climbed, and where, disregarding Socrates' admonition that "He who teaches himself, learns from a fool," taught myself the use of ice ax and crampons and ropes. The Devil's Backbone comes to my mind. It is a two or three hundred yard long knife-edged ridge that is exposed enough so that poles and cables have been placed in an attempt to make it hiker safe. In winter, with both sides iced downslope for a thousand feet and near-gale force winds blowing, it can be really exciting. At its uphill end, lying mostly shaded in winter, is a sixty-degree couloir on the east shoulder of Mount Harwood. All winter long it is filled with snow and ice and the trail cuts right across it. Ah…if my dear old mother had known.

From Baldy's summit, in those ancient days when the glaciers had only just retreated and we still wore animal hides, and smog was unknown, the view from its summit was spectacular. The sixty-five miles west and south to San Jacinto's summit seemed nothing; its mighty scarp as clearly visible as is that of the rounded summit of nearby Baldy is tonight. To the north, the snowy hump of the massive peaks of the Langley and Whitney area of the Sierra, more than one hundred sixty miles away, stood out against the deep blue of the sky. I have stood on Baldy's summit perhaps thirty times, in every season, climbed from every possible angle and route, each time a thrill.

The sun sinks lower; there is a goodly wind blowing across the ridge. Really tired from the long uphill day, I fall immediately into a deep, dreamless sleep.

The next morning finds me on the trail early, anxious and looking forward to town. I eat my last two cheeseburgers, give a good-by wave to Frank, who has roused but is slower to action, and head down the trail. I make the eight uneventful miles in two hours and change. The trail is an easy walk, west along Blue Ridge. I pass by a couple of incongruous looking ponds surrounded by chain link fences. They are reservoirs for the snow making machines of the ski resorts below.

At last the trail reaches the first of its many crossings of the Angeles Crest Highway, at Inspiration Point. By nine o'clock I am once again hanging by my thumb, *PCT Hiker* sign in hand. An hour passes but not a single car has. Frustrated, I begin the eight-mile walk towards town. About half way there, Big Pine Highway joins my road on the left. "Ah...now there will be cars," I think. Little do I know that both of these are roads from Nowhere. Pooped out, pissed off and perplexed, I continue to walk. Ultimately I get close enough to town that side roads from residential areas are vomiting up the occasional car or two as I pass, but no one stops. Finally, a black jeep stops to give me a lift. The driver apologizes for the short ride and stops around the very first corner, maybe a mile down the road, to let me off in mid-town. I ask him about the dearth of traffic on Angeles Crest and he says that the road has not been opened yet for the year. He tells me that a few miles west of the trail at Vincent Gap, there is an avalanche chute that covers the road with snow and boulders virtually every year. Until the snow melts and the road is cleared, it remains closed to traffic. Some years, says he, it might not be until well into June before traffic from LA comes over the hill. On this May day I stood no chance. My next thought is, "Why wasn't this information available from Pizza Man the day before?" Ah well, live and learn...or at least live, that's my motto. No blame.

Wrightwood is a marvelous little town. About the size of Idyllwild and Julian with fewer services than both, it is the first town in the hundred miles since Big Bear. And though its services may be limited, I have yet to see the kindness of its residents surpassed. Of course, this is only my sixth town. I head over to the post office to retrieve my re-supply parcel. That done, I go into the hardware store next door. There is a PCT register there, so I sign in and look for names I recognize. Alas, there are none, for all the hikers I met since the beginning have either left the trail, are behind me, or did not stop in Wrightwood. Then I head up a block off the main street and find the Pines Motel. I am told I can have a room in a couple of hours, so I walk down the block to the Pine Manor Coffee Shop and have a leisurely lunch. Back at the motel, I check in. A lady named Martha stops by. She works down at the recycling station and says she will do any laundry I have and get it back this afternoon. What a deal! I spend a couple of hours kicking back in my motel room and voila! My laundry shows up cleaned and dried.

Then Frank shows up. He is told he can't get a room until maybe this evening, so he hangs out in my room waiting. He has ordered a new, much lighter tent than the one he is carrying. We set it up on the grass outside the room. Unfortunately, the tent poles appear to be for a tent somewhat larger, so we head out to the post office to mail it back and to hit the market. It has a great deli. We head back and Frank checks into his room. Then we hike out to Mile High Pizza to see about a ride back up to the trail tomorrow. The local trail angel is there and says he would be glad to give us a ride back. (I'm sorry now that I didn't write down his name.) All we need to do is show up at eight o'clock tomorrow morning. This day is complete.

In the morning, it's back to the café for an early breakfast. Sitting there is Tony, whom I last saw in Warner Springs eighteen days ago. He has just arrived in town and plans to stay another day. Frank and I have a quick breakfast, say goodbye to Tony and head the two blocks up to the pizza place. Crowded in the back of a Toyota pickup with a camper shell, we ride the eight miles to the trail.

The rest of the day involves seemingly endless circling of the Angeles Crest Highway. I will cross it no fewer than seven times before calling the day quits. In between is the relentless ascent of Mt. Baden-Powell, which involves more than twenty-eight hundred feet of climb through enough snow to make losing the trail no difficult chore. Ultimately I cross the highway at the Eagle's Roost Picnic Area and head down the Rattlesnake Trail. Tonight will be the first night I will not be sleeping in the company of others. In a lifetime of hiking, I have never spent a single evening alone in the wilderness, and I do confess to harboring some bit of fear. In the bottom of the canyon, I find a small flat just above Little Rock Creek. More than the necessary water it represents, I choose it for the unrelenting music it will make throughout the night, thus cloaking the sounds of the "ghoulies and ghosties and long-leggedy beasties and things that go bump in the night."

That said, the night passes peacefully and uneventfully. From here, the next time I will spend a night in another's company (not counting Hiker Heaven, the herd at Kennedy Meadows, the claustrophobic canvas tents of VVR, and the anonymous, crowded campgrounds of Tuolumne

Meadows) will be when I share a motel room with Porter at Buck Lake Lodge, more than 875 miles up the trail.

The following evening finds me camped out on the lawn next to the Mill Creek Ranger Station, nearly twenty-seven miles from my campsite on Little Rock Creek. It is the Friday night of Memorial Day weekend. The guide book says that no camping is allowed in this area, and, upon arriving, I look around, wondering just where I will have to go. I walk around looking for a pay phone... and find none. I am just ready to leave when a ranger drives up. Mary is just checking in before leaving for the weekend. She allows me to use the inside phone while she finishes with the day's business. As she starts to head for her car, she says, "You can sleep on the grassy area around the corner there, if you want to." Hallelujah! The day is done.

The next day begins with clouds covering the sky. To the north, the Antelope Valley is obscured by low clouds, and tendrils of fog creep upward on the Los Angeles side. In two and a half miles, I come to a crossing of Mt. Gleason Road, under which I have been winding. As I approach the road there is a five-foot long arrow in white chalk on the trail. The trail is obvious. I wonder why they have put this here. At the edge of the road are several gallons of water, some Gatorades, and packages of cookies. Ah...trail angels, I think, and help myself. In another three miles I come to a dirt road and more arrows. Following no fewer than four huge arrows across and down the road and through Big Buck Trail Camp, I continue on...still perplexed. In another mile and a half, the trail dives south into a deep, shady ravine, then out of it to the north. Within a few hundred yards I come to another arrow, this time making a u-turn and pointing back the way I have just come. Beyond it are three white lines, completely crossing the trail. I stare at it for a minute. The meaning is clear: "Abandon all hope, ye who pass here." Perhaps this is not the trail. I head back to the ravine and look around. There seems to be a trail of sorts headed up the ravine, but it doesn't look promising. I hike up it a dozen yards and turn around. I decide to sit a spell and ponder the situation.

Within a few minutes a runner passes quickly by and heads up the trail. Just as quickly he returns, so I hail him. It turns out the chalk arrows are directions for a group called The High Desert Runners who frequent these trails. Sheepishly, I wonder if he noticed the missing cookies and Gatorade.

Evening finds me 18.7 miles up the trail, setting up camp at the North Fork Saddle Ranger Station. I meet Yogi and Gottago there. We have dinner together, then they head on down the trail, anxious to make a few more miles in the day. The fog bank from Los Angeles has managed to make its way up the 4,200 feet to this saddle and it begins to drizzle. I set up my tent and call it a day.

The next day dawns, threatening rain. It drizzles a bit throughout the morning as I make my way down Mattox Canyon and into Soledad Canyon. By eight o'clock I cross Soledad Canyon Road, the Santa Clara River and the railroad tracks and head up into the pink, cobbled Vasquez Formation. I pass a cobblestone monument bearing a brass plaque. This is where the PCT was completed on June 5, 1993. Within a mile or so, the rain comes down hard, and the wind is blowing fiercely. I decide to wait it out by going back to the Cypress Park Resort. Sitting in the tiny café, warm and secure, with a steaming cup of coffee in hand, I toast the end of the Mountains of the Saints.

HIKER HEAVEN

I am sitting on the lawn at the home of Jeff and Donna Saufley, near the head of Darling Road in Agua Dulce, trail mile 451. I drag out the two packaged sandwiches and small bottle of Black Label scotch that I purchased just a mile back down the road at the mini-mart. I am at...or is it in?...Hiker Heaven. More than a dozen other hikers are here,[1] some in the large, singlewide trailer nearby, some on the lawn, some poking around in tents that have been set up on the plot below the house. Others are shopping or dining in town. My recline has metamorphosed into supine. With my bare feet resting on my pack, I have lunch and watch the clouds form and reform in the blue sky above. They threaten, but withhold, further rain.

I passed a pleasant hour this morning in the small diner at the Cypress Park Resort, back in Soledad Canyon, waiting out the storm. Doc and Llama, their dog Coy, Grasshopper, Load and D-Low were all there. By mid-morning it was mostly over, so I headed up into the pebbly, pink, concrete-looking formations that mark the beginning of the Vasquez Rocks. The rain was off and on for a while, and the wind was fierce. My hiking poles stowed on my pack, I protected myself with my umbrella, plying it through the vacillating winds like a wind surfer...in reverse.

The rain came and went, came again, then mostly went. By early afternoon I was walking through the wet and only street of Agua Dulce. Near a fence, a couple of blocks before town's center, I looked down, and seeing a wad of green paper, picked it up. It was a five-dollar bill. Taking this as a sign, I looked for someplace to return it to the economy. At the corner of Darling Road, I paused at the mini-mart and then headed up the mile up to Hiker Heaven.

Since 1997, the Saufleys have been opening their home and their hearts to thru-hikers. It has become a haven for the healthy and the injured, the hopeful and the hopeless, the marvelous "wretched refuse" of the thru-hiker world. With only seventeen percent of the trail completed—and often as many as a third or half of the hikers who started now off the trail—it has become a place to retreat and regroup, to enjoy a few days respite before the Mojave Desert and the snowy Sierra to come.

I paused at the gate as a couple of little dogs came running to bark. Donna came out, assuring me they were friendly. A bit dazed, I stumbled in and tried to listen as Donna went through the spiel. Freestanding

---

1 Some new names are Mary from Bellingham, Long Drink from Texas, Strawberry Girl and Blackhawk, and Goof.

shelves filled half of the garage. Here were the resupply boxes. There were the towels and extra clothes. In a hamper went all of your dirty clothes, to be washed and returned in a few hours. A kiosk had information: news on water in the dry section to come between Agua Dulce and Kennedy Meadows; snow conditions in the Sierra; maps to nearby Santa Clarita and the REI further on in Northridge; a sign-up sheet for the two vehicles available to hikers and a hook for the keys. At the moment there were no keys, which was fine since I hoped to travel only a few more feet today.

Next was a tour of the grounds. A long mobilehome is Hiker Central. There one finds the shower, two bedrooms, TV, stereo, internet connection, and full kitchen. There's also an RV, known as the *Honeymoon Suite*, and a number of large family-camping tents spread out on area below the house. It's amazing that the septic tank can withstand the onslaught. A huge hiker barrel, BBQ and hammock made up rest.

I hit the shower and stretched out on the lawn. And so here I am, having lunch. Hikers come and go throughout the afternoon. One of the cars arrives back from civilization and another six hikers pile out. A game of Frisbee takes off and people laze their way into evening. Music pours out of the mobilehome.

In the late afternoon, Jeff arrives from his business over the hill. By then a number of us have contrived to have roast beast for dinner, and the BBQ is being prepared. Later in the evening, with a crowd of twenty or more thru-hikers sitting around, Jeff and Donna tell the story of the beginning of Hiker Heaven. It's a marvelous story of serendipity...of the triumph of kindness over trepidation and doubt. It begins with a tale of poison oak and thru-hikers attempting to take a bath in the pizza parlor restroom and ends amidst late-night slapstick that does justice to the best of comedy...replete with resurgent doubt, locked doors and windows, bachelor parties, and stumbling through darkened halls. Like a Shakespearian comedy, the denouement comes with the words, "Who the hell are you?" Answered in kind by, "Well, who the hell are *you?*" I've heard the story twice and still love it. But I shan't recount it here. If you want to hear it you'll just have to hike the trail. Some things have to be earned to be worthwhile.

The next morning, car keys in hand, four of us, Strawberry Girl, Emily S, and another whose name I fail to remember, make the twelve or so mile drive to Santa Clarita, civilization. Emily is from Alaska, but oddly enough, grew up not far from here, in a little community called Sleepy Valley, and is excited to visit places she hasn't seen for years. She points out the elementary school she attended. Emily started out from Campo without the use of hiking poles. Somewhere along the way she became a convert, and after agonizing over the cost, had a pair delivered to her on the trail at Wrightwood. Unfortunately, almost immediately she lost them by leaving them in a car that had given her a ride back to the trail from town. Word spread along the trail and a collection was taken up. By the time she arrived at Hiker Heaven, a new pair was waiting. Thru-hikers are often the recipients of trail magic but it isn't too often that they get to create it themselves.

We have breakfast enroute. No big deal, except as it will play into events later in the day. We make the rounds, stopping at a couple of grocery stores and a Costco. Ultimately we wind up back at Hiker Heaven for a leisurely afternoon. I plan on leaving tomorrow, so I spend an hour or so checking my gear and packing. It is then that I can't find my glasses. I have been wearing my sunglasses all day, and now my prescription "clearies" are missing. I look everywhere...no luck. Beginning to panic, I take one of the vehicles and head out, retracing our steps from breakfast to market to Costco...no luck. Back at the Saufley's, I try to decide what to do. Hiking without them is not a problem...unless I have to hike at night...or even see at night. I tear my pack completely apart one more time, and unbelievably, they are right there. Sometimes I wonder.

Except for a few hours of panic, the day passes amiably enough, ending with another barbecue. The next morning, I am up early and head down the mile to the trail, which is also the main street of town. Finally, at the end of civilization, the trail takes off, up and into the Sierra Pelona. Only sixty miles remain until the ill-famed Mojave Desert.

THE GHOST OF JACK FAIR[1]

> Who would burdens bear to grunt and sweat under a weary life, but that
> the dread of something after death, the undiscovered country, from whose
> bourn no traveler returns, puzzles the will, and makes us rather bear those
> ills we have, than fly to others we know not of?
> (*Hamlet*, William Shakespeare)

> ...any man's death diminishes me, for I am involved in mankind, and therefore
> never send to know for whom the bell tolls; it tolls for thee."
> (*Meditation XVII*, John Donne)

This day has been filled with both harmony and dissonance. I think most thru-hikers understand the paradox. Coming into town off the trail causes senses to overload, there are too many stimuli, everything is moving too fast. Yet there is great pleasure to be found, sitting quietly in the dark recesses of some restaurant or bar, watching it all spin about you. This is probably more noticeable by those hiking the Pacific Crest Trail than those on the Appalachian Trail, a lot fewer people and a lot less civilization.

Five days ago I came out of the San Gabriel Mountains and, racing the rain, made it to Hiker Heaven, home of Jeff and Donna Saufley. Two days there and two days on the trail has brought me to my next food re-supply point, Lake Hughes. I spend most of the day in town, sorting food and enjoying the hospitality of Harley's Rock Inn. At three-thirty in the afternoon, T.J., waitress and bartender on this day, gives me a ride back to the trailhead on Lake Elizabeth Road. I hike up several miles and come upon a wide, relatively flat spot where the trail cuts back. Stopping for a rest, I check the guide and see that it doesn't appear very optimistic about camping spots for the next several miles. It's heading towards six o'clock—plenty of sunlight left in the day—but I decide to stay here for the night. Feeling lazy and contented, I sit in the shade for more than an hour, looking...at nothing. Strawberry Girl and Blackhawk pass by. "I expected you to be further up the trail," she says. I smile. We chat for a while and they move on. Another hour passes and I begin to set up my evening camp. I notice a beautiful set of mountain lion tracks sliding right across my sandy campsite. Trusting that they are older than not, I photograph them. Not long before sunset, Long Drink stops on his way through. We watch the moon rise, nearly full. We passed by each other in town without knowing, I sitting in the Rock Inn waiting for a ride, he moving by in haste

---

1 Previously published in the Pacific Crest Trail Communicator, Oct. 2002, vol. 14, no. 4

to the post office lest it close. He stops to chat for a while and moves on. I will not see him again, as I unknowingly pass him by the next morning, he being a relatively late starter and I on the trail early. He will leave the trail in Tehachapi and head back to Texas. Normally I am hiking before six, but today, in the pre-dawn moonlight at four o'clock, I hoist my pack and head up the trail; I am on a mission.

I hike all the long day, across Grass Mountain, Sawmill Mountain, and eventually across Liebre Mountain. I stop briefly for an early dinner and hurry down and across Pine Canyon Road and on to Tejon Ranch Property, hastily treading the last tedious miles to Highway 138 and the house of Jack Fair. Jack Fair was, and is, a legend. Last June, at the age of 77, he ended his life...and an era. Tonight is a full moon, and I am looking for the ghost of Jack Fair.

I arrive, exhausted from this long, nearly thirty-mile day, not long before sunset. At the corner of Highway 138 and 270th Street West is a mailbox. It has been smashed, looking like another victim of that timeless, shallow diversion of restless and roaming youth, mailbox baseball. It is severely dented and is held closed by red plastic ribbon. The flag is up, signaling to all the world that there are messages to be sent. I peer inside. If there are messages they will have to be found elsewhere. *Fair, 26803 W. Avenue C-15* it announces. A phone book, still partially shrouded in a sun-shattered plastic bag, lies on the ground; the wind has opened it to the yellow pages. I bend to see that restaurants are waiting and momentarily wish for a phone or a car. A chain link fence surrounds the corner property. The gate is closed but unlocked and sports a sign that says, honk. The faded yellow house with white trim is unoccupied. A realtor's sign in front announces its sale.

Three days earlier, at Hiker Heaven in Agua Dulce, the Saufleys had announced that, even though no longer here, Jack was still providing water if needed. I need it. Tired and thirsty, I open the gate and walk in. The driveway is lined with largish rocks, painted silver and sporting black polka dots. I head directly to the hose bib in front of the house only to discover that alas, the water is shut off. People passing through here only a few days earlier found the water on, but not today. No matter, I had decided in Agua Dulce to spend the night here. I still have a bit more than a liter of water. It will have to do until I pass by Neenach School early tomorrow.

Walking around the grounds, I see a few signs, on a couple of walls and casually stenciled on the water tank. His signs were said to have covered nearly every available wall space. I wonder what happened to them. Those who visited him described him as a poet and a philosopher, albeit one whose swearing would put the proverbial sailor to shame, and the disarray of whose spelling was rivaled only by the disarray in his home. Some remarked on the clutter, piles of cookie and pastry boxes, Coke cans, ashtrays full to overflowing. A large, dingy reclining chair was his throne. People could sit anywhere they wanted...but there. They could cook dinner on his stove, could raid his refrigerator...if they dared. I peer in the window of the nearly empty living room. There's no sign of clutter, no cigarette smoke, no weary looking hikers, indecision on their faces, trying to quickly decide whether to sit back and if not enjoy, at least tolerate the ride, or to follow their instincts and bolt immediately.

I walk over to the well and water tank, hoping to see a switch marked ON/OFF in large, friendly letters. No such luck. On the water tank a sign announces: *I Deserve To Be Crazy, I Work To Get There*. Jack offered services; you could take a shower, if you were willing to brave the bathroom, or just sit around or spend the night. Cost? $5.00...maybe...or $6.00...or $10.00, or nothing at all, depending on who knows what? Some had no cash, so he charged them nothing. Some had no change; he charged them double. For a dollar or two, one could get a ride a few miles east to the West Valley Center, where Lois, the proprietor, would provide ice cream, chips, Snickers bars, packaged sandwiches, Ho-Ho's, beer, tomato juice and all manner of precious commodities. One hiker who had only a credit card found Jack paying for his groceries.

Some accepted the fees Jack charged with good humor; some felt angry and ripped off and left with all due haste. Some were humiliated by his aggressiveness; others found him charming and humorous; some noticed he swore less when ladies were around; most could barely stand his chain smoking; some described him as *half-crazy*, some as *crusty*, some as an *icon*, some as *colorful and shocking*. Some said they felt as though Jack was testing them to see if they were worthy. More than a few found him intolerable. One said it all, calling him *uniquely beautiful*. And to a few, he showed his revolver, saying, "The last bullet's for me," causing them, as they donned their packs in alarm and headed for the gate, to wonder just for whom the other five might be. Some assiduously avoided Jack Fair's place; his history preceded him. Others made it a point to visit, chancing unpleasantness for the sake of experience and stayed on to find the man beneath.

On the wall of a wooden storage building is the life-sized, cutout silhouette of a cowboy, his left leg raised as if resting on the lower rung of a rail fence. White letters on the black figure proclaim: *PCT Hackers 509+ So Far*. This is dated 11-29-99. A true philosopher, some said. Walking around in the failing light, I open the door to an outbuilding. It is totally empty with the exception of one sign[2] on a seat running along the wall.

It's a business deal

No ones needed or needs another

Your born free and respect another Mother

That's true love BROTHER

Stay Free

The Lover

Jack Fair

I hastily set up camp near one of the rows of sadly neglected juniper trees planted around the perimeter of the property in a futile effort to negotiate with the unceasing desert wind. The trees are all straining up and away from the west, home of the prevailing winds. Many are dead or dying. I wonder if he spent time lovingly applying precious water to make them thrive. Visitors described him variously as having been an ex-Navy hard-hat diver, an ex-animal and guard dog trainer for the rich and famous of Hollywood, an ex-motorcycle rider who had ridden the length and breadth of the country. I wonder what stories he would have told me, for I suspect that like all true storytellers, his truths were fluid and his yarns tailored to the audience and the mood in which he found himself.

The sun is going…going…gone…and a radiant full moon rises in the east. The ghost of Jack Fair could not help but stir on this marvelous, beautiful night. The wind, which has been blowing steadily, if tepidly, all afternoon, picks up. The light on the western horizon fades as that in the east brightens. Sitting cross-legged in front of my small tent, watching the moon cast sharp shadows across the land, I think about those final hours. What thoughts went through his mind, what factors calculated, what positives and negatives weighed, what figures summed, what ledgers balanced? Earlier, near the water tank I found the missing signs—a pile of dozens of discarded signs containing statements—poetry, political statements, raillery against the system, against human stupidity, human greed, wry comments on the vagaries of life—haphazardly piled by an heir

---

2 All sign texts, shown in boxes, are quoted with Jack Fair's spelling.

or a real estate agent, no doubt, in an attempt to make the place more saleable. I sorted through the top few in the dying light. That he was thinking of the end is plain, for many signs spoke of life, its worth, its meaning, its beauty, its futility. One read:

The black river of old age.

Who in hell wants to life to a hundred!

Not me, for one I say

Who knows Jack's true story? Someone perhaps. Like all of us, he was born somewhere, had a mother and father, friends and lovers...and enemies, hopes and dreams...and fears. He played the hands dealt to him. The rest is conjecture. Was he afraid in those final hours? I think not. In the pile, partially covered...

Everything is going so good today

The ending I may die and be on my way

27,740 alive today

Just to meet death with open arms, that's a blessing all of its own

That would be the ending of a perfect day

Do not resuscitate

Jack Fair

On a whim, I divide 27,740 by 365, the number of days in the year. It comes out 76—even. On his birthday, a year before his death, he was thinking of the end, as do all of us as time comes calling...as do I, being not so very far from Jack's age, on this haunting, moonlit night. It reminds me of the words of the poet:
  "Do not go gentle into that good night,
  Old age should rave and burn at close of day,

Rage...rage on against the dying of the light."

Dylan Thomas would have approved of Jack Fair, for rage he did, rage against the machine, against the arrogance, the greed, and the stupidity, the folly of man, the dying of the light. Rage as only he knew how, with invective, and poetry...and humor.

His behavior put most hikers off, made them ill at ease, caused them to fill their water bottles and high-tail it for the comparative safety of the desert ahead. But I hope that, of those who left in haste and those who stayed, many came to realize that surely he donned his scaly overcoat of profanity and profundity to protect a poet's heart.

One evening found Meadow Ed, long time PCT hiker and notorious trail angel, and some few others, at Jack's place, watching the movie *Titanic*. Near movie's end, when all is lost and hope is sinking as rapidly as twisted steel in the dark, cold waters, Ed noticed, in the dimly-lit room, that tears were streaming down Jack's face, a face as weatherworn as the bark of the ancient Joshua trees lining the nearby canyon. Noticing he was noticed, Jack quietly explained that he was one of the few survivors on a minesweeper, sunk in the icy North Atlantic during World War II. In the quiet moments that followed, those present felt a wave of vulnerability and pain and innocence, of humanity so great, that as it rolled over them, they felt themselves, in silent accord, likewise burst into tears.

In the bright light of the moon, I walk over to the house once again and peer into the empty living room. In my mind I see Jack in his chair, balancing his ledgers. Failing health, failing spirits...what does it take to make it worth the time? The effort? Fiercely independent, as only a lone desert rat can be, yet in the end faced with the prospect of losing that independence. And alone...always alone. Albert Camus said that judging whether life is or is not worth living amounts to answering the fundamental question of philosophy. All the rest comes afterwards.

Finally, he stands and looks around. Some may say it is a coward's path, but they are wrong. Some may call it a sin, but surely they too must be wrong. The Philosopher takes a Warrior's stance...and says goody-bye. Out in the high desert, amidst a sea of Joshua trees, a lone rider sits silently astride his pale horse. Though the sands are awash in silvery light, he needs none to guide his sure and certain path. To the south, and slightly west, toward the Sierra Pelona he rides...to rendezvous with an old friend.

Back in front of my tent, I sit quietly just a few yards from the house. As the evening lengthens, the wind steadily increases its pace. The nylon flaps noisily. I feel a kinship with Jack Fair, a man I never met...a familiarity like that of a treasured old possession, stored carefully away in some special place, to be brought out and savored on rare occasions, like a wee dram of the finest single malt; something so familiar that it is not necessary to touch it frequently to know that it is there. I feel at home.

You would misconstrue to think that I am thinking of suicide in the sense that Jack Fair did, for I am not Jack Fair. I only wonder if I would have his courage were I in his place. I hope I would, for as Shakespeare's Henry V says, we are all "as men wrecked upon a sand that look to be washed off the next tide"...or the next. The terror of non-existence, that undiscovered country, prowls restlessly among us, and few there are who can stand and stare it in the face and cry, "Enough!"

A wave of emotion, equal parts joy and sorrow, swells up and through me, bursts like a bubble, and is swept away by the wind into the desert night. Life seems such a marvelous gift and so precious, that on this incredible night it is difficult to imagine conditions that would make it not so. May it always be that way.

Not far away a trio of coyotes barks back and forth, engaged in some mysterious tag-team match with the moon. Finally there is the familiar, wailing, three-note call, though I know not if in defeat or victory, then silence. A flash of light comes from the nearby house, and I jerk upright. But then it's only the headlights of a car speeding west through the desert, spreading up and out across the wall, disappearing into the clear desert night... isn't it?

Fare ye well, Jack
"No Way"
Full Moon, May 2002

Epilogue

The following morning, as is my habit, I awaken early. Yesterday still hangs upon my muscles, and last night hangs upon my mind, and knowing that today I will walk a mere seventeen mostly level miles to Cottonwood Creek, feel no need for haste. I sit idly and watch the sun rise, spreading up and out over the desert. Finally I pack my gear, shoulder my pack and head out the gate. I have decided to see if I can get a ride down to a store at the West Valley Center. I cross the street and stick out a thumb. Thirty minutes later I am still standing there. A car coming from the west slows down, signals, and turns into Jack's driveway. The passenger gets out and opens the gate, closing it behind the car. The driver unlocks the front door and the occupants, a man and a woman, start carrying boxes into the house. It appears Jack's Place has new occupants. I wonder what they would have thought had they arrived an hour earlier to find me camping in their front yard.

Another twenty minutes passes. No luck. I have seen myself in mirrors some number of times along this journey, and though not as startling as Shakespeare's Caliban, who was enraged at seeing his own face in a glass, I probably would not pick me up either. I hold no grudges and begin to rationalize that this may not be worth two V8s, a chicken salad sandwich, and a Snickers bar anyway. Most hikers call the distance "a mile or so," but in reality it is four miles even—each way. Eight miles added to today's walk makes me decide to hang it up. I tell myself I will wait for ten more cars to pass. They do, and I head down the road toward Neenach School where I will, hopefully, find sorely needed water, and journey on into the desert.

The prediction is for 105°F today, and the day seems intent on reaching that goal as early as possible. The thought comes to me…Jack is gone. His house has new owners. In a short time no doubt, the last traces of his presence will be gone, and new eyes will look out of his windows, upon the world of sand and sun and sky. Perhaps he led a full and merry life…played bingo at the local church on Thursday nights, danced square and round on Fridays, or had frequent dinner with the locals at the Three Points Roadhouse Café, and so is alive and well in the memories of countless friends. But this is all unknown and I am skeptical. Next year's crop of thru-hikers will notice a house on the corner as they pass by. They will know, perhaps, that in the past it was a place of potential refuge before the onerous desert. The next edition of the hiker's guide will no longer suggest hikers stop by for a shower and an epithet.

All that remains of Jack are in the memories of those hikers who passed through over the years. Whether they passed through in haste or leisure, in tranquility or trepidation, they took some part of Jack with them as they headed out and into the desert. Jack Allen Fair lives on in us all, whose lives he touched, either directly or indirectly, in some small way. What more could anyone ask … to be remembered as long as memory lasts. The early morning sun drives my shadow out and across the road. Momentarily, it eclipses a patch of California poppies, then they burst, brilliant orange-gold into the sunlight. I walk on down the road.

INTO THE DESERT

With an external heat greater than our own internal, may
not cookery properly be said to begin? (*Walden*, Henry David Thoreau)

We are like sheep without a shepherd
We don't know how to be alone
So we wander 'round this desert
And wind up following the wrong gods home
(*Learn To Be Still*, Don Henley)

I am standing on a shoulder projecting down from the north slopes of Liebre Mountain. Looking down through the shimmering heat and haze, I can see the so-called "most infamous" section of the Pacific Crest Trail, the Mojave Desert. Unable to be routed along the crest of the Tehachapi Mountains, because as is common, private interests had more power than the common good, the trail descends down into the westernmost arm of the Mojave Desert, the Antelope Valley, thus avoiding the mammoth Tejon Ranch's mountain property. The author of the southern California section of the PCT guide calls this portion of the trail, "hot, waterless, dangerous and ugly," and so it is to most, I guess, when compared to the better part of the trail to come and some parts already passed. I, on the other hand, have always loved the desert.

Born in the hot sun of summer, growing up on the beach in southern California, and spending virtually all of my adult life climbing and hiking in the High Sierra, I have spent a lifetime reveling in the sun's radiance, as attested to by my yearly bouts with the dermatologist. In high school I discovered rock climbing, and in addition to the granite of the Sierra and the Tahquitz of Mt. San Jacinto, found Joshua Tree National Monument. Many weekends and vacations were spent in the desert, climbing the great boulders of the park and camping beside a roaring campfire at night. In those days, smog was a thing seen only on the western skyline where Los Angeles crept ever outward with its foul air. In the desert, the air carried no hint of the pestilence to come, and the nights were awash in starlight.

That most venerable of desert rats, Edward Abbey, called the desert a place where the "strangeness and wonder of existence are emphasized...by the comparative sparsity of flora and fauna: life not crowded upon life as in other places but scattered abroad in spareness and simplicity, with a generous gift of space." I guess I could say it no better, but there is more to the desert than that, as Abbey well knew. More because of the profound effects that vast emptiness, lying beneath the vault of heaven, has upon the human spirit. Coming, only lately in the grand scheme of things, out of caves, as the metaphor goes, to stare—with good reason—in fear at shadows moving in the night, under skies yet untouched by the cunning of man. The reasons for the fear long gone, our genes have yet to recognize the fact and slowly...slowly we change. More because the desert's spareness and simplicity borders on harsh and reminds us all the more how marvelous it is to live.

Moreover, the conditions that the extreme heat and lack of water place upon our minds and bodies are truly no small threat. The heat we may grudgingly endure, but the lack of water is a serious thing. How much water is enough? Do I have enough? Should I carry more, at eight pounds per gallon, to weigh and slow me down, thus making the duration of the journey longer? Can I make it to the next water? Just where is the next water? These are questions that bother all but the most experienced of desert travelers, and gathering information from a book compares but little with the grim reality of walking through the miles of rock and sand faced by PCT travelers.

But beyond all that, the microcosm of a desert journey contains metaphors of life, there for the exploration. A pearl begins as a grain of sand, a source of irritation, and on this stretch of the Pacific Crest Trail, the stuff of pearls is strewn everywhere. The desert has many lessons to teach, and unlike Moses and his band, who wandered around the Sinai for forty years, I have but two days, and thus must learn what I am able to, if anything, in that short time. Many are the demons that lurk in this waterless land, but angels dwell here as well.

Coming down out of the Sierra Pelona, I cross Pine Creek Road and soon come to a gate, the border of the vast Tejon Ranch. The ranch has magnanimously allowed hikers to travel through the outskirts of its property as long as the traveler agrees to the rules. At the gate there is a sign warning travelers not to stray off the path for any reason. Visions of Yahweh giving similar warnings to the Israelites on their journey out of Egypt make me wonder if the sky will split open and mountains vomit fire should I chance to stray up one of the washes to look at a particularly beguiling rock, or step too far out into a field to examine a wildflower. Feeling like someone is watching me, I circle for several miles through a series of hills that border the Mojave.

Ultimately I drop out onto the sloping floor of the valley and pass the first of many typical desert dwellings. Surrounding what appears to be a pleasantly garbed desert home are piles of...everything. I am reminded of the Pink Motel, so many miles behind. The largest pile is made up of red and blue plastic barrels, other containers, both plastic and metal, and wooden boxes. Nearby are several large, freestanding metal containers for animal feed; no animals are apparent. Many of the piles are construction materials of various sorts, lumber, pipe, sheet metal, coils of wire, and the like. A lot of it looks like plain old trash, and I wonder why these people don't make a well-earned trip to the landfill. Passing down an arrow-straight nearly mile-long section of fence, I parade by the last series of piles, truly the leavings, stored as far from the house as possible and in a small draw, apparently to remain invisible to all but us hikers. Out of their sight, out of their minds, but not ours.

The contents of these last piles are somewhat segregated. The first portion consists of automobile parts, bumpers, two hoods, one red, one green, identical but for their faded colors, carrying that flattened, edgy look of cars of the 1960s, a couple of engine blocks, wheels, etc. Next comes household goods, two kitchen stoves and a refrigerator, a microwave oven (door gone), followed by lawnmowers sans engines (and where in this desert is the grass that needed cutting?), coils of garden hose, some old tractor implements and various tools and odd equipment whose use, even at this short distance, remains unfathomable. Toward the end of this more than one hundred foot series of piles are TV sets, several baby strollers, children's toys, and boxes and boxes of plastic bottles. Finally comes a pile of bicycles and parts, bent wheels, frames and rustless chrome. Lest I make it sound like organization, rest assured that this is only a veneer of order, for the pile is continuous and all available space covered with every manner of artifact.

I don't know what it is about the desert that attracts or creates these vast accumulations of stuff. Perhaps it calls to the kind of personalities that instinctively save everything, somehow believing that it will all be useful for something someday. Acting out some atavistic ritual of survival in a harsh and uncertain environment, they collect and sort and pile and array against the rainy day that never comes.

More likely is that the desert itself creates these personalities. A vast emptiness, the desert reminds us of our insignificance in the scheme of things. Under the bowl of heaven, unhemmed by buildings or trees or mountains, the horizon at infinity, myriad stars strew their dust upon our consciousness. Lights that left their suns while ancient Chinese astronomers, in full daylight, gazed in wonder at the supernova in the Crab Nebula; while Pythagoras drew pictures in the sand and spoke quietly of the transmigration of souls; when Abraham left Ur of the Chaldees to wander a lifetime and spawn all tribes that would ultimately become Jews, Muslims, and Christians; when men found bronze, then iron, to beat into swords; when nomadic Homo sapiens made the discovery that emer, an early form of wheat, when planted, would sprout anew, thus freeing him from a life of wandering and uncertainty; when men first huddled around fire in the African veldt, casting anxious eyes skyward, inventing God to blunt infinity.

Some will no doubt take umbrage with this statement, certain that God invented man. I have no quarrel with that view. But today, armed with greater knowledge of time and distance, in a world of complexity unimagined by earlier men, God often seems not enough. Men surround themselves in the knowable squares of township and range, of village and city, of streets named A to Z and First through Hundreds, in houses boxed and packaged. Few squares exist in nature. Only man, with his fear of the unknown, attempts to box things in, to make them precise and concise, to contain or constrain them, to make them knowable, and thus a thing unfeared.

But the vastness that is desert refuses to be boxed, refuses to be known. Perhaps that makes these dwellers uncomfortable, uneasy on some deep, profound level, dredging up genetic memories of times when man fell from grace and was forced to wander east of Eden, or when African desert lengthened and early man left upon the forty thousand year journey that would people all the world. And so these desert dwellers gather up the wretched refuse of civilization, pile it in rows, neat or disheveled, clumped like the building materials for some new attempt to reconstruct a tower to the gods, a nascent Tower of Babel.

If in that there is solace to be found, so be it. The desert is vast; it contains multitudes; it can take it. But can we interlopers? Perhaps not, for it stymies comprehension. Tomorrow I will pass a dwelling lying several hundred yards off the road. I stand in awe for many minutes, counting no fewer than thirty-five dead automobiles, the remains of several motor homes, travel trailers, and vast piles of, most likely, the usual, mercifully too far from the trail to fully identify. It seems impossible that this is the work of one generation. What can a father say to his son? Monty Python's "Someday, lad, all this will be yours," comes to mind, and I smile. What can they be thinking? Against what future odds is this bulwark laid? A newer, apparently operational car parked in front of the house is the only sign that this is a work in progress. I suppress the urge to interview its owner.

The desert is "the most beautiful place on earth," insists Abbey. He was talking about his sojourn as a park ranger in the then little-known Arches National Monument. Looking out through the less than pristine air of this piece of the Mojave that lies before me, I can see the Tehachapi Mountains, thirty miles to the north, cloaked in haze. Great circles of green, like some alien spawned crop circle in reverse, give evidence, in a land where life fights it out for every last drop of water, that the Tejon

Ranch is hard at work, growing food for cattle by drilling deep into the earth to suck it dry from the inside out. And yet...clean up the air, remove the alfalfa, the deserted and semi-deserted desert homes, and the great piles of accumulated treasure surrounding them, add a few sandstone arches. Ah well, so it's not the same.

I begin to move with purpose down the trail, anxious to enter the desert, to make the acquaintance of this piece of earth, as yet, untrodden, at least by me. Much of the conventional wisdom says to avoid traveling in the desert during the hottest hours, and you might be surprised to learn how many thru-hikers espouse this. Even naturalist Joseph Wood Krutch, that peerless voice of the desert, rarely strayed outside in the heat of the day and made many an observation from the comfort of his air conditioned home. When chided, he replied that even Henry David Thoreau warmed his cabin at Walden Pond, and that, it was "surely no more effete to cool oneself in a hot climate than to warm oneself in a cold one."

For thru-hikers the options are limited, and so the conventional plan entails starting early, not a problem since I always do, and hiking well into the night, the hottest part of the day being waited out under tarp or in convenient shade. Since shade is rarely present in the desert and almost never convenient, and since I carry no tarp and don't want to bear its added burden or that of a brilliant flashlight to rip through the starry night, allowing me to avoid rattlesnakes, but jarring planets from their orbits, and since I have never minded the heat all that much anyway, I plan to walk all through the day, as I have done since the Mexican border. My concession to the Mojave is to carry an umbrella covered with a mirror of Mylar to reflect the light and heat.

This is certainly not the first desert the hikers have come across in their journey from the Mexican border. Most people visualize a desert as a hot, dry, desolate wasteland. To those from other parts of the United States or other countries, I suppose much of the trip so far has truly looked like a desert. Sometimes a desert is defined as land that receives less than ten inches of rain a year. If that be the case, much of southern California fits the bill. Even many parts of the great Central Valley of California could also be labeled desert. But then... there's desert and there's Desert.

For its 2,650 mile length, the Pacific Crest Trail rarely strays more than a hundred fifty miles from its namesake, the Pacific Ocean. Air, heated over land, rises, causing moist marine breezes to work their way inland. When they hit the mountains, they rise and dump their load of moisture. Above a certain height the air has cooled enough, perhaps six or seven thousand feet in this southern California section of the trail. Passing over the ridges, the air falls into the lands below, warming as it falls, and actually sucks moisture from the air and land. This is the rain shadow, and from its effect the vast areas of chaparral of southern California and the true deserts form: the Colorado, the driest desert in the northern hemisphere, touched twice, but briefly, by the trail in the south; the Great Basin Desert, of which the trail has just a taste further north; and the Mojave, stretched out now before me.

Of the roughly six hundred fifty miles of trail, from Campo through the Mojave, three great islands of mountain rise up out of a sea of desert and desert-like chaparral. For a very few miles, no more than a half dozen, in the Laguna Mountains, one strolls through forests of Jeffrey pine and oak. It is distance enough to soothe the mind and cool the body of the traveler, but hardly long enough to fully enjoy and thus not counted among the three. Further north lays the great granite pluton of the San Jacinto Mountains. From the southern slopes of Apache Peak to the end of Fuller Ridge, perhaps twenty-five miles, the hiker meanders through Jeffrey pine, incense cedar, lodgepole pine and a few fir trees. After a torturous twenty-mile downhill run and a two day crossing of the easternmost arm of the Colorado Desert near Palm Springs, comes the next island—the San Bernardino Mountains, which run from the head of Whitewater Creek to some miles past Big Bear, sixty or so pretty dry miles, descending at times low enough to find juniper, sage, and mountain mahogany, and even touches of the Mojave Desert creeping up the mountainside from the north. The largest section is the San Gabriel mountains, where there are nearly seventy-five miles covered with Jeffrey, ponderosa and Coulter pines, incense cedar, and some few others. Of course there are endless microclimates, the heads of shaded canyons, like the west fork of Palm Canyon where stands of white fir are to be found, for example. The Sierra Pelona, through which I have just passed, lies in the rain shadow of the higher San Gabriel and though mountain-like and pleasant, sports few evergreen trees.

Coming down into the desert, all thoughts of cool mountain vistas and shaded, piney trails evaporate like rain drops into the incandescent air. The trail drops down out of the Tejon Ranch, crosses Highway 138 and walks along 270th Street West. Where these two roads cross abides the house where Jack Fair lived. North, down 270th a short mile is Neenach School where I stop for much needed water.

A tall chain-link fence surrounds the school. It is a Saturday, and, as expected, no one is around. The two main gates into the school are closed and locked. I wonder what I will do if all the gates are locked? I am prepared to scale the fence. Fortunately, one of the small gates is unlocked, so visions fade of hanging from the wire, like some jail escape, confused and trying to break in. I walk around the school looking for water. All the hose bibs have the handles removed. In the back there are two water fountains. I try the first and nothing comes out. In growing alarm, I try the second. Cool water flows. Seriously depleted, I drink several liters over a half hour, and then fill my water bottles and head out and down the road. I will find out much later how lucky I am. On this Saturday in late May, it seems like just another weekend, but due to declining population, Neenach permanently closed its doors the year before.

The trail turns east for a mile or so and crosses 280th street, where the Los Angeles Aqueduct, in a ten foot diameter steel pipe, straddles the California Aqueduct, all water hijacked from elsewhere, making an improbable Los Angeles possible. There it turns due north. I look down the road disappearing into the haze in ghastly fulfillment of the prophet Isaiah, "Make straight in the desert a highway." Thankfully I can see the tenuous outlines of the Tehachapi Mountains, so I know that every mountain and hill has not yet been made low, nor the rough places plain.

After a mile or so, the dark pipe is exposed where a wooden trestle carries it across the lowest point in this part of the desert, a dry wash that meanders east-west through the valley. On the right are the first Joshua trees, a vast "forest" that appears to cover several square miles along the north side of this wash and on, in steadily decreasing numbers, into the mountains themselves.

This biome is called the Joshua Tree Woodlands, somewhat of a misnomer, because the Joshua tree is not really a tree at all, but a yucca, a member of the lily family. The view before me includes a few shrub-like Utah juniper, some sage, the ubiquitous rabbit brush, which is blooming in vast yellow clusters throughout the desert, numerous other species I fail to recognize, and of course, the Joshua trees. It seems as though nearly everyone finds them hideous in appearance. In *The Land of Sunshine* (a magazine of southern California published from 1890-1898) one writer said, "Weird, twisted, demoniacal, the (Joshua trees) remind me of those enchanted forests described by Dante, whose trees were human creatures in torment." I have seen Joshua trees referred to in several more recent texts, and oddly enough, every reference to them is prefaced with the adjective grotesque. The author of this section of the PCT Guidebook is no exception. It is a word used to indicate that the natural is distorted into ugliness and absurdity. But I find in them neither ugliness nor absurdity, but a stark beauty, the same craggy elegance, the same coarse perfection beheld in the faces of those peoples of desert and steppe, tundra and taiga, whose lives are forged and tempered by the extreme adversity of the elements, an inner beauty so complete that it seeps out, softening battered exteriors and smoothing weathered features into something baby-like and comforting, something innocent, something found in human faces that the Joshua tree possesses as well, but lacking humanity, is unable to express in terms of leaf and stalk that most travelers appreciate.

Apparently a group of Mormon settlers, leaving San Bernardino for Salt Lake City in 1857, ran into a stand, and one of their number suggested that it looked like the outstretched arms of Joshua, leading the chosen people through the desert and pointing the way to the Promised Land, or back to Salt Lake City. The story varies. It seems a little far-fetched to me. Truly, the message of the Joshua trees, whose multiple arms point in every direction, must be that you are already home. It's a simple lesson in the geometry of our globe, for when all directions lead to the same place, surely you must already be there. I propose that the Joshua trees, clustered and crowded, pointing everywhere at once, be renamed Bodhidharma trees, for this is surely a lesson in Zen, not Christianity.

Although early, it's already quite hot, and I decide to take a break in the shade of the pipe. Sitting in the sand, I look up and see that the pipe is not completely tight; water oozes, drop by drop, slowly, where rivets break the surface, slowly enough so that none drops to the ground, but evaporates away leaving little stalactites of Sierra minerals, less than an inch long.

Looking east, through the arabesque of Joshua trees lining the north side of the wash, I think about Joshua. He was a mighty general, perhaps the greatest of that ancient world, who first becomes known when, fresh from the Land of Goshen and heading into the desert of the Sinai with Moses and the Israelites, he fights and defeats Amalek. It didn't seem to matter that both Moses and Amalek shared the same great-great-grandfather, Isaac. Moses sent Joshua out, and Joshua "discomfited Amalek and his people with the edge of his sword."

After their years of roaming, the Israelites crossed the Jordan River, and leaving Moses behind, Joshua took the reins. He hung a left at the Hill of Foreskins and never looked back. After a bit, he came to Jericho, and as the saying goes, the rest is history. The inhabitants of Jericho, Hazor, Hebron, Ai, Bethel, Jarmuth, Lachich, Eglon, Gezer, Debir, and twenty-three other city-states of the mountainous portion of the ancient land of Canaan felt the edge of his sword, which is another way of saying that the kings and armies of those city-states and all the inhabitants as well, including men, women and children, and on a few occasions even the animals, were slaughtered. "Smitten" and "discomfited" are the words the Bible so carefully uses to describe this. For some reason these thoughts are, in themselves, deeply discomfiting, but I cannot say why at the moment.

I am startled out of my musing as a Jeep station wagon slowly crosses southward across the wash. Vexing thoughts are pushed to the back of my mind. The driver sees me and slows to a stop. Rolling down a window, he says, "Are you a PCT hiker?" Hearing the affirmative, he asks if I could use some ice-cold liquid refreshment, which of course, I can. He introduces himself, Bruce something or other, but being dazed, as I usually am by sudden, incongruous encounters with the "other" world, I forget his name. He is a relative, a cousin, of Black Hawk, who is a bit more than half a day ahead of me. I met Black Hawk and Strawberry Girl a few days back. They are from the east, but Bruce, living in Nevada, is close enough to offer support while they cross the desert. He is spending the day driving around dispensing ice-cold beverages to startled hikers, including me.

We chat for a while. He leaves me with a couple of icy Gatorades and disappears in a cloud of dust. As I watch his car growing steadily smaller down the long washboard of dirt track, I suddenly wish I had asked him to drop me back at the Country Store on the highway, less than ten miles back. I am still longing for a chance to pillage its shelves for goodies not seen in days.

I sit awhile longer, enjoying the shade and the relative cool, mind mostly in idle, thinking alternately of the Country Store and the drops of water slowly forming the stalactites above me. After some time, I shoulder my pack and head north toward the mountains. Eventually the trail/road swings away from its beeline north, to the east in a great sweeping arc. The water has been running in a mostly buried iron pipe until now. Suddenly I encounter a concrete highway snaking its way east and north through the desert.

The day has escalated from hot to HOT. I find that walking on the concrete is noticeably cooler than on the road; no doubt all that icy water I hear rushing tantalizingly out of reach only feet away has much to do with this. Every half-mile or so there is a large concrete box sitting astride the aqueduct, marked as "waterhole" on the map. Waterholes they may be, but not for us hikers, for steel doors secured by hefty padlocks make the issue moot. They do, however, make a marvelously convenient chair for a sit and a sip of water. Now, if they'd just put some shade structures over them, for there is little enough of that commodity to be found on this stretch of the trail.

Bye and bye, after about twelve miles into the day, the aqueduct almost comes out of its hiding place as it crosses the dry wash of Little Oak Canyon Creek. The creek bed has been filled in to contain the concrete tunnel. A spillway runs over the top, in the unlikely case of rain. Another convenient sitting place presents itself and I feel reticent to pass it by. A hot wind is blowing down and across the desert, but it feels cool for the minute or three it takes to evaporate the sweat drenched shirt exposed when I remove my pack. Hiding in the lee of my Mylar-covered umbrella, I check my cheap little thermometer. It reads only 104°F at 1:00 o'clock in the afternoon; this late May day is just a warm-up for the inferno to come.

I sit for some time, staring out over the desert. Finally I rouse and head down the road, through the wash, ever eastward, and a little north. Joshua trees line the hillside, and my thoughts turn Biblical once more, to Abraham, for it all really began with Abraham, and Abraham was a traveling man. Well, it didn't exactly begin with Abraham. First, Adam and Eve had become as gods by eating from the Tree of Knowledge of Good and Evil. But before they could eat from the Tree of Life and live forever, they were given the boot from Eden. Then, to top it off, the agrarian Cain slew his pastoral-herder brother, Able, in a dramatic and terrible foretelling of the revenge of Joshua and the Israelites in the land of Canaan, more than two and a half millennia in the future.

Probably a lot more happened to make God decide that the human race wasn't worth it, for about fifteen hundred years passed between Adam and the Flood. The whole Noah story doesn't use up too many words in the Bible, and none of them are too particular as to what wrongs man committed, and so one can only guess as to what they did that was so bad. The only specific charge was that the world was filled with violence. Welcome to the human race.

The Epic of Gilgamesh, a cycle of heroic poems from ancient Sumer, from the third millennium B.C., thus predating the Bible, gives the first written version of the Great Flood. The Sumerians, who, because both men and women shaved their heads to help fight the heat, were called "the bald ones," and who, just by chance, also invented writing, tell of the teeming masses of humanity, who multiplied and multiplied until the world "bellowed like a wild bull." The "uproar of mankind is intolerable and sleep is no longer possible by reason of the babble," is how the gods put it. And so they destroyed the world—because they couldn't get a decent night's rest. This story was well known, in several versions, throughout the ancient world. It occurs to me that the gods of Sumer must have developed marked patience or perhaps gotten hard of hearing since then, or judging from the uproar these days, we'd all be building boats. Just this morning, one of the ruined, semi-deserted desert dwellings I passed by had a large boat parked in back. I wonder if they know something I don't?

Three centuries after the Flood, Abraham, the twentieth human generation, was born in Ur of the Chaldees, the capital of ancient Sumeria, and as I said, he was a traveling man. Nothing is known of his early life, although many stories were later made up to fill in the gaps. At some point, for reasons unknown, his father loaded up the wagon and left Ur on the banks of the Tigris River, and traveled north to Harran, in what is today in southern Turkey, near the Syrian border. It was in Harran that Abraham, then known as Abram, heard The Voice. Today, if you hear a voice telling you it is the One True God and that you should pack up and leave town and head for a place where you could have all the land for you and your descendants, you might well wind up in the local psychiatric ward. But Abram, at the age of seventy-five, hitched his wagons and headed for The Promised Land. This was the land of Canaan, that slim strip of land between the Jordan River and the Mediterranean Sea.

What was so improbable about all this is that the whole of the ancient world, of the Egyptians, the Akkadians, Sumerians, the Babylonians, Assyrians, Chaldeans, Hittites, the Mycenians, and the Minoans, not to mention a host of other lesser powers, was a world already full of gods. Nobody but Abram in all that time and land suspected that there might be only one (with the exception of Akhenaten in Egypt, some centuries in the future, whose short reign, oddly enough, appears to be within a hundred years or so of the Exodus). And what made the outcome of the story so unlikely is that the land promised to Abram was a land already richly inhabited by others, who had the odd notion that it belonged to them.

In Genesis, the people of Canaan are spoken of as a mild and friendly race. When Abram and his wife, Sarai, traveled and lived there the rest of their lives, he was received as "a mighty prince." Early on in his journeys, a famine forced him into Egypt, where he was also well treated, and parted later a wealthy man. He also spent considerable time in the land of Abimelech, a Philistine king, where he was treated with generosity and kindness. When Sarai, by then known as Sarah, died, she was buried among the Hittites, in the cave of Machelpelah, in the war-torn town today called Hebron. Abram, by then known as Abraham, wound up there too, some forty years later, living to the ripe old age of one hundred seventy-five. In between, he fathered Ishmael, at the age of eighty-six, and Isaac, when he was one hundred, from different mothers. When Sarah gave birth to Isaac, at the age of ninety-one, Ishmael and his mother, Sarah's Egyptian handmaiden Hagar, were mercilessly driven into the desert, without supplies, to survive or not, as they would. Ishmael, whom God told Abraham would be a wild man whose hand would be against all, would become the founder of all the Bedouin tribes, who would become known as the Arabs and ultimately become Moslems, whose hands today are still hard against the seed of Abraham.

Isaac fathered Jacob, later renamed Israel, who became the father of the Israelites. Jacob had twelve sons. One, Judah, became the father of all the Jews. Another was Joseph, who wound up in Egypt through no fault of his own and no acts of kindness by his brothers. Ultimately his brothers and the rest of their kin wound up there too, to become enslaved by a new and untrusting Pharaoh, some say Ramses II. These became the people known as the Israelites, who, four hundred years later, left with Moses and Joshua and wandered in the desert for forty years.

It was there that Yahweh waylaid them. The God of Abraham, who made no other demands on him and his descendants than to make the appropriate offerings and sacrifices, and not to be wicked (though the terms of wickedness are not spelled out in much detail), not to sleep with another man's wife, and not to kill anyone, unless He said it was okay, had found plenty of time to think about it during four or five hundred years between Abraham and Moses. The Ten Commandments were not all he had in mind. Before it was over, he had listed some six hundred thirteen things that needed doing, or not doing.

Lost in thought, I hike a couple of miles beyond the wash of Little Oak Creek Canyon, where the road takes a dip southward and begins to skirt the eastern end of a section of beautifully eroded badlands. Crushed and crenulated, the colorful sediments are sculpted into walls and towers of red and yellow at the edge of the alluvial fan. It is a sharp break in the vast alluvial slopes cascading down out of the Tehachapi. I wonder if it is an earthquake fault scarp, for we are in earthquake country. Not too far to the north, running more or less east-west through Tehachapi Pass, lies the great Garlock Fault, the second largest fault in California. The thought doesn't trouble me much, although many fear earthquakes. Growing up in southern California, the rattling of dishes and shaking of things was a fairly common occurrence, enough of a novelty to cause a momentary pause in dinner or conversation. Considering I have slept astride the mighty San Andreas Fault twice in the past three weeks, in Swarthout Canyon, at Cajon Pass only eleven days ago, and at the feet of Snow Canyon, where the fault cuts across the ten thousand foot scarp of Mount San Jacinto, a week before that. It causes me no consternation.

I come to a junction where three roads meet and cross each other in quick succession. Straight on through, perhaps a half-mile up the hill, I see a hiker. Unfortunately, I assume the hiker is on the correct road. Later that afternoon, when I get around to looking at the Guidebook map,

I will see the mistake I made, a mistake that the Guidebook clearly warns against. But I was paying little attention at the time. The road starts up across the badlands, reaches a ridge and disappears. Ignoring the road to the right, without a thought, off I go.

At the top of the second ridge I see the hiker. He has stopped and is talking to people in a yellow jeep. I hurry on. The hiker is Caveman, who received his name as a result of spending the night in one of the old graphite mine tunnels just west of Elizabeth Lake Canyon Road, three or four nights before. His appellation is a fine one, rolling easily off the tongue, but the thought of spending the night in a mine tunnel leaves me, being slightly claustrophobic, less than enthusiastic. A young man, accompanied by his mother, drives the jeep. She says she is a Pacific Crest Trail Association member and that she is camped out nearby, another trail angel.

Caveman and I learn we are on the wrong road, that the true trail lies about a half mile east, below the badlands, on the desert floor...the road not taken. She says this road will get us to Cottonwood Creek, but only after considerable up and down. Over the second ridge, says she, if we look down the wash, we will see her camp. If we go down the wash there, we can get ice-cold refreshments, which sounds pretty good, and then hit the correct road.

The jeep drives on and we continue down, through the wash, and up the couple of hundred vertical feet to the top of the next ridge. Down the canyon there are a couple of trucks and some tents. But...she said after the second ridge, so we travel on. At the top of the next ridge we look east down the wash—empty. Evidently it was only one ridge not two. But there's no going back. At the top of next ridge, I decide to hike down the wash to the correct road. Caveman allows he will continue on. We part company and I head east and down.

After making it down to the bottom of the wash, I follow the sandy floor as it winds around through the canyon. Not knowing just how far out the road is, I decide to cut across the desert in a more northerly track than I am now following. I make my way across little rolling hills covered with sharply angled rocks, cacti, and creosote bush, and cut by small washes and gullies, making passage a toilsome stroll.

Just when I begin to think the road doesn't exist, about two hundred yards away a car drives by, leaving a cloud of dust in its wake. I hit the road, now the true trail, and follow it eastward. After a mile or so, it makes a turn more northward, and a little later I cross under the twin lines of high voltage electric towers, marching across the desert like a vast column of some iron army. To the north they advance up a wash and over the top of the badlands; to the south they march, smaller and smaller, at last dissolving away into the haze.

It is now the middle of the afternoon, and my thermometer tells me it is 106°F. The Joshua trees have begun to fade, only appearing sporadically here and there. Creosote bush is the main order of business on this section of desert. Graceful and willowy, with tiny, resinous, dark green leaves, it is the most common, wide-ranging of all the desert plants. Consisting of from four to a dozen or more branches, all coming out of the same stem crown, they dot the desert as far as I can see. To most, its name conjures images of black tar oozing out of telephone poles or railroad ties. I pull a few leaves from one nearby and crush them in my fingers. The smell of creosote is there, though this is not the source of the now considered dangerous and banned petro-chemical creosote. Its sticky, resinous leaves aid in limiting water loss, and manufacture a chemical that not only keeps animals from eating it, but when on the ground, act as an herbicide and keep other plants from horning in on the creosote bush's water supply. Here in the desert, where the scant yearly rainfall comes in summer thunderstorm torrents, its deep taproots allow it to live, uncaringly, through seasons and years, wet or dry.

Even more amazing is the life history of this innocuous plant. As the growth of the plant continues, the oldest branches gradually die. Somewhere between thirty and ninety years, the stem crown splits into separate crowns. As time passes, the original crown and branches weather away, as do the connections between the adjoining segments. The plant, now a ring of plants, has become a clone, consisting of several independent plants all descended from one seedling. This outward growth is, as one might suspect of a desert plant, extremely slow, perhaps a bit over a foot in 150 years. In the Lucerne Valley near Victorville, about 70 miles southeast of here, scientists found a clonal ring 45 feet in diameter. Using radiocarbon dating and best guesstimates, they pronounced that *King Clone*, as it is called, is 11,700 years old. Its original seedling was just getting started while glaciers still clogged the Sierra! Just before I hit the road, I passed a clonal circle, about 15 feet in diameter...at perhaps 2,500 years of age, a mere juvenile! Some argue that since the plants are all genetically identical to the original, it is still the same plant, and, hence the oldest living thing on earth. Be that as it may, I still prefer the Methuselah bristlecone pine, hidden high in the Inyo Mountains to the north, at 4,767 years.

Joshua trees may be decreasing in number, but here on the right side of the road there is a single, particularly large Joshua tree surrounded by an ample area of clear sand. It is wide enough and bushy enough to cast the first usable shade I have seen since I crawled out from beneath the Los Angeles Aqueduct, nearly thirteen miles ago. That others have noticed this too is evidenced by footprints and piled rocks. I head off the road and shuck my pack. An hour passes while I stare dreamily into the blue as the one or two wispy clouds on the horizon begin to expand across the sky. Though I have espoused walking all through the day, I have no more than four or five miles yet to travel this day, and at least four hours of sunlight left, so I feel little compunction to leave.

I have to move several times during the hour, as the two-foot wide band of shade marches across the sand in concert with the sun. Another half hour and I rouse...time to move on. Minutes later I find a road branching to the left, which takes me into the canyon bearing Cottonwood Creek. I walk uphill for twenty minutes and the road, making a hard right, runs into the aqueduct again. I assume Caveman must be far ahead of me by now, being younger and having taken, no doubt, the shorter route as I whiled away the afternoon in the shifting shade.

The concrete highway, bearing its precious liquid burden, heads northeast awhile, then runs into the rim of Cottonwood Creek and turns due north. At the end of a long, straight stretch, I turn and look back. Just coming around the corner, a mile back, is a hiker. I wonder if it is Caveman...it must be. Perhaps he too found a place to hide out. At last I see the bridge and the water supply. I find the water, a concrete trough fed by water trickling from a pipe running from the aqueduct above. Carefully avoiding the bees that swarm the wetness, I spend more than a half an hour there. I drink my fill and then some, fill my water bottles, and let the water spilling out of the trough cool my feet. At long last, looking at the map, I see that the road Caveman and I started on made its two hundred foot up, two hundred foot down way through and over a dozen washes. If that is he behind me, no wonder it took him so long, for he has climbed and descended a thousand vertical feet this hellish afternoon. At last I am ready to go, so I saddle up and head out and across the bridge. Day's end is nearing and I begin to look for a place to be.

The trail crosses the bridge, turns left and heads up the north side of Cottonwood Creek. In less than a mile, the trail becomes a trail at last, turning right off the road and up through a ravine. There sits a several hundred pound boulder of white, massive quartz lying alongside the mostly sandy trail. It shines whitely in the late afternoon sun, appearing out of place in the drab duns and grays and greens of the desert. In a little ways, the trail hits the top of the alluvial fan. Suddenly I feel tired and hungry. I abandon the trail and head back across the fan's flat top, back the way I just came. It's a couple of hundred yards to the edge, a hundred feet above Cottonwood Creek. Out on a promontory, back far enough away from its steep sides to be invisible from below, but close enough for a marvelous view, I set up camp and rest awhile. Finally I prepare dinner and sit, looking out over the wash and through the desert.

It is nearing sunset and the ubiquitous desert wind, which has been blowing off and on all day, steadies and picks up. Half surrounded by the Tehachapi Mountains, the desert's heat is still relatively high, while the air in the mountains has begun to cool. The cool, heavier air falls down the mountainside and rushes with seeming purpose across the alluvium into the desert floor below.

I finish my camp for the night, spread out my Tyvek groundsheet, and sit downwind of my small tent to watch the night unfold. High, wispy cirrus clouds, underlain by a few thin patches of altostratus fill the late afternoon sky. To the west, they are almost thick enough to obscure the sun. A blinding silvery patch of sky shows where the sun lies four fingers above the horizon, an hour from setting by my reckoning.

The sky is riddled by trails of sparkling ice crystals, left by jets crisscrossing the sky. Towards the setting sun, there are a number of north-south running bands, evidence of traffic between Los Angeles to the south and San Francisco, Portland, Seattle and all points north. There are a few others lying east-west across the sky.

Sky worms!! The words pop unannounced into my head. It is a phrase I have not thought of in more than twenty-five years. That peerless photographer of the American landscape, Ansel Adams, had no great love of the condensation trails of jet airplanes. Calling them sky worms, he raged at them and cast many an invective skyward when a magic scene was spoiled by their untimely wriggling across the sky.

In another life, I was going to be a photographer. Ansel Adams was my idol. With an old 8x10 view camera, I trudged everywhere I could carry its hefty package. I packed a 4x5 camera and tripod throughout the Sierra Nevada. I poured for hours over his words and pictures, used his techniques and his formulae, spent days hidden away in the darkroom, and do admit, without bragging, that some few of my photographs could sit aside his and suffer no great loss through comparison. I had been accepted to graduate school in art based on my work itself, for my degrees were in Psychology and Anthropology. I planned to go but it was not to be. The ending of a star-crossed marriage and subsequent raising of two young children changed all that, and I never was one to go back, and so...the camera, lo these thirty-five years later, sits in a corner of my basement. No blame.

High up, nearly invisible, a plane, from Salt Lake City or perhaps Denver, makes its way west. I feel no resentment, loft no invectives into the evening wind at its passage, for it is the sole sign that I am not, at this moment, the only living creature in the entire world. I wonder what the passengers are thinking, strapped tightly in their too small seats, finishing up a miniature bag of peanuts and one last cocktail before returning to the upright position and heading down into the nightmare that, to my way of thinking, is Los Angeles.

Having spent more than a month now, mostly solitary by day, alone with my thoughts, making irregular forays into civilization, and then only for hours or a day at most, I find it nearly impossible to put myself in their place, to be thinking about being disgorged, like Jonah, from the belly of a great aluminum whale, finding myself on a freeway, sandwiched in lines of cars, close enough to clearly see the grimacing faces of their occupants, hurtling terrifyingly down the road at seventy-five miles an hour, or worse, parked in seemingly infinite lines of land-locked vehicles, inching forward slowly...slowly. All of this with the goal of visiting either Grandma or Disneyland, or wandering through the back lot scenes of some movieland or the other, perhaps anointing themselves with sun screen and standing in herds on the beaches, or worse...going home. It seems to me as foreign as walking on the sun.

At last the sun reaches the Tehachapi Mountains. Still partially hazed by the clouds, it appears as a brilliant orb attached to the top of the mountains by an equally brilliant shaft of light, looking for all the world like the blazing silver mushroom cloud of some far distant atomic explosion, inexplicably detonated on the top of a mountain peak. And then, as seems common enough in lonely places, the night rushes in. Silver turns to molten pink, then angry red. Further from the horizon, the lower stratus clouds race through shades of gray. I find it a curious coincidence that the German test pilot who flew the first military jet described it as "being pushed by angels," and far above, my only connection to the world of humans, a single band of white, blazes ever west and slightly south, toward the City of the Angels.

Within the hour after the sun sets, a nearly full moon rises up through the haze and clouds. This first night after the full moon, no diminishing of its shape or size is yet apparent, especially since its light, through distant cloud, is fuzzed and gossamer. Westward, the highest clouds still show the faintest trace of pink along their lower edges. Goosebumps pop up all over my arms and legs and neck, the result of an incredible day, followed by this incredible evening...either that, or the wind is getting colder by the minute.

Down the canyon, perhaps a quarter mile away, I see a small stationary light spring up, faintly winking and flickering among the dark, barely perceptible shapes of the Joshua trees lining the canyon. Caveman perhaps, seeking refuge for the night. I wonder if he feels the same fear sleeping under infinite skies that I felt, thinking of sleeping in an old, abandoned graphite mine? I trust not.

Sitting in front of my tent, I think one last time of Joshua and the Israelites. Joshua smote and smote until he could smite no more. This smiting appears to have lasted maybe six or seven years or so, and at the end Joshua was old and feeble—"well stricken with age," as they say. I guess all that smiting took its toll. He called all the tribes together and divvied up the land. Unfortunately, he had not conquered it all, only some of the city-states. Leaving much smiting to be done, he died. His successors faced various tribes of the Canaanites, who inhabited the coastal plains and valleys, and, further south and four hundred years later, the Philistines, from whom comes the word Palestine, when Solomon became king.

The Canaanites were buddies with the Hittites, who were the rulers of most of the land to the north and east—the Egyptians being the power elsewhere—and shared in their knowledge of iron. In the valleys and coastal plains, the Bronze-Age Israelites were no match for them, not having the advantage of "chariots of iron," and wound up having to make treaties. They began to live amongst the Canaanites and adopted much of their culture, including their gods. This was the source of much of their trouble for the next four hundred years: the time of The Judges, when, as punishment for their failures, they were conquered and subjugated again and again.

The Philistines were of particular trouble. Known to the Egyptians as *The Sea People*, they are spoken of in the Bible, in the Book of Amos, as refugees from Caphtor, probably Greeks from the Island of Crete where the Minoan Civilization flourished and died, the first wave arriving about six hundred years before Joshua. Like all of the tribes under Hittite rule, the Philistines too, are spoken well of in Genesis, but by the time of The Judges, they appear to be beyond bellicose, most likely because of the considerable smiting and attempted smiting undertaken by Joshua and his successors. For more than a hundred years it was all the Israelites could do to hold their own against the Philistines. Before the Israelites are done, neither the Hittites nor the Philistines, nor any other peoples of Canaan, for that matter, will think kindly of the seed of Abraham.

Yahweh, an ascetic, harsh, demanding, and above all, an unforgiving god, had left explicit instructions; they were to smite these infidels every one, not hang out with them. Yahweh knew that the Israelites would find it difficult not to backslide, because the gods of that ancient world were, by and large, a joyous lot, given to venerating the earth and its renewal, dancing and celebrating, drinking wine, and fornicating. Even seven hundred years after the time of the Exodus, Solomon the Wise would fall prey to those joyous earth-venerating agrarian gods, Bäal and the Earth Mother, Ashtoreth, gods knowable and close, not transcendent and beyond all knowledge. The temples of the high places and groves came again, for a while, into popularity. Of course he had six hundred wives and three hundred concubines, so he shouldn't get too much criticism for his backsliding. After all, who could resist the power of nine hundred women whispering of the Earth Mother in his ears?

The great story of the Old Testament, really, is that of the struggle of Yahweh to overcome the gods of the ancient world, who had thousands of years head start on him, and without annihilating them, overcome the Israelites, who were a *stiff-necked* lot. *Stiff-necked* is an agrarian term describing an ox that refuses to be yoked, an apt description of the Israelites. Ultimately, Yahweh and the Israelites learned to live together. They submitting to the yoke, mostly, and he not destroying them every time they failed one of his tests, which were many, and which they frequently did. And in the end, the Israelites managed to hang on long enough to take over the Promised Land, and it is an interesting world we live in today.

Suddenly I realize just what it was that bothered me this morning when I was thinking about Joshua and the Israelites. I am no historian, but sitting here in the desert, my mind floating free, it occurs to me we have a word today for what the Bible describes as Israel's entrance into The Promised Land. It is an act that reverberates down through all of Western history, including the Crusades, the Inquisition, five hundred years of strife in Ireland, the Muslim Ottoman Empire's murder of more than a million Christian Armenians in the early 1900s, Hitler's appropriation of this idea and subsequent extermination of six million Jews and perhaps five million other undesirables during World War II. Today we call it genocide...and it startles me to think that Joshua and the Israelites may well have been the first perpetrators in recorded history.

The idea of karma flits across my mind, troubling thoughts that startle me, considering the persecution that has been waged upon the Jews throughout the course of history. But of course, it *is* karma. Most think that karma means getting what you deserve, but it does not. It simply means *doing*. What happens to you is your doing, be it good or ill. The concept carries no connotations of blame or justice. Be that as it may, I feel momentarily guilty, as perhaps, sadly, necessarily befits one in these politically correct times.

That champion of liberty, former Supreme Court Justice William O. Douglas, always insisted that there be no limits on thought, that no subject be taboo. And anyway, my thoughts are often their own masters, going where they will, juxtaposing the sacred and the profane, the trivial and the profound, the dolorous and the joyous, with equal alacrity.

The winds, which seemed to be practicing all day for this, their day's hurrah, are steady in force and direction. I begin to feel cold, a delicious sensation after the heat of this long day. Discounting momentary thoughts of night-roaming tarantula and scorpion and scaly rattlesnake, I drag my bag out onto the ground and crawl in. The night is too fine to waste enclosed in the double nylon cocoon of tent and bag. The moon rides high in the evening sky.

I have spent many years traveling through wild places, but really never alone. Even on this trip of now more than five hundred miles, I have spent few nights alone. I think back, counting; this is my sixth solitary night. I always thought I would be afraid. Visions of the giant ants and tarantulas and praying mantises and scorpions, memories of marauding desert monsters of the science fiction movies of my youth, float through my mind. This is the desert...where monsters roam and flying saucers land to transact their fiendish, alien business. I laugh quietly to myself.

Feeling relaxed and at peace with this marvelous, benign desert world, I lie in my bag, listening to the wind and watching the sky. From my Lake Hughes mail drop, I have a few ounces of Oban, a fine, sweet, lightly smoky, single malt scotch from the edge of the Hebrides Islands. It has been secreted in my pack, waiting for just the right time—which is now, my last night in the Mojave. Eventually I fall asleep, to awaken, however briefly, several times throughout the night to chart the progress of the moon across the sky.

The next morning finds me up early facing the prospect of a slightly more than twenty-two mile day, with more than thirty-one hundred vertical feet to climb, all the way to Willow Springs Road, and hopefully a quick hitch to Mojave, with its restaurants and its...well...restaurants. Oh yes, and a food drop at White's Motel. I shoulder my pack and begin the long steady climb, due north up the sandy, southern, alluvial slopes of the Tehachapi Mountains. The trail comes to and navigates for some distance along a barbed wire fence, evidence left by the Tejon Ranch, again. Finally the trail starts up in earnest into the mountains.

Throughout virtually all of the canyons and washes I have passed this morning are tracks left by motorcycles. I will see them for miles to come. Some of the tracks go up the heads of ravines so steep that it seems certain no machine, let alone mortal, could make the climb. Late in the day, riding in a truck into Mojave, I will mention this to my host. He says these tracks are only followed by *advanced* riders. I wonder how many miles of ruin must lie behind a motorcycle, before its rider becomes *advanced*? In places, like still distant Gamble Spring Canyon, the tracks will be so numerous and destructive that it will not always be apparent where my trail lies. The destruction is savage, and I know that if motorcycles were banned tomorrow, it would take decades, if not centuries, to heal itself in this dry, tender land.

When I was younger man, I would be ready to rant and rave to anyone who would listen—and many who would not—about these horrible people and their horrible machines, but old age brings, if not forbearance or resignation, at least more than one thought about nearly every subject, which I suppose, some might regard as indecision. I look sadly at the damage, then say to myself, "Ah well, this *is* a pretty remote and desolate place, and think how I would feel if even one percent of these motorcycleers or off-road vehicleers or motorboaters or snowmobileers or jet skiers, no longer having a chariot to ride or a place to ride it, wound up hiking in the mountains, or walking the PCT?" I shrug, feeling the presence of the ghost of that champion of the desert, Edward Abbey, chiding me for my acceptance. But let riding dogs lie, say I, for they, no doubt, live lives as filled with joy and sorrow as the quietest, solitary thru-hiker, and deserve as much as any to enjoy their momentary respite from the drudgery that occasionally allows them, in spite of the obnoxious, damaging mode they choose, to recreate and hence, re-create themselves.

Just as the trail makes a serious foray uphill, only to drop down into Tylerhorse Canyon, I cross one of the many dirt roads. The trail follows it up and out of sight. I hear gunshots. Looking around, I see a pickup truck parked on top of a hill down to my right, perhaps a quarter of a mile away. The truck begins to move and heads up the road I am walking on. I am certainly no enemy of firearms, for I own a number and engage in competitions on a regular basis, but surrounded by a veritable freeway of evidence left by city dwellers, I must admit I feel a tinge of fear, no longer alone in the wilderness, as I am. I pick up my speed. The truck is only a few hundred yards behind me when I reach the point where the road crosses the crest of the ridge; the trail breaks from the road and starts down under the ridge. I walk a hundred yards, and feeling winded, but now safe, I stop to rest a minute. Suddenly, I hear a "Hello!" and look up.

A dozen yards above me is the pickup. There are six Latinos, four with rifles. The two in the cab of the truck are adults and the four in the back—with the rifles—are evidently their teenage children. One of the kids says, "Hey, did your partner leave you?" I'm not certain what he is talking about, so I tell him no, I am walking...alone. I bite my tongue; why did I say that? I tell them I am hiking the Pacific Crest Trail, that I started at the Mexican border. We discuss that curiosity a minute or two, and then they ask me if I have seen any wild pigs? I say no, but that I've seen plenty of quail. They laugh, saying it is not quail season. The men get out of the truck. One, wearing multiple tattoos, which I take as evidence of gangs and growing up rough in some inner city, smiles and says, "You better be careful or the coyote will get you." I interpret his words with double meaning, the wily four-leggeds of the desert, and the wily, dangerous two-leggeds who guide illegals in their hurried journey to the United States across deserts further south. Is this a threat? I reply that I haven't had a good meal for days and the coyote might just be my dinner. They all laugh. The Tattooed Man says quietly, "Vaya con Dios"...go with God. The two men pile back into the truck, and it disappears.

Struck with shame over my baseless paranoia, I pick up my pack. Intolerance, and its dark brother, prejudice, it seems, recognizes neither age nor avocation, riding cheerfully on the brow of young and old, doctor or drayer, savant or simpleton...or solitary thru-hiker. I wonder when we humans will lose these seemingly unshakable fears, a throwback to the times when men lived in bands and learned to distrust, for good or ill, all those not of their own kind? I am reminded of the words of George Aiken, longtime U.S. Senator from Vermont: "If we were to wake up some morning and find that everyone was the same race, creed, and color, we would find some other cause for prejudice by noon."

Another round of the wheel, reminding me again of the distance I have yet to travel, not only in miles upon the ground, but within myself, I walk on down into Tylerhorse Canyon.

The Guidebook says that most likely the creek will be dry this time of year, but eight days ago a pretty good set of storms blew through, and the creek is beautifully wet. I spend a quick half hour, drinking and drinking...and soaking my feet. The trail switchbacks upward and eastward, then down into dry Gambel Springs Canyon, then up and out again, sixteen hundred feet up, to the summit of the Tehachapi Mountains. Joshua trees have now vanished, to be replaced by juniper and a few Coulter pines, and a little higher, the piñon pines.

Reaching, at last, the top of the ridge, just before the trail swings more northerly around the edge and begins its journey down, I stop and look back toward the desert. Soon it will be gone, out of sight but never out of mind. I sit on a convenient rock and stare a long while, looking south. Behind me are all the mountains through which I have been treading these last weeks, San Jacinto, San Gorgonio, San Bernardino, San Gabriel, Sierra Pelona. I can see them clearly, but only in my mind's eye, for the haze makes the distant mountains just a barely discernible darker zone across the horizon. Only the Sierra Pelona are clearly visible, more or less. I trace my route along their ridges and down into the flat, past the place where Jack Fair lived and died, where I passed through washes and over alluvial fans to Cottonwood Creek and spent last night, and up the hill to where I now sit.

Suddenly I wish the desert had been a lot wider, had presented a lot more difficulty than it did. Surely the terrain from the slopes of Granite Mountain, down, across, and up the San Felipe traverse, through the edge of the Anza-Borrego Desert, presented equal, if not greater hardship. And, the trip across the Colorado Desert, from Snow Creek and up into the San Bernardino Mountains was truly difficult. From Jack Fair's house to where I now stand is hardly more than thirty miles. It was over too soon. In my mind's eye, I can see the sand-filled waddis, the spine-choked hillsides, the plateaus, with their mosaic *pavement*, the serrated mountains, and above all the sun...whose brilliance distills life to its very essence.

I understand, for the first time, really, that the desert is a lens of unequaled power. It brings into sharp focus the image of your existence, makes clear that often blurry line between the important and the trivial, and reminds you that there is much that can only be understood in solitude. The English Renaissance philosopher, Francis Bacon, who said, "Whoever is delighted in solitude is either a wild beast or a god," was wrong, for though I love this solitude with a passion that, from this high hill of old age, seems no less powerful than that I had for my first love, the girl next door, I am neither wild beast nor god, being nothing more than an old man, a solitary thru-hiker...with miles to go before I sleep.

At last, I head down the remaining seven or so miles to the road...and civilization.

I make good time down to where the trail crosses Tehachapi-Willow Springs Road. Not too long before the road are lines of wind generators. The trail passes close to them and the eerie whooshing noise they make fills the air. I finally hit the road at its intersection with

Cameron Road. I head south-east a couple of hundred yards to Oak Creek Road, which goes into Mojave, a good intersection, I think, at which to hang by my thumb, hopefully for just a short time. I have yet found only one place where I could not get a ride, from where the trail crosses the Angeles Crest Highway, just west of Wrightwood. On the other hand, I have yet to get a quick ride, and this day proves no exception. There is a steady stream of traffic headed into and away from Tehachapi, but few cars turn off towards Mojave. Those that do, as usual, fail to heed my request.

After a long while, a Volvo station wagon, heading in the wrong direction, passes by. The driver, evidently seeing my Tyvek groundsheet sign, saying *PCT Hiker, Mojave, Please*, slows down and turns around. His car is loaded to the gunnels—kids and groceries—but he stops, opens an ice chest and gives me a bottle of ice-cold water and a banana. His son gets out too, and we all talk a few minutes. He's done some hiking, knows about the trail. He says I won't have too much trouble getting a ride the fifteen miles to town, for the traffic is steady. I thank him, and they drive away. A *lot* he knows about getting rides, I think.

But not much later, a man in a pickup bearing the logo of a wind generation company pulls over. I pile my gear in and off we go townward, toward showers and salads and bunches of grapes. I glance in alarm at the speedometer, for we appear to be flying down the highway at terrifying speed, but it reads only fifty. Although I have experienced the shock of this phenomenon many times, moving from days of foot travel to instant freeway speed, it never fails to take me by surprise. He is talking about hiking and the Tehachapi prison and who knows what, but I barely hear him.

Tired from the long day, and momentarily lost in reverie, I think about my trip through the desert. I wonder what the world would be like today, if somewhere along the path of history, things had worked out differently? If Abraham had disregarded orders from an unseen god to pull up stakes and leave Harran. Or if, instead of allowing Ishmael and Hagar to be cast out when Isaac was born, Abraham had kept them and cherished them, would there be no nation of Islam today to be at odds with the rest of Abraham's issue and place the world at the brink of chaos? What if Moses had taken a left turn, traveling the scenic coastal path instead of the terrible wilderness of the Sinai, thus avoiding Yahweh, lying in ambush in the mountains? Would there never have been a signal that it is right to slaughter all who believe differently? Would the Thousand Gods of Hatti still rule in strange accord? What if the Philistines had wiped out the marauding Israelites? No Islam, no Judaism, no Christianity...would we still worship the joyful gods of field and forest, the earth goddess, Ashtaroth, or one her many incarnations, Ishtar, Astarte, Aphrodite, or Venus? What would the world be like if our religion bade us take care of the earth and nurture it, instead of telling us right off that we have dominion over the fish and fowl and cattle and every thing that creepeth, giving, to some, the notion that it is ours for the rape? Surely it would be a curious world, where men sang and drank wine, dancing around altars of burnt or sin offerings, only to be found in expensive suits headed for the office with its computers next morn.

And, there's no saying it would be a better world, for all religion, it seems, has its dark side, its faces of war and evil and death, its Shiva, dancing the Tandava at the destruction of the universe. It is easy to look back along the long corridor of history and say, " Ah...look what might have been," but there is no second guessing history, and what might have been is just that, what might have been. And what is...is. And today is all that matters.

You would misconstrue to think that I lay all the ills of western civilization, ills ancient and present, at the feet of Abraham, the father of those three great monotheistic religions, forged out of the history of one desert people. Surely his crime was only that of being human, of proudly wearing that imperfect brain that still calls us to listen, even in these times when gods no longer deign to talk to men and prove themselves with deeds miraculous, to listen to One who surely made us in his image, for we bear His fatal flaw, that of a jealousy so great it allows for nothing else.

There is a story, so prophetic, that it would seem impossible for men not to have learned its lesson, were not their flaw so deeply impressed in wrinkled brain matter that perhaps five times the five thousand years since it was told would be inadequate. We bear the mark of Cain as if it were a banner, proclaiming to all the world that, though our deeds be beyond redemption and our punishment incalculable, we will still kill our brothers, kill them for trivial things, for genetics or religion or philosophy, for a culture different than our own, for thoughts and beliefs, and for skin color.

Suddenly I hear something about new windmills and kilowatts, and I nod, as if I had heard every word. The truck speeds on.

IS IT IS, OR IS IT AIN'T?

Don White, owner and proprietor of White's Motel, Mojave, drops Potato Picker and me off at the Cameron Road overpass where the trail intersects the Highway 58 at Tehachapi Pass. It's eight o'clock in the morning. The trail heads east, along the slopes of Pajeula Peak and parallels the freeway for a mile or so, undulating up and down and around rocky desert washes. In the washes are stands of brushy juniper. Joshua trees grow in profusion here, and many are in bloom. There are a few yucca too, the same Chaparral Yucca, also known as Our Lord's Candles, that were growing in Soledad Canyon, nine days to the south.

Eventually the trail cuts across the bottom of Waterwheel Canyon. It hits the eastern ridge and starts steeply north, switchbacking up and across. Although neither as great in number, nor in degree of severity, nor remotely as scenic as the infamous switchbacks up Mount Whitney from Trail Camp to Trail Crest, they do call them to my mind and remind me that the high mountains are not far away.

After about twelve hundred feet of climbing along the eastern edge of vast Waterwheel Canyon, the trail crosses it at its head and treads over smoother terrain. To the west is Red Mountain. There are at least twenty-six other Red Mountains in California, and although I don't know how this one stacks up, it is fairly unimpressive at something less than 5,700 feet in elevation, a minor bump on a long ridge.

The foliage now is predominantly sagebrush, but eventually I come into the piñon forests. Before the highway disappears from sight, I look down searching for the Garlock Fault, the second largest in California, through which the highway passes, but nothing out of the ordinary catches my eye, just the interminable passing by of trucks and cars, and the blades of the wind generators, glinting in the morning sun as they turn and turn.

The Guidebook says that I am now officially in the Sierra Nevada, but is it or isn't it? It doesn't look very Sierra-like to me. In fact, to the casual observer it doesn't look much different than the Tehachapi Mountains, through which I made my way just two days ago. But the Tehachapi have an entirely different geological history from the Sierra, and although there is some granite near the eastern end, the fact that there are great cement works nearby, telling tales of limestone and its watery birth, should be a clue that they are not the Sierra.

The sage and rabbitbrush-covered hills roll and sprawl before me. In the canyons are scrub oak and Utah juniper. Here and there, along ridges, are solitary outcrops of granite that hint of the Sierra, jutting up into the desert sky, but it all looks muted and subdued, and the foliage is all wrong. That these mountains are granite is true, but it is the discolored granite of the desert, water and wind pounded and rounded, looking far more like the rocks of Joshua Tree National Park, and the Sierran Alabama Hills, and even the outcrops of Hauser Mountain back at the beginning of the Trail, not the shining, ice-shattered rock of the High Sierra that caused John Muir to exclaim, "Never before had I seen so glorious a landscape, so boundless an affluence of sublime mountain beauty. I shouted and gesticulated in a burst of wild ecstasy." However, I am happy to be back in the mountains and on the trail again. Like a thrilled tourist spying the tail of the Loch Ness Monster, these hills give me hope that the rest of the critter, the High Sierra, will soon show its head.

About half way up the switchbacks, Potato Picker pulls away and disappears. I won't see him again until Golden Oak Spring, late in the day. I met Potato Picker for the first time yesterday at White's Motel. I arrived there beat down by the long run from Cottonwood Creek, out of the Mojave, up and over the Tehachapi Mountains, and down to Tehachapi-Willow Springs Road, a 22.7 mile day with more than three thousand feet of ascent and then back down again. The previously described hitchhike dropped me off right at the motel. I checked in and was given a room way out and around the back. "Ah, put the hiker trash out of sight and mind," thought I, but I was wrong, for others were checked in right next to the pool. The room was really hot, so I cranked the air conditioner up to "blizzard" and fell onto the bed for a few minutes. Then, dragging myself up, I headed for the shower. Being a Leo, I am no lover of long showers, but I did my best to run the hot water tank dry. I dressed in my grimy togs, for I carry "town clothes." Disregarding the admonition by William Brewer, of Professor Whitney's California Geological Survey in 1863, that "our camp shirts did not dine in public places," I headed across the street to the gas station, which also housed a mini-mart and a Burger King. Two quarts of V8, and a double cheeseburger with extra onion and fries later, having ignored the guarded stares and wrinkled noses of wary tourists in the restaurant, I arrived back at my room. It had cooled down considerably in my absence. I fell into bed and slept soundly till late the next morning, six o'clock.

From Cameron Overpass to the first water, Golden Oaks Spring, is 16.1 miles and 2,700 feet up. So I had decided to take a well-deserved zero day. I needed time to sort my re-supply package, and mainly just to laze about. Tomorrow Don will drop me off at the overpass early in the

Life on the Trail

Ray begins his Pacific Crest Trail hike at the
Mexican border, April 27, 2001

Granite Mountain,
Anza-Borrego Desert

No Way Ray and
Fallingwater,
2002 Kickoff'

Cabazon
Country Store

Ray after discovering the Pink Motel, Mount San Jacinto in the background

Yogi and Gottago near the North Fork Ranger Station on a rainy day, 2002

Desert dweller's
treasures,
near Highway 138

Sign at Jack Fair's house,
middle of the Mojave Desert

All alone, near Wyley's Knob, southern Sierra

Meadow Ed hosting thru-hikers at Kennedy Meadows campground, 2003

Doc, Florida Bob and No Way Ray at
Kennedy Meadows campground

Ray's pilfered headgear,
Golden Trout Wilderness

Ray hitchhikes out to resupply at
Horseshoe Meadow Trailhead

Ray on top of Mount Whitney
after completing his first
John Muir Trail hike, 1972

Siberian Outpost

Snowfield on the approach to Mather Pass, 12,100 feet

Rae Lakes and the Painted Lady,
below Glen Pass

Fishermen who gave No Way Ray a
ride across Lake Thomas Edison to
Vermillion Valley Resort

Tuolumne River in Tuolumne Meadows

The sparkling pond just below Seavey Pass, Yosemite National Park

View north towards Sonora Pass, Emigrant Wilderness

Indian paintbrush

Trail angels—Bill, Janie, Beth and
Mike—set up the Animal House for
hiker respite near Lost Lakes, 2004

The Spiritmobile giving hikers a lift
near Lake Almanor, Highway 36, 2004

Sunset clouds from Hat Creek Rim, northeast California

Trail angel, Georgie Heitman (Firefly), at Hat Creek Rim overlook with Mount Lassen in the distance

Gourmet salmon dinner at Drakesbad Resort, more trail magic

No Way Ray toasts the California-Oregon border, 1,700 miles from Mexico

Crater Lake

Skin diving through Oregon, near Six Horse Springs

North face of Three-Fingered Jack, Oregon

Most excellent buffet breakfast at Timberline Lodge on Mount Hood, Oregon

Wild huckleberries, the hiker's reward for 2,200 miles completed, Indian Heaven Wilderness, Washington

A moody Mount Rainier

Bus and dock at Stehekin on Lake Chelan, WA, the last resupply point in Washington before the border

McCall Glacier with Mount Rainier in the distance, Washington

Monument at the Canadian border

morning. A zero day is not the same as a day off, for what would one call a day off from paradise? Hell? So it's called a zero day, a day when no miles are hiked on the PCT itself. In theory, it's day of relaxing, enjoying the comforts of civilization, and its attendant clamor, just long enough to know that it's time to leave them behind as rapidly as possible. Sometimes, however, it seems to me that the "attendant clamor" can be overpowering. And it can be a hectic time, if tasks are many. Thus far I have taken only three zero days, one each in Idyllwild, Big Bear, and at Hiker Heaven in Agua Dulce. This will be my fourth in five hundred sixty miles.

I hiked out in the morning in search of the elusive breakfast banquet. It was a nice, cool (for here) morning, so I walked about a half mile down the road to the local Denny's and ordered two Grand Slam breakfasts, and a huge glass of orange juice. I laughed to myself, picturing Tony-The-Brit's legendary breakfasts. A slight man with a marvelous story, I last saw him nine days ago, having breakfast in Wrightwood, he having just arrived in town as I was headed out. I took a great picture of a smiling Tony, surrounded by eggs, hash browns, bacon, ham, toast, pancakes, milk, orange juice, coffee, and water.

I had a leisurely breakfast and headed back to White's. My re-supply package was being held in the office. Don got it for me and I made arrangements to spend one more night. I asked him about a laundromat; he replied that the nearest one was some distance away. I forget how far, but it must have seemed too far, for I decided to do my hiker-trash laundry routine, especially since the day was going to be a hot one.

Back in the room, I spread out the contents of my re-supply box and relaxed. After a bit, with all my clothes on, except for shoes, I stepped into the shower. Using a small bottle of shampoo that I bought the night before at the mini-mart, I started the wash cycle. First I washed my long-sleeved nylon shirt. In the five days since I left Hiker Heaven, it had become so grimy and salt-encrusted that it would nearly stand by itself. Crinkling audibly, I was afraid it would just crack and fall to the floor in shards. And so, still wearing it, I shampooed it up and scrubbed it down. I did likewise with my shorts, spandex cycling shorts, which I wear under the shorts, and socks, removing the garments one at a time, as they were washed and rinsed. This took a while, as you might imagine. At the Tahquitz Inn in Idyllwild twenty-four days ago, there was a bathtub, so I just soaked them for an hour, did a grape-stomping dance on them, then rinsed. Putting on my Frog Toggs, the tops and bottoms of a lightweight, windproof, mostly-waterproof Tyvek-like material suit, I hung the wet clothes outside my door, over some withered bushes trying desperately to grow in this inferno. Likewise, I draped my sleeping bag. Afraid that they might be pilfered, even though the huge parking lot in this back corner of the motel had but two cars in it, I cracked a curtain in the window and kept a nervous eye on them for the hour or so that it took them to dry in the rapidly heating desert air.

While they were drying, I surfed the TV, discovering as usual, that the news was the same as it always seems to be, mostly bad. It reminded me of my first hike of the John Muir Trail, in 1972. Having just finished our first long trail, my wife and I came out of the mountains at Whitney Portal, to lodge in the Dow Villa motel in Lone Pine and watch John Dean spill his guts about the burglary of the Democratic Headquarters to the Watergate Commission. Of course, in those ancient days I was far more liberal than I am today, so I'm sure it was good news to me at the time.

I began sorting through my re-supply box and discovered that I had not packed the Guidebook pages for Section F, Tehachapi Pass to Walker Pass. Not having the pages does not make it impossible to hike, but being a solo hiker, I would prefer to have them…just in case. Yesterday, Don mentioned that there were several other hikers about, so I pulled in my now mostly-dry clothes, dressed, and strolled over to the office. He pointed out the room, number 138, across the way and upstairs, where I headed and knocked. The door opened. The first thing I noticed was a pyramid of ten Gatorade bottles sitting on the television. The television was on but the volume was muted. Then I saw and introduced myself to four people, Potato Picker, Teatree, Leprechaun, and The One, all except Potato Picker, who answered the door, were lying down. They had been sick for two days and called this the "SARS Room." Making the crossed-finger sign-of-the-cross to ward off the vampires, and, staying near the door, I asked about taking someone's Guidebook pages to run myself a copy. Potato Picker, allowing he had some errands to run as well, offered his. We both went over to the office where Don gave us the keys to his old Chevy pick-up. Off we went.

If you don't know about trail names, some of the people I have been mentioning may sound a bit odd. Trail names, a tradition derived from the Appalachian Trail, are pretty common on thru-hikes. I guess about 80% of the people I met had them. It seems as though some good percentage of these people pick their own names, perhaps before they start out, perhaps a name to make a statement about themselves as they begin a new life and travel into a totally new environment. There is one faction that claims a person's trail name must come from others while on the trail, but I have no quarrel with those who choose their own. And why not? Reinventing themselves in a group that cares little for titles, college degrees, job descriptions, mortgage payments, and the names, games, and chores that define a person's existence back in the other world, seems as natural as walking all day, every day, for months and sleeping on the ground at night.

Many, similar to the naming process among a number of American Indian tribes, have their name bestowed on them by others as a result of some incident along the trail, or a physical characteristic or mannerism. One hiker, at Kennedy Meadows, after a marvelous Meadow Ed spaghetti dinner and a beer or three, starts dancing around the evening fire, and becomes Firedancer. Another, found pounding ten stakes into the ground with a hatchet (ignore the air rifle he was carrying), becomes Hatchet (John). Wildflower from New Hampshire, the black sheep in a family of classical archaeologists, got her degree in botany. One Gallon blames his name on a certain large container of ice cream that he magically made disappear. And so it goes.

My own trail name, *No Way*, came to me at Hiker Heaven in Agua Dulce, although I cannot remember who actually did the bestowing. Sitting around a table on the lawn, several of us introduced ourselves. I said my name is Ray...because it is. One said, "Is that your name or a trail name? Do you follow the Ray Way?" The *Ray Way* is the backpacking philosophy espoused by ultralight backpacking guru, Ray Jardine. I replied, making a Zen joke, that I didn't follow the Ray Way; "I follow the Path of No Path, the Way of No Way." To which, the person exclaimed, "Ah, I see, you're 'No Way Ray!'" And it stuck. It's an euphonious name, although some may think it describes a negative attitude, as in "no-freakin'-way!" Nearly eleven hundred miles up the trail, in the Marble Mountain Wilderness of Section Q, I will meet several southbound ladies doing a section hike. Asking of and hearing my trail name, one says, "We say, 'Yes Way'," and so I am forced to explain. Seven days from now, Stormy will find me sitting, invisibly, with my white Kelty Cloud pack amidst a field of huge, white, prickly poppies, near the end of the vast Manter Fire devastated area at the head of Rockhouse Basin. She allows as how, since my white pack makes me almost invisible among the flowers, that my name should be Prickly Poppy. I argue against such a move, since the name does not exactly roll off the tongue, and thru-hikers, being thru-hikers, would no doubt quickly shorten "Prickly" to a less than genteel reference to an obnoxious or contemptible person...or to a portion of a man's anatomy.

Back at the supermarket in Mojave, the Picker picked up some Pedialite, a nasty tasting (as it turns out) electrolytic fluid for babies. Don had recommended it for fluid replacement for the SARS group, who had been attempting to deplete theirs in various ways...the details of which should probably remain unchronicled. I got a few goodies, and headed off to the stationery store to get the Guidebook pages copied. That done, and back at the motel, I had an inspiration. Don had warned that he needed the truck to pick up some hikers at three o'clock. I asked him if it would be possible to drop me off when he got the hikers and pick me up at Cameron Overpass about three hours later. Though it was getting late in the day, he nodded in the affirmative, so I grabbed a bit of gear and off we went. I had decided to slack pack the 8.6 miles from Tehachapi-Willow Springs Rd. to the Cameron Road overpass, thereby not missing that section of the trail when I hike out from Tehachapi tomorrow. And I must start at Cameron road, for I felt that the 24.7 miles from Tehachapi-Willow Pass Road to water at Golden Oak Springs might be too much for one day. And so, my zero day becomes a nero day, a day of nearly-no-trail-miles.

The miles between these two roads are not much to talk about, plenty of sagebrush and some few Utah juniper, of the kind that I saw in the upper Mojave. There is a low ridge that separates this canyon from the one through which the highway that crosses over Tehachapi Pass runs, and the trail ascends it north until it reaches the crest, then meanders east, through forests of eerie sounding wind generators, and drops down to the freeway. Though it was hot, the miles passed quickly. Before dark, I was back in the shower at White's. A quick dinner of two quarts of V8 and a chicken salad sandwich, and I called it quits for the day.

The next morning finds me standing at the trailhead with Potato Picker, headed the 84.1 miles to Walker Pass and my next re-supply. By the time I reach what passes for level walking, Potato Picker is long gone. Hikers spend a lot of time looking at the ground, and I am no exception. On this morning, I have been noticing an abundance of a singular species of beetle along the last few miles of trail. As kids we erroneously called them "stinkbugs," for, when tampered with, they hiked their posterior high into the air and emitted, at least to my memory, a disagreeable smell. Actual stinkbugs have a soft, shield-shaped body and emit a smell that is considered to be among the top ten "worst smells" in the animal world, or so the Discovery Channel tells me. These before me are shiny, black ground beetles with a tapered abdomen. I tamper with one. Up comes the rear. I watch for a while, wondering just how long it will retain the posture. It does so for a couple of minutes. I see more and more of them, so I repeat the experiment a couple of more times. It is almost as though they have a built-in timer, for they all retain the defensive posture about the same time before hitching up and hiking on. I get closer but cannot smell anything untoward. Perhaps my memory is faulty. I pick one up and hold it close to my nose. There is a smell, acrid, but not terribly stinky.

I continue trekking among the beetles. My foot moves forward and heads down; a beetle lies in its path. I stop and look at it. Suddenly I get an eerie feeling. I am looking down on this shiny fellow who is intent on whatever mysterious quest this morning has brought and walking in what no doubt passes for a straight line in the insect world. This beetle has no eyes to see me, no senses to record my presence, and moves tirelessly on, busily scanning the horizons of its own small universe as if I do not exist, and for him, I don't. I look down on him, godlike, knowing I hold life and death in my hands, foot actually, and thinking that either choice lacks importance...to me. Suddenly I feel as if I am being stretched out and sucked high into the sky. The earth flattens out below me and features become as if twigs and pebbles. I see myself, far below and beetle-like in size. What if some Other, sharing my height in the same proportion that I do to the beetle, and hence, more than 800 feet tall, strides across these dry mountain tops, living an existence undetectable to my puny senses, intent on some purpose as incomprehensible to me as my twenty-six hundred mile jaunt is to a beetle. In my mind, a monstrous foot hangs in the air above me. The hair on the back of my neck stands up. The feeling, and it is nothing but a feeling, lasts but a moment and is gone. And, although I am neither Hindu, thus eschewing the most insignificant death, nor vegetarian, for I will attack the meanest hamburger when in town, carefully avoiding the beetle, I make my own incomprehensible way along the mountain.

By two o'clock, the beginning of the five-mile-long string of Sky River's wind generators comes into view. I make my way toward Sweet Ridge. The trail crosses its southern end and circles around the east side. Where it crosses a northeast ridge and heads down into some canyons, I catch a view of Olancha Peak. Far to the north, six days hike from here, the PCT will wind right across the ridge I can see.

Not long after four o'clock and more than sixteen miles into the day, lying in a cool, shaded canyon, Golden Oaks Spring comes into view. Potato Picker and two others are resting among the live oaks. I meet Paul from England, and Hatchet John. The spring at Golden Oaks is piped through galvanized lines, where it drops into a concrete tank, faced in rock. The tank is about four by six feet and about two feet deep. Fortunately, the pipes drop the water some two feet above the water's surface, so that unlike the water at Pioneer Mail Picnic Grounds way back in the Laguna Mountains, I am able to capture the water before it falls into the tank. I say fortunately, because the tank is loaded with dead insects, pollywogs, bird droppings, some slimy things defying identification, and who knows what else.

I decide to cook dinner here before hiking on into the evening. While I make preparations, Paul and Hatchet contrive to assemble their gear, which is spread out around them. Hatchet takes an air rifle out of his gear! He plinks a few shots and packs it back into his gear. I am flabbergasted! I have hiked for a good many years and seen a lot of bizarre gear in the mountains, an eight pound full-sized altimeter out of a World War II bomber and a pressure cooker on Mount Whitney come immediately to mind, not to mention the thirty-inch Japanese sword I once took to the top a Sierra peak, to practice kata,[1] but I have yet to see a hunter's weapon. I ask him about it. Both he and Paul have one, somehow thinking it to be a good idea. He is from Georgia and says he plans to hunt along the way. He shot a rabbit in the Mojave Desert, supplementing his fare. I suggest that he might want to get rid of it before he gets into the national parks, since wrapped up along side his pack frame it looks, at the very least, like a fishing pole, and he will almost certainly be queried about it somewhere along the way. He allows as how this may be a good idea. They finish packing and move on out. Shortly after that, Potato Picker leaves too. I sit for an hour before doing the same. The day is closing and I begin to think about a place to be.

I hike on and eventually come to a wide road running along the crest of Sweet Ridge. Crossing it, I circle through ravines and ultimately find a relatively flat spot off the trail. The day is done. I am lying in my bag. Cache Peak looming a few miles south. I can see a line of wind generators several hundred yards up the hillside. Their sound, floating through the darkening sky, is eerie. It seems to rise and fall in pitch, and periodically get louder. I listen awhile, wondering just what causes the variation in sound. The only thing I can think of is that they are moving at different speeds, and that every once in a while, their periods of rotation synchronize, and so harmonize. I time the rotation period of several of the towers, trying to divine the pattern, but it doesn't concern me too long, since it's been a long day. Listening to a wind-generator lullaby, sleep comes quickly and pleasantly after twenty-one long miles.

Next morning, within ten minutes of hitting the trail, I pass two small tents a few yards off the trail, Paul and Hatchet. They didn't get much farther than I did. This day turns out to be long, difficult and HOT! Since I came about four miles beyond Golden Oaks Spring, today I have only about fourteen miles to water, but they are a difficult fourteen miles. For a while, the trail stays in terrain similar to that of yesterday afternoon. Piñon pines are the dominant tree and are smeared thickly across the

---

1 A kata is a pattern of steps, thrusts and blocks used in martial arts training

mountains. Scattered here and there are the scrubby Utah juniper and not a small number of yucca, blooming in large, tubular heads of cream-colored flowers, some as long as four feet. But within three miles or so, walking along a ridge, I come to grasslands and massive blue oak trees, and gates and fences and signs warning of private property...and abominable cows.

Then, ascending 500 feet, I find myself among Jeffrey pines once again. The change is heartening, but it is still hot...and getting hotter. I begin to cross dirt roads and even see a cabin or two. Then, a dirt road and a sign that says *Robin Bird Spring*. The Guidebook briefly tells the story of its 1994 rescue and renovation, ending with the note that after all the work was done, with "a deserved sense of pride," it was given its name.

I can only imagine what the spring looked like before. I look around at the piles of downed timber and cow pies, and the spring dribbling down the hillside through it all, under a barbed wire fence surrounding it, in this oak-shaded canyon. Working my way around the wire to a gate, I make my way the thirty yards or so to the spring catchment. It is a large, deep concrete tank with a loose-fitting wooden lid. I peer inside, expecting to see floating mice and things unspeakable, but it is too dark. The water runs out and down in a tiny creek. I go about halfway down and filter several liters of water. I wonder if the author of the Guidebook was speaking tongue-in-cheek about this place. Ah well, beggars and choosers and all that. And since I don't know what it looked like before, and I didn't do any of the work, certainly I have no desire to denigrate the work done to provide me with this marvelous, essential water.

There are four people resting in the shade where the water runs out and down the canyon. I meet Cliffhanger, Steady, and Stitches. Potato Picker is there too. I have lunch and chat a while as they prepare to leave. The water runs through a small pool, so I remove my shoes and soak my feet. It feels heavenly. Suddenly my ankle and calf start to burn, and to my great distress, I discover I have brushed up against some nettles that I failed to notice. This will bother me for rest of the day and part of the next. It is one o'clock and the others pull out. I relax, enjoying the cool. Just about two o'clock, when I am ready to leave, Paul arrives. He says Hatchet is somewhere behind him. We talk, and I delay my departure half an hour, waiting for Hatchet. Finally, I am tired of waiting and start to leave. There is a yell from somewhere off and down the trail. Paul takes a water bottle and trots off down the trail. Twenty minutes later he and Hatchet return. Hatchet has been out of water for several hours and has been feeling ill. He has eaten only a single Power Bar all day...and threw that up. He is sweating profusely and looks pale. I am no doctor, so I know not how serious is his condition, but he doesn't look good. He tells us he'll be fine, and after drinking more water than a man should be able to hold, he relaxes to take a nap. It's good to be young and strong. Paul assures me all will be well, and that they will spend the night there, so, now late in the day, I head out.

Day's end finds me only a bit more than three miles further, on a saddle between Cottonwood Creek (from whence I came) and Lander Creek. I find a suitable spot and hastily eat a light dinner. I remove my shoes, putting on my one-ounce camp slippers (made from old shoe insoles), and put my socks on a large rock to dry and air. Then I unload my pack and likewise put my sleeping bag on the rock to air and loft. I set up my small tent, and within fifteen minutes, throw my bag inside. I go back to repack my gear and get my socks. That's when I notice that they are literally crawling with ants. A second later I make the connection and bolt for my tent. My fears come true and I spend the last minutes of light trying to clear all the ants out of my tent, searching out the last few holdouts by flashlight. After that, I'm ready for bed.

The next morning, I cross Lander Creek within two miles and a mile later hit Piute Mountain Road, a large, well-graded access road. Here, I find Cliff, Steady and Stitches. They are just breaking camp. I wave and walk on through. The trail, which has come nearly true north since Tehachapi, now makes a hard right, to run east onto and down St. John Ridge. In a mile or so, just as I walk by, I notice a three foot rattlesnake stretched in the grass out along the trail. This causes me to leap forward about six feet and come down, heart pounding. But, the early morning cold has made the snake torpid, and it remains motionless. As I approach the bottom, nearing Kelso Valley Road, the numbers of Joshua trees increases. I come to a particularly shapely Joshua tree, which calls to me to take a short break.

Sitting in the sand, I gaze east at Mayan Peak, an isolated peak shaped like one of the great Mayan pyramids at Chichen Itza or Palenque. I first saw it more than eighteen miles ago, just before going up to Hamp Williams Pass. Now, at a distance of perhaps four miles, it looks much more imposing. Stitches passes me by and heads on down toward Kelso Valley Road and the water cache. I stare awhile at the Joshua trees, enjoying their spiny company. Not nearly so large as many of its Mojave brothers, this incomparable yucca under which I sit is a marvelous plant. Like all members of the yucca family it relies on the help of a moth, each species of yucca surviving only with the help of a particular species of moth, which is particular to it. The details of this dance are well recorded and should be read by all desert travelers. Alan Watts, the Zen philosopher, argued that when a plant and an insect are mutually dependent on each other for their existence, they are in reality just one organism. I lazily think about that curiosity.

Moreover, six feet below the surface there is neither season nor drought. The amount of water is nearly constant through wet and dry seasons as well as wet and dry years. And so the Joshua tree sends its roots deep into the earth to seek out its water of life. A Joshua tree of no more than eight or ten feet in height, much like the one under which I sit, may send a root forty or more feet below the surface in search of water.

Eventually, I re-shoulder my pack and head the last mile or two to Kelso Valley Road. Stitches is there, as is a large cache of gallon water jugs. There is a note from the trail angel, one Mary Barcik, who lives in nearby Weldon on this very road, and a plastic peanut butter jar with pages and names of those who have already passed through. Some have called this angel Moto Mary, telling the story of her delivery of water by motorcycle, but the number of containers here tells a tale of other vehicles. Her note indicates that a similar cache is to be found at Bird Spring Pass, 15.4 miles up the trail. I hope it is true, otherwise it will be another long thirteen miles to McIver's Spring, the next water. The water here is still relatively cool in mid-morning. I gratefully fill my containers and drink deeply. This kindness eliminates the necessity of me hiking steeply downhill for a mile to obtain water later in the day. We sit in the sand and chat.

Stitches tells me about her companions, Cliffhanger and Steady. Steady is from Texas, and while she spends four or five months hiking, her husband Dave, supports her by living in motels and driving to trailheads to deliver supplies. He has some business that allows him to work through the internet. His next scheduled rendezvous is Walker Pass, so he is not supposed to show up here, but she says she wouldn't be surprised if he did. This no more than said, up he drives, dispensing candy bars and ice-cold sodas. Do you believe in magic?

Within the hour Cliff and Steady arrive, and we all hang out and gab for a while. They don't seem inclined to leave, so I say my goodbyes and head on toward Mayan Peak. I won't see them again until Kennedy Meadows, nearly ninety miles up the trail. Circling around the east side of Mayan Peak, I wade in and out of rocky washes. The heat is stifling. Suddenly I am in shade and glance up to the sky in surprise. A solitary cloud has formed in just the right spot to block the sun. Walking in and out of shade for the next several miles, once being lightly sprinkled with rain, I make my way through the day.

At length, having navigated up and down four ridges, I begin to look for a place to end the day. The Guidebook tells of a place where there are "good campsites among the boulders," and this is where I finish a nearly twenty-one mile day.

I set up camp and have dinner. As the sun sinks lower, the desert takes on a ruddy hue. Standing on one of the boulders, I look in all directions. To the north lies a ridge with more outcrops of bouldery granite. To the east, the land stretches out and down more than two thousand feet and thirty miles to the town of Ridgecrest and the Naval Weapons Testing Center at China Lake, all invisible from here, and the mountains beyond. The wind is blowing strongly and whistles through the rocks and sage. There is no other sound...no sign of life. I keep glancing toward the ridge a mile to the south-west. Cliff, Steady and Stitches should be close. The sun is nearly to the horizon in the west and the evening blossoms. Suddenly I feel very lonely. There is not a living creature to be seen or heard, no birds singing in the brush or chasing insects for evening meal, no humans, no sky worms left by high-flying jet, no nothing. I am reminded of the words of the poet Keats,

> Oh what can ail thee, knight-at-arms,
>
> Alone and palely loitering?
>
> The sedge has withered from the lake,
>
> And no birds sing.

As the sun sinks lower and lower in the west, I palely loiter among the boulders, vainly searching for signs of life. On this, my forty-second night, I feel small and insignificant...and alone.

But alone, I am in fine company, for even that paragon of solitary wilderness travel, John Muir, was not immune to loneliness. In a letter from the foothills of the Sierra in 1868, he wrote to Jeanne C. Carr, who was his botanical and spiritual mentor and confidant, complaining that "I am very lonesome and hunger terribly for the communion of friends." I keep looking back at the ridge to the south, expecting to see the group winding their way down, but no... Suddenly, to the east, down the mountainside and away, across the desert, there is a flash of light. A few seconds later it repeats. I look carefully and see, for just moments, a miniscule shape moving south along the desert. The sunlight is reflecting off of a truck, out on Highway 14 fifteen miles away, and headed south, to Los Angeles no doubt. I breathe a sigh of relief. I am not alone in the world. Far and away, in the gloaming, the lights of Ridgecrest begin to twinkle.

I crawl into my little tent, noisily flapping in the wind, and among the boulders, fall asleep.

The next day finds me up early and on the trail to Robin Bird Pass and a water cache, hopefully. The trip is short and rapid in the desert morning. A few miles along the trail, I once again gelandesprung over a rattlesnake. This one, small and docile in the morning cool, is beautifully coiled into a bowl it has scoured out in the sandy trail. Its scaly form so matches the texture and pattern and color of the sand that it is nearly invisible.

By noon I reach the pass and find gallons and gallons of water. Thank you Mary Barcik! As I fill my containers and lounge contentedly for a few minutes, I look at my Guidebook pages to see what lies ahead. It is then that I find the last few pages are missing. Somehow the lady at the stationary store in Mojave failed to copy them...and I failed to notice. Now I do not know where McIver Spring will be found. I chance to look across the road and see, not fifty feet away, a huge green-tinged Mojave rattlesnake slither out of the sage, across the road, and slowly disappear south into the canyon. Taking this as a cue to leave, I hoist my pack and head up, trusting that thirteen miles up the road the spring will not be hard to find.

The trail makes its way through a canyon and around and up across the slopes of Skinner Peak, continuing north, ridge after ridge. From the slopes of Skinner Peak the true Sierra, far to the north, make a first appearance. At last!! It won't be long now. After several miles the trail walks along a dirt road, then finally, at a sign directs me west and up a canyon. By the time I get to the top of the canyon, I can see that McIver Spring must be in the patch of green trees an hour back down the trail. I stop and cook dinner, sitting right in the middle of the trail, then deciding that one liter of water will be enough, head north. After nearly twenty-three hot miles, I spend the night on a small ridge, looking down on Walker Pass. In the morning I will have only a few miles to go.

I arrive at the BLM-managed Walker Pass Campground by seven o'clock. Without much ado, I walk through to the highway and cast my thumb into the traffic waters. Between cars, I delve into my pack and drag out my Tyvek ground cloth, turning to the square that says *PCT Hiker, Onyx Please* in large, friendly letters. This is my fifth hitch and I am prepared for the worst, as usual. My hitches at Scissors Crossing, Baldwin Lake, Wrightwood, Palmdale, and into Mojave have taught me one thing...people don't like my looks. Unable, perhaps, to decide whether it is Kris Kringle or Charles Manson standing on the highway in front of them, they are long past by the time they decide.

That being said, within ten minutes, Cheryl, on her daily drive from Inyokern on the east side, to Lake Isabella and her job at the post office, swerves to stop and pick me up. I feel like my luck is changing for the better.

Onyx is really nothing but a post office and a gas station-mini mart, so I decide to skip my re-supply parcel at the post office and take a ride into Lake Isabella, some twenty miles to the west. She drops me off at the Isabella Motel, a long, flat-roofed, 1950-ish, white stucco building on the north side of the freeway. The manager allows me to check in, even though it is early. I suspect part of the reason is that there are only two cars parked in the lot. Down across the freeway and in the valley to the south lies the town...and breakfast. A ten-minute walk finds me at the Dam Korner, having the huge three egg, bacon, sausage, hash brown, and pancake breakfast, a veritable bargain at only $4.99.

The laundromat is about a mile to the west, along the main and only street. As I walk on, I see a war surplus store. It opens at nine o'clock, and with perfect timing, I walk in moments thereafter. I am looking for cheap town clothes, so I won't have to sit around in the heat of the laundromat in my rain gear. There is a long rack of Hawaiian shirts, and I find one, blue with red hibiscus flowers all over it, for only four dollars. The shorts are another matter. The shirt, I plan to keep in my pack for future town use, but I have no need for another pair of shorts. I find plenty, but all too expensive. Finally I spy a pair of bright orange shorts for six dollars. I explain to the proprietor that I only need shorts in order to do laundry and that they will be left behind when I leave town, and since these orange shorts are so hideous that he has no doubt had them for years, that perhaps he would consider a deal. And so with a bag containing a brilliant blue and red shirt and orange shorts (bought for the princely sum of $3), I walk the remaining half-mile to the laundromat. There, I run into Potato Picker, and meet Brent, Stormy, and Bryan.

We chat a while. I learn that Potato had run into someone who was hiking north from Walker Pass. Potato offered to drive the car to Kennedy Meadows so it would be waiting when the owner arrived. And so, he and Brent, Stormy, and Bryan are cruising around town eating and doing laundry and eating. Alas, it is a small car without room for one extra. So they leave, and I sit around in my blue and red and orange town clothes and watch the dryer as it completes its tedious circles. I will run into Brent and Stormy and Bryan the next day, but the Potato Picker, by then two days ahead, disappears forever. I learn much later that he will leave the trail at Crater Lake, in Oregon.

The next morning finds me back at the Dam Korner for a breakfast encore, then on a bus that ultimately drops me off at the Onyx Post Office and my re-supply box. I sit in the grass at the side of the gas station and sort and pack. It is nearly 18 miles back to the trail at Walker Pass, so out goes my thumb and my *PCT Hiker, To Trail Please* sign. Time passes, as do all the cars. After an hour I walk over to the post office and ask the postmistress if by chance she knows anyone nearby that would be willing to take me to Walker Pass, for a nominal fee. She calls her daughter-in-law and within thirty minutes I am at the trailhead. Although I offer to pay, for the gas at the least, she will take none. I thank her profusely, hoist my pack and hit the trail. It is 49.9 miles to Kennedy Meadows, and I had planned to make it in two long days. It is nearly eleven o'clock, so that plan turns into two and a half days. Ah well.

Eleven and a half miles later, having run into Brent, Stormy and Bryan during the course of the day, we all find sleeping places on the hillside above Joshua Tree Springs to watch a nearly-full moon rise. Joshua Tree Springs comes with the warning that it contains greater than allowable levels of uranium. However, virtually all hikers avail themselves to the few liters they will need to get them up the trail.

The next morning finds me on the trail early, as is my custom. In order to utilize the watershed of Spanish Needle Creek, the trail makes a series of torturous twists and dives down into the canyon, all lost altitude that is far more torturously regained than lost. By noon I catch up with Bryan, Brent and Stormy as they take lunch and dry their gear. Perched on a ridge, down Sand Canyon and to the east, the multi-hued desert spreads out. Across dry China Lake are the Argus Mountains, and more than fifty miles to the northeast, the snowy summit of Telescope Peak, riding the skyline above Death Valley, is faintly visible.

Eventually, I hoist my pack and head on along the ridge. The trail circles north of Lamont Point, then drops down to Canebrake Road. A half-mile along the road brings me to the end of the day at Chimney Creek campground with flat ground and piped water. A quick meal and I roll out my bag. Tomorrow will bring me to Kennedy Meadows and the true Sierra.

Early in the morning, I pass Brent and Stormy. They hiked a couple of miles on across Canebrake Road, rather than come up to the campground. They are camped near the remains of an old mine and its equipment. By the time I have traveled three or so miles, I come to a withered, blackened forest with its skeleton trees. For the next fourteen miles I walk through the remains of the Manter Fire. The largest fire in the history of Sequoia National forest, it burned 74,000 acres in 1997. Somewhere along the way, a view of Olancha Peak breaks out from behind a ridge. Twenty-five miles north, at more than 12,000 feet high, it is the southernmost of the High Sierra peaks. To the west of them, and further still, I can see a snowy blur, the peaks of Mt. Langley and its neighbors. Mt. Whitney might be visible, but I can't separate the individual peaks at this distance.

At long last I come into Rockhouse Basin, and by late afternoon I am sitting on the porch of the store at Kennedy Meadows, ice-cold beer in hand and happily contemplating a day of rest on the morrow. Life is good!

AN ANGEL LOOKS AT SIXTY[1]

"You go over and fill this with pot water," he says, pointing one hiker to the faucet up the road a bit. To another he says, "Take these vegetables and cut them up." Forcing Chowdah to own up to his trail name, he says, "You're making the clam chowder today. Get the cans of clams out of that box, and the half and half out of that green cooler. You need to make a roux." "What's a roux?" enquires Chowdah. Meadow Ed stands imperially at the head of a campground table, surrounded by hikers. Like the conductor of a symphony orchestra, he shrugs in this direction, points in that, nods in agreement or clucks disapproval as hikers ebb and flow around him. He gives orders effortlessly, and magically they are followed. Well, not so magically, for without so much as a "by your leave," his orders truly are orders.

It's late afternoon June 19, and I am in the campground at Kennedy Meadows, gateway to the High Sierra. Enthralled by the vision of a table, covered with pots and pans and silverware and spices and half-empty bottles of beer and cans of peaches and yams and olives, a dozen or more thru-hikers mill uncertainly about. Anxious to help, yet feeling reticent, perhaps even shy, they walk this way and that, uncomfortable with just standing around and not quite certain what is expected or required, yet unable to tear themselves away from the allure of such vast amounts of food.

A two-burner cook stove covers one end of the table. Nearby, three ice chests sit in the shade. One is filled with beer and wine, another vegetables and perishables. The third, more beer and wine...and sodas. Hikers paw through them, eschewing "diet" sodas...looking for the *real* stuff.

A group of three new hikers walks down the road, casting about for something that makes sense. From across the road, other hikers yell out their names. It's Brian or Remy; H, or Hatchet; Whoop Ass or Whippin' Stick; Black Hawk or Hawkeye; Billygoat or Mountaingoat; Weather Carrot or Walking Carrot; Nowhere Man, No One, or No Way Ray (that would be me)...and on it goes.

A smile lights up their faces and indecision fades. A happy reunion takes place. "Where have you been since we saw you at Hiker Heaven?" "Did you hear, so-and-so got off the trail at Tehachapi?" This one and that spent four days sick in Mojave! What's-his-name pushed on into the Sierra

1 Previously published in the Pacific Crest Trail Association *Communicator*, August 2006, vol. 18, no 4

yesterday. Minutes pass as people catch up on all the gossip of the trail. Then Meadow Ed calls them over and chants the monologue. "We have these four campsites," he says, pointing this way and that. "You can camp anywhere...but don't go too far that way." "These coolers are full, help yourself." "Dinner will be in an hour, so you better go get set up. Don't worry, I'll volunteer you to help wash dishes later."

Most thru-hikers first meet him at the Kick-Off party at Lake Morena, near the trail's beginning. For the past seven years, near the end of April, a shindig is held that celebrates the Hiking of The Trail. Known as the ADZPCTKO party (Annual Day Zero Pacific Crest Trail Kick Off Party), it features workshops, contests, slide shows, feasts, and a general howling at the moon in honor of The Trail. There, Meadow Ed dispenses water information for the long, hot, desiccated miles of southern California, a subject hard in the minds of all. But his story predates the Kick-Off.

In 1971, Meadow Ed left his Massachusetts home and headed west. He discovered the Sierra Nevada, and as do all who visit, fell in love with the shining granite and blue-black sky. Ten years ago to this day, Meadow Ed woke up in Kennedy Meadows. He had decided he did not want to awaken on his 50th birthday in Los Angeles, and so there he was. During the course of the day, he met a group of seven thru-hikers. He had extra food and offered to cook it for them. A nascent trail angel appeared that day.

Two weeks later, in Reds Meadow, he ran into the same hikers, and again a few days later in Tuolumne Meadows. As they headed north, one hiker said, "When will we see you again? His reply was, "Where's the next meadow?" Thus became Meadow Ed.

For the past ten years, Meadow Ed, full time poet, sometimes chef, sometimes hiker, oftentimes trail angel, has set up camp here in the Kennedy Meadows Campground, catering to thru-hikers for a week or two in the middle of June. The week before may find him fifty miles south at Walker Pass Campground, set up there and doing the same. A week or two later he might be in Reds Meadow, or Tuolumne Meadows, at the end of the High Sierra. You might find him sitting casually next to the highway heading into Chester, nearly six hundred miles up the trail, staring out over a Crater Lake overlook, or amidst the clouds and rain, he could be standing next to Monument 78, miles from nowhere, at trail's end.

Here at Kennedy Meadows there will be something for lunch, but most hikers make their way back to the Kennedy Meadows store for an afternoon of laundry and eating and welcoming new hikers as they trudge in from the trail. Back at the campground, dinner is a grand affair, with

BBQ chicken and baked beans, or spaghetti and French bread. There are usually a few vegetarians in the crowd, so accommodations are made for them too.

Yesterday he drove a load of hikers down to Ridgecrest, more than an hour away and nearly a mile lower. Some needed new shoes, some to buy food for the coming Sierra, some just to sightsee and get lunch (that would be me). The day passed cheerfully and ends with a bonfire and dinner.

After dinner, there's clean-up and sit-down. Meadow Ed sat, watching the hikers ebb and flow. You might say like a king watching his subjects, but it's not that. You might say like a parent watching his children, but it's not that either. The kindness and concern is palpable, but Meadow Ed doesn't necessarily like all hikers. "Some people are just takers," he says. "They're first in line for food, but always seem to disappear when it's time to clean up." I try to stand up for them a little, suggesting perhaps they just don't know what to do, but he is adamant. "No, they're just takers and that's that." So be it. I bow to his years of experience and shut up.

And so finally, here it is, Sunday, June 19.[2] By early afternoon, there are more than fifty people milling pleasantly around. Meadow Ed introduces me to some of his friends who have come up from Los Angeles. Friends, who although they know he has another life, have never experienced it. Jeff and Donna Saufley from Hiker Heaven arrive, and it's hugs and gossip all around.

And suddenly, it's time. Two birthday cakes, replete with balloons, songs, and wild applause materialize. Happy birthday is sung and tales and testimonials chanted. A card, surreptitiously circulated among the hikers throughout the day, is produced. From it, a poem is read:

A scholar with a camp stove for a lectern,
A preacher with a church 2,650 miles long and two feet wide,
and a congregation of scraggly thru-hikers.
A poet with the wilderness for an audience.
Overflowing with kindness and compassion,
What else could anyone ask to be....Meadow Ed

Meadow Ed smiles; the party goes on.

---

2 June 19, 2005

THE SIERRA NEVADA

In the midst of such beauty, pierced with its rays, one's body in all one tingling palate. Who wouldn't be a mountaineer! Up here all the world's prizes seem nothing. (*My First Summer in the Sierra*, John Muir)

Leaving Kennedy Meadows, I look to the north in anticipation, the familiar thrill of walking once more with an old friend, the mountains of the Sierra Nevada. It has been a lifelong love affair.

For a day and a half I hung around the store, camping two nights in the campgrounds. Meadow Ed had set up his usual marvelous hiker camp at the Kennedy Meadows Campground, and twenty or more hikers were to be found...eating, drinking, singing around the evening campfire, and in general, having a grand time.

In the pre-dawn darkness on the morning of June 15th,[1] I quietly rise, pack my gear and head out. No one else is stirring. At the end of the campground, I realize I do not have my hat. My youth was spent reveling— and burning—in the southern California sun, so my dermatologist and I have come to an agreement. I can continue on with these jaunts...if I cover up. I stop at a picnic table and tear my pack apart...no hat. I repack and head back to the camp. In the dim light, I look everywhere...no hat. As I reconstruct the day before, I realize I must have left it in the motor home that gave Bryan and me a ride back from the store. We spent most of the day there waiting patiently for our turn at the phone. Since so many hikers want to use the phone to check in, there is a sign-up sheet at the phone. I was number five on the list; Bryan was sixth.

I met Bryan in the laundromat at Lake Isabella, at Joshua Tree Springs, and again at Chimney Creek Campground. Recently out of the Navy, he lives in San Diego, in southern California. He was an engineer on the carrier USS Constellation and is celebrating his re-entry into the civilian world with a long walk. Back on the porch at the store, we waited for the phone...and waited...and waited. One fine lady, whose name I will omit—ah, what the hell, it was Stormy—spent three hours on the phone! She must have talked to everyone west of the Mississippi. This, say I, was rude and thoughtless. Ah well, the beers were cold and the company fine. No blame.

But as a result, we started late back to the campground, having missed any drivers heading that way. At length, two men and a woman with a baby picked us up in their rented motor home. Looking for the

Kings Canyon Big Trees, they were just a little off track, since the canyon of the Kern River and about ninety miles of road lay between the them and their destination. The two men were in the front, speaking quietly, until near the campground the road narrowed, and the branches of a tree rudely thumped the side of the motor home. The driver exclaimed, "Merde!" So I say, "Vous etes français?" He replied in the affirmative. I said, in what to them, no doubt, was laughable French, that I studied French in high school and college, but had never much used it. We chatted a bit, mercifully in English, for theirs was much better than my French. I realize that when we arrived at the campground, to a chorus of applause from our fellow campers as we stepped out of the door, that I left my hat sitting on the seat. Meadow Ed, I apologize for stealing one of your dishtowels, but my need was great and you were still fast asleep. I use a spare shoelace and tie it around my head. Now, looking perhaps too middle-eastern for these times, I head up the trail.

Several years ago, before my ultralight days, a friend from Alaska and I hiked this trail from Kennedy Meadows to Trail Pass. We hiked out with the usual fifty-pound packs and made our four-day trip to Horseshoe Meadows. By nine o'clock I pass the place where we spent the first night. By one in the afternoon, three thousand feet higher at the head of Cow Canyon, I pass the place where we spent the second night. By the end of the day, I am 19.3 miles from Kennedy Meadows and almost 5,000 feet above it, on the shoulder of Olancha Peak, and looking for a place to be.

Gradually, through the course of the day, it has gotten cloudy. High, wispy cirrus clouds, underlain by thin sheets of altostratus, cover the western sky. I set up my tent, fix dinner, then walk over to a bouldery granite ledge. Climbing it, I sit for half an hour, watching the sun, fuzzed and silvery, sink towards the Great Western Divide. At last it arrives just above the horizon, its color changing from silver to orange as it sinks low enough to encounter the tainted air of the Central Valley to the west. The clouds thin, and Olancha Peak glows red-gold. A wind is blowing up the crest. I crawl into my bag and sleep dreamlessly through the night.

By noon the next day, I am more than thirteen miles up the trail, at a saddle on the crest that looks down on the Owens Valley below. This is a wind-blown, dry, harsh spot...the sort of place where foxtail pines do what, I suppose, is considered thriving in their vernacular. There is a nice flat spot in the sand, right on the crest, so I traipse over to have lunch. My Alaskan friend and I arrived at this very spot in the late afternoon of the third day, and decided that the view was too good to waste, so we spent the rest of the day and that night right here. I had secreted Stolichnaya vodka and raspberry Crystal Lite in my pack, and we made snow cones all afternoon. Camped out in the sand right at the edge of the precipice, I watched the headlights of cars and trucks ply their way along Highway 395, only six miles distant but more than 6,500 feet below.

I pull out my ground pad and sit comfortably with my back resting against a tortured foxtail pine. Out across the canyon, the great salt flats of what was once Owens Lake shimmer in the heat. The story of the City of Los Angeles' pirating of the water of the Owens Valley and its lake is history that every hiker in these mountains should know. It was engineered by William Mulholland, that shallow mechanic who saw no beauty in the world other than the works of man and once commented, un-jokingly, that Yosemite Valley would make a great reservoir. It was a sad and shameless business that turned a garden into a desert. There were times that I have railed and ranted and wished to revisit the days of dynamiting the Lone Pine gates and spilling the water back into its natural course. But times change. Ten days in the future, nearing Reds Meadow, I will run into a solitary hiker, the only person I will see in seven days in the High Sierra, until I get beyond Muir Pass. An old man like me, he says he has recently retired from Los Angeles Water and Power, the pirate overseers. He asks me not to hate him. But I have had years to think about it, so I tell him that his former bosses deserve praise, for if they had not slunk into town and furtively bought up all the land, today the Owens Valley would look like Los Angeles, with endless strip malls and houses and private property, with paradise going to the highest bidder, and the air quality sinking to the lowest common denominator. He looks amazed, then relieved. "I've never thought about it that way," he says. "Thanks!"

But meanwhile, I am sitting with my back to the tree, looking down on the otherworldly view of reds and grays and greens that was once a lake. On its northeastern shore, I can make out the buildings that are the remnants of Keeler, a ghost town from the silver days. Further still, in the hazy air, I can see the summit of Cerro Gordo Peak, more than twenty-five miles away.

Cerro Gordo was the scene of a silver strike so rich as to be almost unimaginable. Silver was first found near Independence in 1865, and by January 1, 1870, nearly a thousand locations had been filed on, among them, Cerro Gordo. By 1871, the mountain boasted eleven producing mines. Two stage lines ran daily between Lone Pine and Keeler, and the stories are that they were always full. With silver worth around $1.30 per ounce, the mines of Cerro Gordo produced perhaps 17 million dollars. Of the ore, nearly half was lead, which was worth 5 cents a pound in those days. Later, both zinc and gold were produced. Silver was smelted at such a rate that it could not be transported. One mine, the Union, reported in 1872 that it was producing 100 to 150 bars of silver, weighing eighty-three pounds each, every twenty-four hours. The Cerro Gordo Freighting Company had fifty-six wagon teams on the road, each huge wagon being pulled by sixteen to twenty animals, and could not keep up with the production. A small 85-foot steamer, the Bessie Brady, was built to run the bullion from the smelters at Keeler to Cartago, across the lake and on the south-west shore. Still, it was produced faster than it could be transported. Bullion piled up at various places along the route, so much so that bars were stacked into walls and covered with canvas to make temporary housing for workers.

I pass a leisurely, dreamy hour before I realize it. Repacking my gear, I head on, and by dusk find myself at Dutch Meadows. A small stream flows listlessly at the meadow's edge. Replenishing my water supply and making dinner occupy a few minutes. For the first time since I started the trail, I find myself bothered by mosquitoes, and so I set up my small tent and amuse myself for awhile by blowing my carbon-dioxide laden breath on them through the netting and watching them go crazy.

Next morning I am on the trail early and headed for civilization. As I come to Trail Pass, a view of Horseshoe Meadows is offered up and the desire to head down to the meadows and the trailhead is tempting. However, I will hike the additional 4.8 miles to Cottonwood Pass, descend, and arrive at the same trailhead only a couple of hours later.

By ten o'clock, I arrive at Cottonwood Pass. My ride into Lone Pine, the same friend (now formerly) from Alaska who hiked these miles with me years ago, is not supposed to arrive until around three in the afternoon, so I have several hours to kill. I sit on the sandy ground in the shadow of a wind-gnarled lodgepole pine and look out to the east. The vast horseshoe-shaped meadow stretches out below me. Through the gap at its end, the southern end of the Inyo Mountains looms through the haze. I look at the trail as it switchbacks down the ridge below me and into the head of a fork of Cottonwood Creek. Suddenly, I remember coming up this trail thirty years ago to the month. We were on a trip with Karen and Miles and their brand new baby. Near this pass was as far as they got, unfortunately. The time and distance and loads turned out to be more than they were prepared for, and so they turned back.

A year later those dear friends disappeared from my life, under shaming circumstances not entirely of my own making. Miles, if you're out there, I hope that eventually you came to understand that I was more the seduced than the seducer, and that much of my crime was a failure of character, of not being wise enough to say no, of not realizing that true friendship is more precious than many things. Over the years I have searched you out. Technology is marvelous. It allows an aging, graying man to spend his increasingly sleepless nights listening to a whisky lullaby and searching the internet...sometimes for the past. First in Portland, Oregon, then in Vancouver, Washington, now, in the past few years, you have disappeared even from the aether. I found your last name, some kin no doubt, in Detroit City from whence you came, but I never quite got the courage to contact them to see if you were still in the world.

I often think of you, and I hope life has been good to you these thirty past years and that happiness and love have refilled that well which was emptied so long ago. Of the small handful of things in my life that I deeply regret, the loss of your friendship ranks among the highest. I have not had so good a friend since, nor will I again, most likely.

I know that the sorrow caused by such deep anger and pain never truly disappears, for I too have known it. But it is couched away in some dim recess of the mind, to be brought forth on long nights when the second hand ticks slowly, rolled across the mind, and gingerly sampled, like the bitter-sweet raw apple wine drunk so long ago by two dear friends, much younger and far less wise. Suddenly, it feels as though a great weight has been lifted from my spirit, a weight that truly I was not even much aware of until just now, when it disappeared. Long have I blamed myself for those events, but enough time has passed...enough penance been paid. If the truth be known, perhaps we were both played the fool.

The noise of a jet passing high overhead rouses me from my reverie, so I hoist my pack and head down the trail. I am standing in the parking lot before noon. Now I have three hours to kill, so I look for a tree under which to sit and while away the hours. I am no sooner packless when, miraculously repeating his re-appearing act from Kelso Valley Road and Kennedy Meadows, up drives Dave, the husband and support team for Steady. He has beers in his cooler, so we chat awhile before he heads up to the trailhead to wait. He is no more than out of sight when my ride, more than two hours early, shows up.

This and the next two days go by in the kind of blur that wilderness travelers, suddenly plopped down in civilization, are only too familiar with. A road trip three hundred miles south to the Saufley's Hiker Heaven in Agua Dulce, a quick side trip to REI in San Fernando, Los Angeles, for a hat to replace Meadow Ed's towel, a return trip all the way to Mammoth and back to Lone Pine, and suddenly, I'm dumped out at the Cottonwood Pass trailhead and ready, if dazed.

Retracing my steps to Cottonwood Pass, I head north around Cirque Peak and into the canyon bearing Rock Creek. On the exposed, southern, sandy slopes of this mountain are to be found stands of foxtail pine. They seem to grow only in the starkest of sites, their trunks gnarled and foliage compact. Unlike the lodgepole pine, which follows the dictates of its names, lodgepole and <u>Pinus contorta</u>, growing tall and straight when they can, but willing to writhe across the ground as tree-line shrubs if they must, the foxtail remain erect and proud, braving the harshest of conditions. Those in the most exposed places are stripped of much of their bark and foliage on the windward side. On the leeward side of one, only a thin strip of living tissue runs from ground to branches, bearing proof of the stubbornness of life. Some of these trees, like the truly ancient bristlecone pines of the White Mountains to the east, barely appear to be alive, yet they often live a thousand years or more.

The trail circles around the shoulder of the peak, at last hitting a westward running ridge and following it down to Rock Creek, more than nine miles later. The creek is running hard, and it is apparent that the trail crew constructed this crossing later in the summer, when what is now a torrent was but a trickle. I look around, and only yards downstream, see a large tree that, no doubt with hikers in mind, had the courtesy to fall, neatly bridging the riotous creek.

Just across the creek, the trail begins to wind up the slopes of Mount Guyot toward a pass on its east flank. Ultimately I arrive at the nearly 11,000-foot pass and stop for a rest. Years ago, when my children were young, they and my wife and I, did a several day loop, over Cottonwood Pass, down into Big Whitney Meadow, north over Siberian Pass into Siberian Outpost (the PCT was once routed through this beautiful, bleak, sandy flat) down into Rock Creek and up over this same pass to Mount Whitney and down. We all rested somewhere near this very spot. Suddenly our silence was shattered by a roar like that which might presage the end of the world. No more than yards away, an F4 Phantom jet materialized, up and out of Guyot Flat, over the ridge and disappeared south. We could see the pilot's face, and in retrospect, I think it surely must have been smiling. A naval air station at China Lake, some miles south and east into the desert was its home, no doubt.

I hoist my pack and start down the short three hundred vertical feet, where I spend the night at Guyot Flat on the north side of Guyot Peak. It is a huge, wind-swept, sandy flat, sparsely populated with lodgepole pines. I set up my tent in the lee of a long-downed log. Even though the flat is open to the west, and the sun, sinking near the Great Western Divide and the Kaweahs, still shines brilliantly, it is cold. I prepare a quick dinner, and lying comfortably in my sleeping bag, watch the shadows stretch out across the flat.

To the west, the sun disappears behind Triple Divide Peak. In the gloaming, I snuggle down into my bag and think about tomorrow, for tomorrow I will reach Crabtree Meadow and make the climb of Mount Whitney. My first visit to the Sierra, so many years ago, was an attempt to climb Mount Whitney.

I can recall, almost as if it was yesterday, my introduction to that which I consider among two or three most important things in my life. More than forty years ago I began a lifetime love affair with the sparkling granite, the blue-black sky, and the sharp, crystalline air of the high country of the Sierra Nevada. Since that time, there have been no more than a few summers that I have failed to wander and climb somewhere in their heights. I have hiked every trail, crossed every pass, made my way over scores of cross-country routes, and climbed nearly every significant peak. Like the call of the Sirens, as Homer said, the allure of this place has been "beyond all conjecture."

My mind travels effortlessly back to that day. I set my alarm clock for 1:30 AM and arose, waiting for my friend to arrive. By two o'clock, we were on the highway, headed out of southern California towards Lone Pine; Mount Whitney was our goal. It was a Saturday in late May, 1958. The era of muscle cars loomed on the horizon and gas was cheap. Radar for controlling speed had yet to be invented; our trip was rapid and riotous. A bit before dawn we rounded the corner of then partially wet Owens Lake. In the nearly full moonlight, the wall of mountains glowed whitely. To me it seemed as if they were snow covered, and I thought my first trip to the Sierra would end in the Owens Valley lowlands. An early breakfast of eggs and bacon, hash browns, and toast at Jack's Gateway Café, all food normally shunned these days by a health-conscious old man, and we were on the road to Whitney Portal.

The rising sun made it abundantly clear why John Muir called the Sierra the Range of Light. Breathtaking color, red-black, like an ember at first, then deep red, lightening by degrees through blazing gold, to yellow, then white, showed that the mountains were not, in fact, covered with snow. It was just the polished granite of Lone Pine Peak, Wotan's Throne, Mount Whitney itself, and the other peaks, reflecting the moonlight so brightly that I mistook it for snow.

At the Portal, we shuffled gear and were on the trail by nine o'clock. A sign at the start of the trail announced 10.5 miles to the summit. We figured to make it by early afternoon. Ah, the arrogance and ignorance of youth!

We stopped along the way and ate a prodigious lunch...mine including a can of kippered herring that came back to haunt me again and again throughout the remainder of the day and that night. By day's end we had advanced a whole four miles to Mirror Lake, which in those days allowed camping and fires.

That first attempted climb of Mount Whitney ended the following morning after spending a horrendous, sleepless night with a violent mountain-sickness headache. Our gear was so heavy and our experience so light that it took literally all day to hike those few miles. Engrossed in the pain of my headache and the recurring flavor of the kippered herring of lunch, I had planted myself in the near dark, only to be awakened the following morning by horses stepping over me. In my agony, I had camped right in the trail, to be rudely aroused by an early-morning pack train. We packed our gear and made a hasty retreat. Although I did not realize it at the time, some resonant chord had been struck in my being, and I would return again and again.

Many times over the next years I would repeat this venture, on similar weekend trips, arising at dark-thirty, driving pell-mell through the desert, to be on a trail by sunrise and atop some peak or the other and back in the car by Sunday evening, to repeat the trip home, and ready or not, be ready for school the next morning. Summers always found time for a week or two trip. Even when I left southern California for college, and even when, for a period of some few years I lived in Oregon and New Mexico, I returned again and again. I have hiked the Cascades of Oregon, the Rockies, the Swiss Alps, and the Torridon and Cuillin Hills of Scotland, have traveled through the Karakorum, Tien Shan, and Kun Lun of Pakistan and Western China, but I have never found a place of rock and sky that fills my heart like the Sierra Nevada. To roughly paraphrase Shakespeare's Romeo, there is no world outside Sierra walls.

Gradually the evening deepens and stars appear above my sandy little camp in Guyot Flat. I fall peacefully asleep. The next morning I break camp extra early and in the dim pre-dawn light, head north the two miles to Crabtree Meadow. I hope to make it most of the way to Forester Pass today. With a side trip to Mount Whitney, it will involve walking nearly thirty miles today…a hefty number, even if more than half will be without the encumbering backpack. I move rapidly and arrive at the John Muir Trail junction before six o'clock. I turn west and uphill about a mile, along Whitney Creek to the Crabtree Ranger Station. There, removing my pack's top pouch, which I picked up at Lone Pine and am using for the first time on the trail, and which doubles as a fanny pack, I stash my gear in a bear box[2] and head eagerly east. With only water, lunch, and precautionary rain gear (even though foul weather in mid-June is almost unheard of), I push on toward Guitar Lake.

The trail heads up along Whitney Creek, through a narrow canyon between Mount Young and Mount Hitchcock, named in 1881 for two Dartmouth College professors, the former of mathematics and astronomy, the latter of geology. Past Guitar Lake, which from above looks like one, the trail pushes southeast and up...and up. Ascending through patches of snow to the Sierra crest just a couple of hundred yards below Trail Crest, at 13,600 feet, the highest trail pass in Sierra. From there, the trail winds due north, right along the crest.

Seen from the west, the summit of Mount Whitney is a huge, rounded hump at the end of a two-mile long ridge that is broken by a number of pinnacles. The stupendous chasms between these pinnacles are kissed several times by the trail, and the view down the fifteen hundred foot cliff is thrilling. Ultimately the summit block is before me.

I zigzag my way up over fields of snow, arriving at the summit just before eleven o'clock. The rock hut is a small, two-roomed building with a corrugated tin roof. This early in the year, the windows are covered with steel plates and the doors are closed and locked. Later, when the snow has melted, it will be opened up and provide a death trap for inexperienced hikers caught in the ubiquitous Sierra summer thunderstorms, even though there is a warning sign. Oddly enough, the idea for construction of the hut was conceived after the first recorded death by lightning on the mountain, on July 26, 1904. One Bryd Surby and two other employees of the U.S. Bureau of Fisheries had climbed the then brand new trail to the summit. The three sat upon the summit, having lunch, when Bryd was struck by lightning and killed. Dr. William Campbell designed it in 1908, and by 1909, with funding from the Smithsonian Institute, the hut was completed. Of course, these days, conventional wisdom says stay out of shallow caves, which of course, is just what this massive stone shelter resembles.

From the top of Mount Whitney, I look out over the Owens Valley. I cannot immediately recall exactly how many times I have viewed this incredible scene...perhaps a dozen. In May 1959, I made my second trip to Mount Whitney, this time successfully climbing it by trail. Over the intervening years, I have climbed it from every angle on every route.

Below, the Alabama Hills stretch out, their eroded, bouldery shapes in stark contrast to the angular, fractured granite of the Sierra. I

---

2 A metal storage box provided by the Forest Service to prevent bears from accessing hiker food.

have camped and climbed in them many times over the years. Their name is inextricably woven into the history of California, of gold and the Civil War. During the Civil War, California, too far away to be involved, was far from uninterested. While predominantly pro Union, the state was rife with Confederate sympathy. When placer gold was discovered in the hills by sympathizers, they named their mine the Alabama, after the Confederate cruiser, which, with its Confederate officers and British crew, sank 64 ships in the Atlantic and Indian Oceans. In June 1864, she was sunk off the coast of France by the Union ship USS Kearsarge, causing joyous northerners, when they heard the news later in the year, to name a mining district to the north of the Alabama Mine, the Kearsarge District, a name which passed on to an early mining town, some lakes and pinnacles, a pass, and a mountain peak, in order to taunt the southerners.

The name Alabama came to cover the whole of the hills. Once they were thought to be much older than the Sierra, the remnants of a previous mountain range, but science has shown them to be the same age as their towering neighbors. Only the weathering effects of wind and heat have altered them so.

I stay on the summit only an hour, lunch and a rest, for considerable progress has yet to be made today. I look out over the Inyo Mountains. The view is considerably different this day than it was in 1959. I still have a photo from that second trip, of a young me standing on the summit, grimacing in the cruel sunlight. In the background, against a blue-black sky, mountain range upon mountain range can be seen. We counted five mountain ranges off toward the horizon far into Nevada—the Inyo, the Panamint, the Funeral, the Coso, the Last Change—more than a hundred miles.

Looking out over this land that I know so well and love, I see it with those same eyes that squinted in the fierce sunlight a lifetime ago. The sky is still that deep blue-black that hangs over all high places, and the morning is still filled with that special Sierra light that makes the world of sky and granite glow from within. I take a last look at Cerro Gordo, where men toiled for a chance at treasure, and rode ore buckets down the mountain, ducking to avoid the cross-arms, and gambled and loved and died, to leave nothing but a ghost town and a chapter of history.

All that is gone now...and so, almost is Cerro Gordo Peak...lost in a wave of smog that fills the valley and crawls toward the mountain summits. But in my mind's eye, I see it as it looked that June morning so long ago. Through the crystalline air I could see to the edge of the world.

I grab my water bottle and head down the switchbacks that lead to the trail to Guitar Lake, Crabtree Meadows, and my gear. With the rest of the Sierra to come, I grow impatient and nervous, as if renewing acquaintance with an old lover.

By the end of a long day, I am setting up camp not too far from one of the half dozen, small, unnamed lakes below Forester Pass. The first three fords, Wallace Creek, Wright Creek, and Tyndall Creek passed without incident. The water was cold and flowing strongly, but not terribly deep, perhaps two feet. As the sun rides lower, I set up my small shelter amid the boulders and sand, and patches of snow. The sky deepens in color, making greater the contrast of the thin, wispy cirrus clouds. Crawling into my sleeping bag, I see, high above in the distant, deep notch of Forester Pass, two figures appear in the fading light. Silhouetted against the sky, they look small and insignificant. Knowing what the other side will look like and how far they will have to go to find shelter for the night, I feel glad to be up to my ears in down. The wind weaves its way through boulders and violently shakes my tent, a mountaineer's lullaby.

Dawn finds me headed towards Forester Pass. Just before the trail starts up the steep east wall of the canyon, I see another hiker, down and a few hundred yards away. He is sitting in front of a dome tent and appears to be lacing up his shoes. All of a sudden a blast of wind forces its way down the canyon and in a flash his tent is headed towards a cliff that drops down to a lake below. And, while it looks hilarious to see him pounding across the rocks in hot pursuit, it is no joke, for he could easily lose his tent, or, worse, injure himself. But within a hundred yards he has overtaken it and trudges back to his campsite. He sees me and waves, the no doubt sheepish look on his face invisible in the distance.

Forester Pass has a bad reputation among thru-hikers, perhaps deservedly, perhaps not. The trail is hacked out of the side of a rock wall, and in years of great snow, it presents a formidable challenge. Fortunately, this year has been mild and the trail is mostly clear. To top it off, there is an incredibly steep couloir that one must cross, right below the pass. The steps across the snow are few, perhaps a dozen, but the consequences of a misstep would appear to be inevitably terminal. A number of people have already made their way across, so it is just a matter of carefully stepping across the icy slope. It takes but a few moments. On the other side lie about two miles of snow, a long trip down into Bubbs Creek and then up again to Glen Pass.

Glen Pass actually offers more danger than did Forester, for there is a mile of high angle snow to negotiate. After yesterday's nearly thirty miles, today yields only eighteen and fortunately so, for it has taken me most of the day to get here. The snow is soft and traction good, although my trail runners are scant protection from the water, and my feet are soon soaking wet. By the end of the day, I am camped near Rae Lakes.

The next day yields approximately the same mileage as I make my way down into Woods Creek and up over Pinchot Pass. So far the trail has been relatively easy to follow and the snow light and of no real consequence. I am beginning to curse my decision to bear the added weight of an ice ax through the Sierra.

A day later, the deep U-shaped notch of Mather Pass looms on the horizon. The trail winds more than two miles through gently sloping Upper Basin, a vast, glaciated wasteland more than 11,000 high. There is enough snow to make route finding a bit of a problem. In fact, I lose the trail several times in the snow and rock. I have been over it a number of times, though, and know how it heads up to the east before it crosses under the pass, from east to west, and finally switchbacks its way up and across. Within a few hundred yards of the pass, I hear the sound of an airplane, and it's not too far away. Looking towards the south, I see the black, angular shape of a stealth fighter, coming right up the canyon. I am only a few hundred feet lower than 12,100 foot Mather Pass and am actually looking down on it! Neither invisible nor quiet, it cruises right past me, takes a little jump up, and glides right through the notch that is the pass. Within seconds the whole show is over. I probably wouldn't have had time to grab my camera and get a picture…but I'll never know, since I just stood there open-mouthed and watched.

Just below the crest there is one last short, high-angled patch of snow. I have been carrying an ice ax since Kennedy Meadows and am bound and determined to use it. And this is probably the last chance I will have to rationalize the extra weight. I unhitch it from my pack and tie my hiking poles down. The few hundred feet of snow pass without incident.

The north side is not so easy. The snow is more extensive, running along the ridge to the north, and the route is difficult to follow, for everyone, it seems, knows a different way. Eschewing the tracks that go straight down, punctuated by the occasional, wider twin smears made by buttocks in either fall or glissade, I follow those across the less steep north ridge. I am no stranger to the techniques of glissade. Long ago I made the now non-existent but once infamous thousand-foot glissade down the north slope of Mount St. Helens, but traveling alone, I hesitate at the far simpler prospects below me now. An injury here would be no small matter. And so, unfortunately, I go too far north and descend too little, and as a result, have to make my way down nearly 800 feet of high angle talus and scree. Not a problem, really, but tiring and time consuming. It is nearly 2 PM by the time I make it to the lower of the two Palisade Lakes. I hurry on, anxious to get a run at Muir Pass for the morrow. Down the interminable Golden Staircase and into the canyon I pound.

The trail goes along Palisade Creek, through several miles of patchily burned forest, mostly lodgepole pine, that seem, with their papery-thin bark, to have little resistance to fire. A toasting that would be little more than an inconvenience to the ponderosa pine that surround my home in the western Sierra foothills has left a vast stretch of blackened, soon to be lodgepole-less forest. To top this day off, the storms of late April caused many of these dead and dying trees to topple. Time and again I must route my way around trees, in singles and multiples, that block the trail.

More than ten miles past Mather Pass, I run out of steam. I had hoped to make it a few miles beyond Big Pete Meadow, putting me short miles, perhaps six, from Muir Pass, but here I am, setting up my solitary camp at Grouse Meadow, more than five miles short of my goal, and eleven miles from the pass. Ah well.

In the late afternoon, the mosquitoes become ferocious, so I hastily set up my shelter. Grouse Meadow could as well be named Grouse Swamp. I crawl in and begin to shuffle gear around, when I notice I have set up directly under the fall line of a large dead tree not too far away. Considering how many downed trees I have seen in the last few hours, it makes me nervous enough to crawl out, fight the mosquitoes for a little while longer, and set up on the side where the tree leans away. If it goes, it will be a heart-pounding experience...but I will be safe.

On the trail early the next morning, I run into fairly heavy snow by the time I come to the small, unnamed lake a mile before Helen Lake. I think this lake is Helen and the snowy ridge above is the pass, a mistake I have made before, in less snowy conditions. By the time I reach Helen, the snow cover is complete, except for exposed ridges. I make my way up steep snowfields. Ultimately I see the top of the Muir Hut, peeking over a ridge of snow, only a few hundred yards away. I arrive at eleven-thirty in the morning on this twenty-third day of June.

The scene is unbelievably beautiful. Snow pack is almost solid as far as the eye can see. Wanda Lake and the closer Lake MacDermand are still frozen, although a patch of bluish-white appears at the lowest end of Wanda, indicating the melt is not long off. At the west end of the lake is a towering peak, only forty feet short of 13,000, but unnamed and dominated by massive Mount Goddard, a few miles to its south. The cloudless sky is that deep blue-black that is the trademark of all high places.

I have been at this place a number of times since I first came here in 1972, have climbed most of the peaks of the area, traveled its trails and cross country routes, including twice through the fabled Ionian Basin and Enchanted Gorge, guarded by the twin peaks of Scylla and Charybdis, only a short mile and a half from here, but totally invisible behind nearby Mount Solomons and the peaks of the Goddard Divide. I have never stood in anything but mute awe in this wild place. I do so again, but only for a few minutes, for the clock is ticking, and more than two miles of snow are softening in the blazing sun.

West, and below me, halfway to Wanda Lake, are two dots, hikers. With the exception of the LA Water & Power man at Piute Creek, these are the first people I have seen since two hikers briefly silhouetted themselves on Forester Pass, five days ago. Knowing time is critical because of the softening snow, I hurry on. Sadly I am not early enough; I knew I wouldn't be. The great, almost flat snowfield between Muir Pass and Wanda Lake and on down to Sapphire Lake absorbs the sun's heat marvelously well, and the two miles of treading gingerly on the crusty snow, only to posthole repeatedly, take their toll. I am wearing shorts and scree gaiters, which keep the snow out, but are little protection against moisture. My shoes and socks are soaked, no big deal really, but the inside of both of my calves are snow burned, repeated breaking through the crust and plunging knee to thigh deep in the snow has scraped away something more than just the surface layer of skin.

In about an hour, I catch up with the hikers, Wahoo and Lou, a young couple, curiously enough, vegetarians from Des Moines, Iowa, where on any given week upwards of half a million cattle give their all for steak houses and fast food joints across the land. With them, invisible from the pass, is friend Alice, who has met them for a portion of the trip.

I met them last at Kennedy Meadows, where they were waiting, to no avail, for a resupply package. When I left Kennedy Meadows on Sunday morning, they were waiting for Monday's post. My two and a half day sojourn in civilization must have allowed them to pass me by. I marvel at the curiosity that we could travel along for so many days, perhaps no more than a few miles apart, each unaware of the other.

We make it to Sapphire Lake, where I stop to dry out my gear and cook an early supper. They disappear on down the trail. In the bright sun, I enjoy noodle-delight and look up at the summits of Mounts Huxley, Fiske, Haeckel, Wallace, Spencer, Darwin, and Mendel, the peaks of Evolution Basin. I have stood on all their summits at one time or another over the years. I feel at home.

A bit more than two hours later and four and a half miles down the trail, I pass Wahoo and Lou and Alice having their dinner at the outlet of Lower Evolution Lake. I stop and chat a few moments and then hurry on.

I have been traveling light and am technically out of food. I will be having a small serving of noodle-something for dinner and breakfast the next two days and have but two ounces of jerky, two granola bars, and a Snickers bar left for lunch materials. Only two days more separate me from the Vermillion Valley Resort and real food. I make it to Colby Meadows by six that evening, a twelve-hour hiking day and only seventeen miles traveled. Only Selden Pass and Bear Ridge separate me from VVR…oh yeah, I forgot…and the 3,900 foot drop down and 2,900 foot climb up to the pass and down the hill to a campsite at Marie Lake, a mere twenty-one miles.

I make it over Selden Pass, which is one of the lower Sierra passes, and find virtually no snow. Then, it's down to Marie Lake by late afternoon. I rest a spell and fix what meager food I have left. I wander about a bit, looking for a room with a view and ultimately find it well above the trail.

Twelve miles to the north, the 12,000 foot peaks of the Silver Divide begin to take on the rosy glow of a Sierra evening. Looking out across Marie Lake, to the east, I see a couple of campers on its far shores. I watch them walk about for a bit…feeling a kinship with someone I will never meet or see again. The truncated top of Mount Izaac Walton pales from rose to lavender. Izaac Walton lived at the beginning of the 15th century. He witnessed the untimely deaths of all of his seven children and wife, and struggled on and became a wealthy businessman. He carried on until he was just over fifty, until he, by his own admission, had "…laid aside business, and gone afishing," publishing *The Compleat Angler* some nine years later.

Rose turns to lavender as evening rushes in. Mount Izaac Walton shares a few last moments with the sun and retires for the night. Darkness spreads across the mountains, and one by two, stars erupt. I fall asleep thinking, "Tomorrow is feast day!"

And so it is. I rise in the darkness and sprint the fourteen remaining miles to the boat dock at Lake Thomas Edison. I arrive shortly after noon and am faced with the prospect of a several hour wait for the afternoon boat. I pull up at the bear box and tiredly remove my pack. About thirty feet away, there is a couple sitting under a tree, close to the water. I say, "It won't disturb your picnic if I rest here awhile, will it?" and a conversation begins. Minutes later, with an ice-cold beer and a luscious turkey, cheese, tomato, lettuce and onion sandwich in hand, my new friends offer to take me to VVR in their boat. By one o'clock, I am sitting in the bow of a small boat, spray in my face, and at peace with the world.

By two o'clock, I am ensconced in the restaurant having desert, a huge slab of hot, fresh peach pie covered with vanilla ice cream and an ice cold Sierra Nevada Pale Ale (the first one was free!).

Vermillion Valley Resort, commonly called VVR, is one of the finest stops on the PCT. It receives some bad press among the hiker community, for reasons that need no elaboration. Needless to say, no operation catering to hiker trash and fishermen could hope to boast 100% satisfaction...and so it is here. And, after all, some of the complaints may well be valid. But all of that aside, after seven days of solitude and struggle, Paradise could make no better claim than does VVR. After lunch, I spend the afternoon sitting in the shade with Chef Paul, once President Jimmy Carter's chef at the White House...now retired to a comfortable chair and a cold beer. He is off duty until dinner. We chat amiably and drink cold beers.

The afternoon boat arrives, bringing Lou, Wahoo, and Crazy Alice. Brent and Stormy, whom I had not seen since Kennedy Meadows, ten days ago, are also aboard. We all congregate at the tent cabin that is reserved, free, for thru-hikers. Lou and Wahoo have retrieved their food drop, and Lou is busy sorting and grumbling. She had instructed their resupply agent, a mother or mother-in-law, to include a 12-pack of Twinkies. A slight mix-up causes 12 12-packs to be shipped...to everyone's amusement but Lou's. It's beer and Twinkies all around. I had planned to buy enough food in VVR's small store to get me to Tuolumne Meadows, four days up the trail, but serendipity trampolines into play. A group of Brits from Her Majesty's 6th Signal Corps are SoBo-ing[3] the John Muir Trail. Two have decided to leave, so they have filled the bear box at Tent 7 with Her Majesty's finest MREs, Meals Ready to Eat. Beef Wellington, chicken and dumplings, and several others will provide my dinner for the next four nights. A bit heavy, but after the 35 pound pack I carried through the Sierra, it amounts to little.

The next day passes quickly. By three o'clock, I decide to catch the outgoing boat. At the restaurant, the outdoor barbecues are fired up and tri-tip and chicken, tonight's dinner, are beginning to sizzle. Ah well... By three-thirty, I am sitting on the boat, feeling the spray in my face, and headed for the trail.

I decide to camp next to the lake and get an early start in the morning. I idle away the three or four hours of sunlight watching the clouds form and dissipate over Bear Ridge. The next morning finds me on the trail early and headed for Silver Pass. Near the pass, I have a close encounter of the weird kind with a couple of southbound hikers...more of which will be said later. By evening I am well on my way. Tuolumne Meadows awaits.

---

3 SoBo = southbound. As opposed to NoBo, northbound.

JUST ANOTHER THRU-HIKER[1]

Master Po: "Ah, but Grasshopper, can any man afford such arrogance?"
(explaining to his young student why he, a Shaolin monk
whose life was dedicated to peace, had fought.)
(*The Arrogant Dragon*, Kung Fu, a 1970s television series)

Editor's note: The story flashes back here to Bear Creek, a day's hike before Vermillion Valley Resort described in the last chapter.

I am standing, somewhat confused, near the edge of Rosemarie Meadow, at a crossing of the west fork of Bear Creek, Section H, mile 858.9. Across the creek, the trail clearly takes up again. It is barely light, and in the cold, brightening morning, indecision hangs upon me like a frosty rime.

The last few days have been...well, trying. Both Mather and Muir Passes offered their own difficulties, particularly Muir Pass. Postholing across its two-mile snowfield on the northern side sanded my calves to the quick. Yesterday, a long twenty-one-plus-mile day brought me to Marie Lake. Short on food, come hell or high water, today I will be at Vermillion Valley Resort for some real food. And so, I break camp at dark-thirty and am on the trail, standing at the crossing of the West Fork of Bear Creek, vexed at the prospect of fording this early in the morning.

I hear a voice say, "If you're headed to Vermillion Valley, the trail is to your right." I glance to the right, and there is the trail, at my feet and as plain as near-day. The voice is coming from behind me, in a flat above the creek. Three hikers are stowing their gear. I say "Good Morning." They reply in kind, revealing they are Brits, headed south on the John Muir Trail. One says, "So you're a thru-hiker, then." It is not a question. "Pretty obvious, I guess. We *are* a scruffy lot," I say, practicing conversation, a skill, rusty from my days of solitary travel, that will come in handy at VVR later today. "It's not that alone," says he. "You're easy to spot, especially you solo chaps, you have a hunger...a fire."

We chat a few minutes. With a warning to cross Muir Pass early, I bid them farewell and travel on down the creekside. A hunger. A fire. For some reason, it pleases me to have such, and I wonder what this fire looks like that it is so easily recognized. I have no mirror, or I would check, even though I suspect that I would see nothing out of the ordinary, nothing apparent...to me. But I understand, for I *have* felt a fire of late, and

1 Previously published in the Pacific Crest Trail Communicator, April 2004, vol. 16, no. 2

although I am uncertain what it means, I have felt it, for it has driven me along this trail more than eight hundred miles.

I walk on beside the creek, thinking about fire and hunger. The ford is upon me, and Bear Creek is running hard. Here is the high water. Hopefully Hell, its trusty companion, is not nearby. It's about thirty feet across and appears, near the middle, to be nearly waist deep, not a pleasant prospect this early in the morning, or at any time, for that matter.

As I sit down on a convenient rock to remove my shoes, I pause and look around. The sky, just at dawn, is of the deepest blue and cloudless. The sun has not risen high enough to put me in its warming light, but a massive, turreted mountain, just more than a mile to the east, is outlined in brilliant, silvery light. Theodore Solomons traveled through here in 1894, the year before he pioneered a trail through and named the peaks of the Evolution Basin, through which I traveled only yesterday. The peak has a number of oddly shaped ridges that run down from its more than 13,000 foot summit, and for this reason he gave it its name, Seven Gables. Years ago, retracing his steps during a tour of the spectacular Lake Italy region, I stood on its summit. The breathtaking view was burned forever into my memory. The Sierra crest was only a few miles to the east and on it lay the glaciated summits of Mts. Hilgard, Dade, Abbot, Bear Creek Spire, and Mt. Julius Caesar. Twenty-five miles to the south, the huge massifs of Mt. Goddard, Mt. Darwin, and Mt. Mendel, all peaks just a few hundred feet shy of fourteen thousand, were etched against the sky. I sit for several minutes lost in the memory.

But crossing this creek is the business at hand, so I rouse myself and look around. Downstream, and to my north, lies the huge glacier-gouged canyon through which Bear Creek runs until it hits Bear Ridge and is forced west. Towering over me to the west is a long granite ridge sporting several minor unnamed peaks. In the direct rays of the early morning sun, it incandesces and reminds me that the Sierra truly is the Range of Light. I know these Sierra mornings...utterly still and quiet, pregnant with the infinite possibilities of a new day, as if the whole universe is holding its breath to see what comes next. And so it is here, with the minor exception of the roar of Bear Creek at my feet.

It occurs to me that much of my hunger has been about this solitude. I thought the trip would mostly be a solitary one and was not certain how I would react, for I have had but little experience in total solitude in a lifetime of wilderness travel. All right, I confess, I've virtually none. I was surprised though, for at the beginning, fresh out of Campo, the herd runs strong. It takes a long time for the starting pack to thin out, for people to lag behind or drop out, or for the faster hikers to forge far ahead. You see and travel with many of the same people over and over again as the weeks pass by and you move up the trail. Truly, in the first month or so, I don't think there was ever more than a few hours, half a day at most, between me and some other hiker. Terrain and mileage, and above all water, often conspire in those fiery southern sections to put several people together at day's end. Recall that my first night alone came nearly 400 miles into the trail, one day out of Wrightwood.

Needless to say, that night passed quietly and uneventfully, and so by the time I reached the Sierra Pelona, six days later, solitary evenings had become the norm. During the month that has passed since that night, with the exception of brief stops in civilization, in Mojave, Lake Isabella, Kennedy Meadows and Lone Pine, I have been virtually alone.

This solitude has become important to me, and it is as though I somehow knew all along that it would be. Ian-The-Brit, are you out there? If perchance you ever read this, forgive me, my dear friend. We traveled together, since our hiking speeds were similar, from the Laguna Mountains to Big Bear, fifteen days. One day past Big Bear when you came up lame, I ditched you. It would have cost me nothing to wait another day, and yet, perhaps cost me everything, for even then I must have known that I truly needed to be alone. And though I know not why, that has been my hunger...my fire.

The ford of Bear Creek is uneventful and not quite as deep as it had appeared, but the current is the strongest I have yet encountered. It is exceedingly cold, and about mid-thigh level, not that all-important few inches higher where the term frigid takes on new meaning. I put my shoes back on and travel down the trail.

The trail winds up the seven hundred foot hump of Bear Ridge and then goes down...and down. Descending more two thousand feet over fifty-three switchbacks to Mono Creek, I race on. That, and the mile to the end of Lake Thomas Edison, and the boat to civilization, was my quest on that morning.

———————

Two days later, after that great stay at VVR, I am back on the trail and on my way towards Silver Pass. Just above Pocket Meadow the trail makes its final ford of the north fork of Mono Creek and starts up the west canyon wall. The trail flattens out and heads for the pass. Above, I see two hikers coming down. As they near, I step off to the side and wait for them.

"Where you headed?" I ask in reply to their greeting. They stop for a chat. They are hiking the John Muir Trail and headed for VVR to re-supply. The lead hiker of the two, a man perhaps in his early fifties, offers that he has hiked the JMT three times before. "How about you?" he queries. "North," I reply. He takes a moment and looks me up and down. "You're hiking the PCT." Dejà hear....recognized again. And again, no rising inflection indicating a question. There *is* something different in his voice, but I brush it off and offer, "Pretty easy to spot, I guess. We *are* a scruffy lot." The line worked only two days ago. Ignoring my comment, he says off-handedly, almost as if to himself. "Tennis shoes...no gear." There's no mistaking the condescension in his voice.

I take a close look at him. He sports a large, exterior frame backpack; sleeping bag hung outside, off the bottom; full-length Thermarest ground pad rolled up and stuffed under the top fly; four bulging side pockets. Glancing down, I see marvelous, monstrous, thick leather boots. Until this past spring, I had a pair in my gear, just for old time's sake, mind you. They broke in my feet for the first thousand miles I put on them. Ten years ago I swore never to wear them again, but just couldn't seem to give them up—a reminder of my years of servitude, I guess. I hadn't thought of them for years and hope never to again. I recognize all his gear. For most of my long hiking career I looked just like him, and much of it, or the like, still hangs in my garage, just in case I lose my mind at some future date and decide to hike once more with a fifty- or sixty-pound pack.

"Why would you want to do that?" he asks. "You travel so fast you never have time to enjoy yourself, to see anything."

I can't understand this antagonism. Surely it is not me personally, for I am being amiable. I took a long shower just yesterday. My clothes, proudly confessing to evidence of seven and a half days on the trail, served time in the outdoor washer and drier at VVR. So it can't be that. Nor can it be that he knows that my pack, fully loaded, probably weighs a mere thirty percent of his, can it? In the past, did some ultralight backpacker dance around him, laughing and taunting? This is not what I had expected, and my hackles are raised.

"Why would you want to do that? You travel so fast you never have time to enjoy yourself, to see anything." His words sink in. My mouth hangs open as I start to answer, but no sound emerges. Why indeed? There are probably as many reasons for hiking the PCT as there are people who hike it. Certainly I don't speak for them, and without warning, I find it difficult to speak for myself.

Suddenly the events of three days ago flood through my mind. The hunger. The fire. The solitude. My entire life, it seems, has been guided by responsibility—often, I think, even shackled by it. Barely at the age of twenty, a shy, introspective, inexperienced, nerdy youth, I married the girl next door. She was sixteen and pregnant, and I was *responsible*. That marriage ended most unkindly, leaving two young children without a mother, and a father to raise them on his own, more or less, at least for the few years until I remarried.

For more than forty years thereafter, responsibility for and to others has been the watchword…until now. And truly, I am not voicing great complaint, for much of the responsibility was self-chosen. Nor by any stretch of the imagination, am I trying to say that I have lived a life devoid of freedom and joy. Even now, though, as an old man, retired from work and ostensibly free, I still have responsibilities, commitments to others. Welcome to life, I guess, and, perhaps, after all, it is only the days and weeks of solitude that have caused this to loom so largely in my mind.

But I think this *has* been much of my fire…a need to be totally on my own, to be responsible to and for no one but myself; to eat when I am hungry; to drink when I am thirsty; to rest when I am tired; and with no goal other than to walk and gawk. Kaleidoscopic visions flash through my mind: of that first nervous night in the San Gabriel Mountains, alone in Rattlesnake Canyon under the brooding brow of Eagle's Roost; of sitting by my tent near Jack Fair's empty house in the Mojave, as the winds howled through the desert and a full moon rose; of standing on top of weathered granite boulders in the Jawbone Wilderness with only my shadow, cast by the setting sun on nearby boulders and glints of sunlight flashing off windshields on Highway 14, twenty miles down and across the desert, for company; of glimpsing two miniscule hikers lingering, but briefly, in the notch of Forester Pass, as the sun faded, and I scurried out of chilling winds and into my small shelter amid snow and boulders at its base; of sitting quietly beside the trail, surrounded by the towering peaks of Evolution Basin, listening to the silence, and making the marvelous discovery of how unlonely being alone can be.

The solitary thru-hiker has absolutely no responsibility to anyone in the world but himself, and therein lies the magic, for those who need it…for those that are ready for it. Even so, after days of travel, though relishing the solitude, he appreciates the occasional reassurance when he becomes uncertain that he is not alone in the world. Brief encounters with other hikers along the trail are pleasant diversions and should never be angst-ridden and unpleasant, as is this current one.

How can I explain all this to the hostile stranger standing in front of me, when I barely understand it myself? My mouth hangs open. After an eternity, perhaps six seconds, I shrug and say the first thing that comes to mind. "Gotta do something…can't dance."

The inanity of my statement causes *his* mouth to fall open, so he changes the subject and says, probably, the first thing that comes to his mind. He asks about snow conditions further south. I recite the pass-litany...Selden, Muir, Mather, Pinchot, Glen, Forester, Trail Crest. I tell him of my problems on Mather and Muir, adding that it should have been easy, since I've been over the Muir Trail seven or eight times. Nonplussed by his attitude, and neither for the first, nor probably for the last time, forgetting all I have learned, I am sucked into his one-upsmanship game. Ah well, sucked into is not quite true, for I am rankled and eagerly enter the fray. Only three times on the Muir Trail, eh...beginner!

We exchange Sierra info on most favorite places, mountains climbed, hardest trips, each trying to outdo the other, he caviling my every statement. Suddenly I come to my senses and realize it's time to extricate myself from this pointless conversation. I am allowing myself to be controlled by someone whom, blessedly, I will never see again, and for reasons unclear, doesn't like thru-hikers.

Perhaps sensing that I will imbrue myself no further, he asks me if I know what time it is. I reach into my shirt and pull out the watch-Photon light combo, the thru-hiker's Antikythera Machine, telling me all I need to know about this world of ceaseless trail, hanging around my neck by a lanyard. I glance at both of these hikers...no watches are in evidence. I know these watchless people, for I was, and mostly still am, one of them. When one's whole working life is wedded to the time clock, a trip into the wilderness means the watch, that premier evidence of slavery, is the first thing to be tossed aside when freedom beckons. The main function my watch serves is give me a clue to what day of the week it is, in case I have to hit a post office for a food drop, and to time that interminable ten minute waiting period for boiled water noodle-something to metamorphose into that delectable substance all hikers know and love. I glance at my watch, putting it back into my shirt. "It's a bit after seven-thirty," I say. "Are you planning on catching the morning boat into VVR?" The game is afoot. Hearing the affirmative, I add, "You'll have to hump it then, it's nearly six miles."

"The boat gets there at 9:45 and hangs out for about ten minutes," he counters, "we'll make it." They turn to start down the trail. "You'll never make it," I say, just loud enough so that I could be talking to myself, but loud enough, too, for him to hear it. He doesn't turn around, but I see his head twitch. Now I am no fisherman, but I am suddenly aware of the meaning of "hook, line, and sinker." The gauntlet thrown, the challenge taken, I see his pace quicken.

In my mind, I see them charging, helter-skelter, down the mountain, splashing through five creek crossings, two requiring fords, and two sketchy boulder hops, in their heavy chrome-tanned leather boots, dancing carefully over slippery rocks (they have no walking poles), sprinting that last mile to the dock, coming breathlessly over the last hump down to the lake, just in time to see the boat round the corner.

Sometimes I am amazed by the old cortical computer on my shoulders, and sometimes I am shamed by it...sometimes both. As I stand there, watching them disappear, and I compute mileage and probable hiking times, tempered by stream crossings, I am convinced that they will, in fact, make it just in time to see that boat...as it rounds the corner heading *back* to the resort. For you see, when he asked me the time, in that split second, without noticeable pause, and without malice of forethought—well, at least without forethought—I cheerfully subtracted forty-five minutes from the true time. It was really a quarter past eight.

Suddenly I feel embarrassed by my behavior, for surely he will ultimately figure it out, and neither his consciousness nor his opinion of thru-hikers will be much raised. Then a cool breeze flows down from Silver Pass, bearing with it the mellifluous sound of Master Po's voice. "Ah...but Grasshopper, can any man afford such arrogance?" As I turn and head on up, my laughter chases down the canyon, floating past two hikers, heads invisible, but doubtless down, behind huge packs, speeding along the trail.

To the End of the Sierra

The clouds have been building today, and as I sit on the ground in front of the Tuolumne Meadows store, drinking a beer and eating dinner, thunder warbles across the mountaintops. I arrived here early in the morning after a marvelous four days from VVR and have been lounging around all day, watching the hubbub of the tourons. Not a very flattering word...tourons. A melding of tourist and moron. In the bathroom, some Park Slave, no doubt, had inscribed it in bold letters on the wall, for all the world to see. At any rate, after spending so much time alone, I find it both entertaining and mesmerizing to watch it all.

Thunder sounds again. Come to think of it, for the last three days the clouds have been building and dissipating. I know these Sierra storms, and it won't be long before rain will be more than threatening. But most likely not today. Tomorrow morning I will be headed out, to the end of the Sierra and into northern California...land of lava and fire.

Spending the night in the campground is a noisy affair. The hiker campsites are clumped in the middle of the regular weekender-RV camps. I look forward to getting out of civilization. This morning I am up early, but wait for breakfast at the little café. It opens at seven o'clock. I am coffee'd and fed and on the trail by eight.

Editor's Note: The manuscript for this chapter ended here. The missing section covers approximately 110 miles and 5 days from Tuolumne Meadows to Ebbetts Pass. The trail covers the stream-swollen northern section of Yosemite National Park, and the Emigrant and Carson-Iceberg Wildernesses. Ray hiked through this area in early July in both 2003 and 2004.

A SIERRA STORM

The lightning splinters on the peaks, and rocks shiver, and great crashes split
the air and go rolling and tumbling into every cave and hollow; and the
darkness is filled with overwhelming noise and sudden light.
(*The Hobbit*, J.R.R. Tolkien)

It always amazes me...how quietly it begins, with the smallest and simplest of things...like the gentle brush of a butterfly's wings or the first rays of sunrise. It's early morning, and I notice a small puff of a cloud, a nascent cumulus, riding low and all alone on the southern horizon. In more than forty years of meandering through the Sierra, I have seen this many times and know well what it portends. Further, I have experienced this same drama for the past six days, since I left Tuolumne Meadows in Yosemite National Park.

By mid-morning the larger brothers of this insignificant, nearly unnoticeable cotton ball have gathered to fill half of the sky. I walk towards Ebbetts Pass, sometimes in windy, chilling shade, sometimes in glaring sun. Suddenly, clouds sweep over the sun and a biting wind drives a light rain across me. For the fifth time in six days, I have experienced this early, ephemeral shower. The first couple of days out of Tuolumne, I donned my rain gear, only to remove it minutes later as the clouds and sun again played hide-and-seek, at least for a few hours, until playing ceased. And so I know this momentary rain is but a taste of what is to come.

I cross Wolf Springs Pass and travel on down the seven miles to Ebbetts Pass. By now the clouds have coalesced and cover most of the sky. To the northeast, virga—trailing rain that evaporates before it hits the ground—reaches its gray, gossamer fingers down towards the summits of Highland and Silver Peaks, both nearly 11,000 feet tall.

I arrive at the highway near Ebbetts Pass, mile 1044.8, section J, a little after 1:30. Sitting on a large, friendly rock just above the trail, I watch the cars roar by. Civilization is too noisy...too fast. No more than twenty feet away, I can clearly see the faces of the occupants, but lost in their own worlds, no one notices me. I wonder what they are thinking, where they are going in such a hurry. Perhaps they, too, feel the coming storm. A faint rumble of distant thunder reminds me that I also should be hurrying, so I gather up my gear and head up and around Ebbetts Peak. Within minutes, the trail breaks into the open, and the view sweeps out and around me in full circle.

By now, it's hide-and-seek in earnest. The clouds are definitely it, and the sun is busy hiding. Dark and foreboding, they cover the heavens. A second rumble undulates across the sky, tumbling and reverberating among the peaks. A minute later the thunder is louder and seems closer, so I stop to look for lightning. To the south, from where I have just come, over the Dardanelles, and Hiram, Airola and Iceberg Peaks, I see a flash and count...thirty seconds, about six miles. More to the west, lightning flashes over some closer unnamed peaks...fifteen seconds, three miles.

It's coming on fast, so I stop to check my pack. My gear is protected from the elements by an *innie*, a tough, plastic trash-compactor bag inside my pack. With all my gear stowed inside it, the pack itself will get wet, but the contents stay nice and dry. Over a lifetime of hiking, I had always used a "rain-proof" cover for my pack, hence an "outtie," and always with mixed results. A single storm, on the last day of May, the day I came out of the San Gabriel Mountains and into Agua Dulce, and these past five days of rain have convinced me that I needlessly spent a lot of years with wet gear.

Now the trail begins to descend and wind its way through a maze of granite slopes, ledges, and boulders. The rain begins, not yet in earnest, but with obvious intent, so I stop next to Sherrold Lake, more of a pond really, and don my rain gear. The lightning and thunder are five seconds apart...a mile and counting. And I lose the trail. I walk back and forth and range outward and back - no trail. Checking the Guidebook, I see it says the "often faint" trail "snakes northwest...ducking in and around obstacles," and I can't find it - no *ducks* and too many obstacles.[1]

The rain has now decided to get serious, and actual lightning bolts are visible, though still a mile or so away. I begin to feel some concern, more for my inability to find the trail than from the storm. The Guidebook says the trail follows the "path of least resistance," and somehow I convince myself that must mean down. Kinney Reservoir is visible, four hundred vertical feet below me, and *that's* down, so I drop into a steep ravine that falls towards its dark waters. After descending a hundred or so ticklish vertical feet, I come to my senses and head back up to where I know the trail must surely be.

Now back where I began, I look around. The rain is coming hard, and lightning and thunder are only two and three seconds apart. The area is dotted with savagely gnarled lodgepole pine trees, none very tall, but many of respectable girth. I pick one, which must be nearly five feet in diameter, and about eight feet away from its base, sit down on my pack. The wind, blowing strongly out of the west, drives the rain aslant, and here, sheltered in the lee of this venerable tree, I am fairly well protected. Hunched down, I look around and see that, of the dozens of trees about, including the one giving me shelter, all have tops that are split and

---

1 A duck is a trail marker of piled stones.

shattered and dead...signs of lightning strikes. Truly, it's not the most comforting of sights.

Lightning terrifies most people I think. I, on the other hand, have always loved the storms, the fierce winds and raging elements, and although not much afraid, I confess to feeling some small disquiet as light and sound edge closer to becoming one. Over the years, I have waited out these mountain storms many times and have come to accept that there isn't really much one can do about them other than stay home, of course, but that has never been an option. Obviously there are certain precautions that may be taken: don't hang onto metal, try to get off of ridges and peaks early, don't be the highest thing around, don't hide under tall trees, don't go into caves, try to contact the ground as little as possible, try to camouflage yourself in a grove of moderate-sized trees, don't fly a kite...and so on. Wisdom changes though, for the rock hut on the summit of Mount Whitney was constructed in 1909 as a shelter from lightning as a direct result of a death on its top, three years earlier. Now, caves are right out, and a rock hut and a cave differ in little more than name. An old mountaineering book of mine from the 1950s suggests lying down on the ground; now the recommendation is to squat down, contacting the ground with as little of one's self as possible.

All precautions aside, by and large you are, as Homer says, in the hands of Zeus Who Loves the Thunder. You will either be struck or not, die or not, so you may as well sit back and enjoy the marvelous show. It's out of your hands. It seems that much of our pain in life comes from a fear of death. I have found that there is great serenity to be gained in knowing that, although death may be at hand, there is nothing that needs to be said, nothing that can be done. And, after all, the probability of being struck is remotely small. That being said, I recall the wry statement of writer Douglas Adams, "The more unlikely an event is, the more likely it is to happen immediately," and make a passing nod to St. Barbara, patron saint of those besieged by lightning. Life is full of incongruities. Isn't it marvelous?

Head down and supported by elbows on knees, my seated position feels comfortable, so I close my eyes and begin to...not doze really, but...withdraw from it all. My mind travels back to other places and times, to other storms. One from long ago comes to mind, a beautiful series of rolling cells that raged up the Sierra crest south of Mount Whitney. My wife and I were camped in a little dome tent below New Army Pass. The cells were coming from the south, and bumped along the crest about every half hour for three or four hours. You could hear them coming...thunder at first distant and lightning faint. Then, they would become brighter and louder until the crescendo, and it was upon us in all its fury. Passing on and to the north, it would gradually fade and give way to a new set from the south. The lightning was so fierce that I could see the fiberglass poles of the tent...through closed eyes.

Before that even, in 1972, my wife and I hiked the John Muir Trail. Coming up and out of LeConte Canyon, on the middle fork of the Kings River, we traversed Dusy Basin and went over Bishop Pass, out and down to a food re-supply at Parcher's Camp, below South Lake. Just over and down from the pass, a storm began in earnest. At the base of the pass, we saw a small tent over by Saddlerock Lake. Nestled among the rocks on a tiny peninsula that jutted out toward one of two islands, it looked small and insignificant below storm-wracked Mount Goode, towering nearly two thousand feet above. Ultimately we made it down to the trailhead and got a ride (with former Olympic skier Jill Kinmont and a National Geographic photographer, but that's another story) down to civilization and took a zero day on the next.

The day after that, Tuesday, found us returning to the trailhead. At road's end there were ten or fifteen cars with people swarming everywhere, checking gear and shouldering packs. Asking what was the matter, we learned that two hikers were overdue. They were to have been out on Sunday and failed to show. Five days later, we heard from other hikers that the two had been found...struck by lightning and killed and lying in a small, insignificant tent on the shores of Saddlerock Lake.

A bright flash, followed in only two seconds by the thunderclap, startles me momentarily. Still adequately distant...almost. I hunker down and let my mind float free again. Another time, on another hike of the John Muir Trail, my son and I endured six days of the most ferocious thunderstorms I have yet to see. A side-trip found us on the summit of Mount Tyndall, some six miles north of Mount Whitney. We summited early, for this was the third day of storms. By the time it struck, we were back and semi-safely in our tent. We learned later that a number of people had been on Mount Whitney at the time and sought shelter in the hut. A man and his son were struck that day, as lightning entered and ricocheted around inside.

Three days later, going over Pinchot Pass, the storm caught my son and me down a couple of miles on its north side. We sought cover in a sparse, stunted forest near the Taboose Pass trail junction. North and down across the south fork of the Kings River, the trail broke out of the trees and traced a clear track up a long moraine to Mather Pass. Fully a mile away, we could see the tiny, dark forms of three hikers coming down the trail. Suddenly, there was a burst of lightning. It came down seemingly directly toward the hikers, and to this day I swear that I saw it abruptly change direction so that it appeared to travel level with the ground and right over their heads. The hikers ran jerkily in all directions, scurrying about like Keystone Cops in an old movie. We hunkered down on the side of a ridge, camouflaged among the trees, and I counted forty-three lightning strikes that were three seconds (less than half a mile) or closer within a half hour.

Another year, we climbed Mount Whitney by the Mountaineer's Route, a stingingly steep couloir on the northeast face of the mountain. We arrived in mid-afternoon, but didn't stay long for the clouds were gathering. Whitney, being Whitney, had a dozen or two people lounging around on its top. We took the trail down and got onto the long south ridge. Within a few minutes, we felt every hair on our bodies begin to stand up. There was a raw humming in the air. Throwing off my all-metal Kelty pack frame, I bounded west down the bouldery slopes. Within seconds there was a thunderclap so loud that my ears rang. The sharp smell of ozone cut the air. I looked to the summit and saw a dozen people, apparently auditioning for a part in St. Vitus' Dance, the musical.

Moments after thinking of that time, I feel a familiar sensation as I begin to tingle over my entire body. Like the scarcely perceived sounds of a distant ringing telephone that somehow instantly and seamlessly become incorporated in your dream, Zeus has sculpted my reverie to warn me. Barely having time to act, I cram my fingers in my ears and hope for the best. Immediately, it goes off. If you've ever spent time in a foxhole, or gone fishing with dynamite, or had lightning strike right on top of you, you know the feeling—the light and sound and pressure. Stunned, I look around, expecting to see a nearby tree smoldering, standing in a shower of bark with a long scar winding around its trunk to the ground. But no, I can't see much, nor am I much inclined to explore.

This last seems to be the storm's hurrah, for no more strikes come closer than two or three seconds, and they begin to travel further afield. Mighty Zeus, having proofed me, no doubt searches for other hikers to assay.

In minutes, the rain begins to lessen, and within a quarter hour I am up and looking for the trail. And here it is, plain for those less harried to see. Another hour passes, and I am walking along the base of a stark, serried, volcanic ridge, headed toward Reynolds Peak. The sun, newly coaxed from its hiding place, illuminates the land. Everything is wet and luminescent. A beautiful pink Indian paintbrush glows in the gray sage. A little further and I come to a field of dusky, green mule-ears, their golden-yellow flowers shining fiercely in the sun's lambent rays. Among them, white and blue lupine sway in the late afternoon breeze. Another Sierra storm has come and gone. The world has been created anew. Nearby, a bird makes a few tentative inquiries and, apparently satisfied with the answer, bursts into song. I head on up the trail.

DO YOU BELIEVE IN MAGIC?

Don't look for the silver lining, just wait for it.
(Ogden Nash)

In the summer of 1972, my wife and I made our first long hike, the two hundred plus miles of the Sierra Nevada's John Muir Trail, from Yosemite Valley to the top of Mount Whitney. We took nearly a month to hike those miles. On the last full day, we climbed up Mount Whitney, having decided to spend that early August night, the last night on the trail, on the summit. Arriving on top not more than an hour before sunset, I found that someone had left an unopened can of beer on a handy rock. Ecstatic over my good fortune, I hastened down the backside toward the Mountaineer's Route, and filled a plastic bag with snow.

We ate dinner as the sun reached for the horizon and the beer chilled. The great, pyramid-like shadow of Mount Whitney spread out over the Owens Valley, and a full moon began to rise above the shadow's apex. As the moon rose a little higher, it began to pale and redden. At the end of a marvelous, magical trip, sitting on the summit of Mount Whitney, ice-cold beer in hand, I watched an eclipse of the moon! Although in those ancient days I had no name to give it, I had, for the first time, experienced trail magic! In a lifetime of hiking and mountaineering, we experienced this magic on more than one occasion, but for thru-hikers it is at once something both common and special, for the trail takes care of its own.

Every thru-hiker knows about trail magic. It is what they call all those marvelous, unexpected things that happen as they move, day after day, along the trail. They can regale you with story after story, often of the kindness of strangers. More likely than not, the tales revolve around food, a subject never far from our minds, or getting unexpected rides from or to the trailhead. But magic is what you make of it, and in one form or another, it can occur when you stand at a crowded trailhead or miles from another living soul.

The memories of trail magic hang like sparkling ornaments on the trail. A bit over sixteen miles from Hiker Heaven in Agua Dulce, after a long, hot walk through the Sierra Pelona, I was suddenly brought to a standstill. Just to the left of the trail, underneath the tree-like ceanothus, an area had been cleared out. There sat nearly a dozen 2-gallon water containers, and more importantly, an ice chest filled with sodas and beers—The Oasis—all treasure left by the Andersons of the Casa de Luna.

On the morning of the third of July, after weathering that typically fierce Sierra thunderstorm near Ebbetts Pass the day before, I left a ridge above the headwaters of Raymond Meadows Creek. My destination for the day was Lost Lakes, nearly 18 miles up the trail. The Guidebook suggests avoiding them because they are spoiled by myriad car campers. Be that as it may, there was water to be had. The storms held off, and late afternoon found me at the Lost Lakes road junction. There, attached to a tree was a paper plate proclaiming *PCT Animal House, Food, Drinks*. I walked slowly through the campground. From a couple of hundred yards away a lady yelled at me and waved me over.

For the past five years, over the week encompassing July 4th, Bill, Janie, Beth and Mike, from Placerville, have set up their white 10x20 shelter and entertained thru-hikers. I was led inside the shelter where chairs and tables and barbecues and ice chests and bowls of fruit awaited me. Rain came and went as I whiled away the rest of the afternoon.

There are trail angels out there, people who know you are coming, who are plotting good against you. Some, like the Hiker's Oasis in Anza, the Pink Motel in San Gorgonio Pass, Hiker Heaven in Agua Dulce, Casa de Luna in Green Valley, Pooh Corners in Truckee, Little Haven in Belden, the Heitmans of Old Station, and the Dinsmores in Skykomish are well known. Others, like the Animal House, are marvelous surprises.

Coming up that last little hill before Highway 36 and a hitch into Chester, I hastened to get respectable looking (no small chore!). I collapsed my hiking poles and tied them to my pack. Trying to walk and stuff my hat into a pocket and comb my hair at the same time, I stumbled towards the road. Word was out that, due to a recent ill-received inundation by the Rainbow Family, locals were not picking up hikers. Whoever the folks of the Rainbow Family are, we must bear a resemblance to them in some untoward way.

As I blundered onto the Highway, scrabbling at my *PCT Hiker, To Chester Please!* sign, there, parked, was the Spiritmobile, with Spirit (Old Steady's support) sitting patiently on a log, waiting to likewise support other hikers. I first ran into her in Sierra City, when she took a load of us back to the trail, and again at Belden Town Resort. Days from now, she will be patiently sitting at the trailhead in Dunsmuir. Further on, in Etna, she will carry seven of us back to the trail, where Captain Mike will produce one of his famous watermelons, and we will all share it on the roadside.

After spending the night on a bouldery ridge high above Lake Tahoe on the 4th of July (and watching four simultaneous fireworks shows!), I made my way to Highway 50. Just before the highway in the Little Norway parking lot, a man standing next to a white van bearing Missouri license plates halloed me and invited me over for some fresh fruit. Gordon Lockwood and his sister Sue had been supporting a thru-hiker who left the trail weeks before, but they decided to continue on anyway and support others along the trail. And on it goes.

There are supporters out there, looking for you...waiting for you.

━━━━➤●◄━━━━

Given the numbers of hikers on long trails, the numbers of trail angels, supporters, friends, family, and knowledgeable locals, I think it not so surprising that all manner of wonderful things happen, for there are people lurking out there whose goal is to make them happen. But there is something beyond that, something deeper.

Leatherfeet and I sat on the side of an intersection of the Quincy-LaPorte Road and Kenzie Ravine Road, Section M, mile 1229.5. Porter had walked the mile or so down the road to a water source. While we waited, Buzz and Izzy showed up. We all sat awhile. Porter returned and everyone saddled up to head out. I am not a crowd hiker, so I waited a while longer.

In a bit less than three miles, the trail made another crossing of paved Kenzie Ravine Road. Standing on the edge of the road, I paused to check for a water source on my map. The next water for a number of miles was on Bear Wallow Trail, a jeep trail a mile and a half ahead, and off the trail another half mile. In the few seconds I stood there, a car drove by and stopped. The driver asked me if I needed any help. I told him a brief thru-hiker's tale, and hoping not to hike a half mile off trail for water, asked him if he had any to spare. John and his wife, son, daughter and daughter's friend were on their way to Little Grass Valley Reservoir for the weekend. Not only did they have extra water, they had some ice cold beers, and within a few minutes Sylvia had made up two huge carne asada burritos. A picnic on the side of the road! How likely? If I had been thirty seconds earlier or later, I would have come to an empty road, crossed it, and walked on. Mere chance you say...and yet.

There *is* something deeper, something indefinable, that hinges not on sheer chance alone, but on synchronicity, that involves seemingly unlikely encounters with strangers, that speaks, above all, of serendipity and a state of grace, and truly, magic. It seems to happen with improbable regularity when the path ahead is clear, and the mind rests empty of expectation, and is child-like in its acceptance. When *now* is all there is and all that is needed. When you're neither looking for nor expecting the cloud with the silver lining.

In Chester, just about the halfway point on the PCT, I leave the Seneca Motel at six AM. I have a parcel to mail when the post office opens at seven-thirty, and I want to make certain that I have a good, long time for breakfast. I walk down to the Kopper Kettle Restaurant (along with Jan's "World Famous" Red Kettle Restaurant in Idyllwild and the Breakfast Buffet at Timberline Lodge, arguably the best breakfasts on the trail) and order coffee and a massive breakfast. By eight o'clock I am on the road and hanging by my thumb. I continue to walk westward, through the town, as I hold my *PCT Hiker, To Trail Please* sign out...to no avail. Within a few minutes I am at the end of town, so I stop. About ten minutes pass when an old Toyota pickup stops. I marvel over my change in hitchhiking luck from those early days on the trail, when it was an onerous and ugly chore at best.

The driver, Michael, has just worked the night shift at the hospital and now is headed out to join the local search and rescue. A hiker is missing in the Humbug Summit area on the other side of Butt Mountain, through which I passed just yesterday. He says that he and his wife, the town veterinarian, have a contest every year, to see who can pick up the most PCT hikers. Yesterday she scored five and a dog, so he is behind. He drops me off and I head north. My destination for today is Drakesbad Guest Ranch, 18.4 miles up the trail.

Edward Drake, trapper and guide, came west from the Rockies in the 1860s. He prospected up and down the Feather River, and by accounts, must have struck it semi-rich. At Bidwell Bar he opened a saloon that was big enough to employ three or four bartenders. As the diggings wore out, he moved on up the river, and ultimately, came upon what became known as Hot Springs Valley. By as early as 1875 he had begun to live in the area, and records show that in the 1880s he began to purchase the property, eventually totaling four hundred acres. He constructed a log cabin and a barn. Then came a bathhouse, well, and latrines for campers. The guest ranch was born. It was shown on one of the first maps of Plumas County, in 1892.

In 1900, when he was seventy, he sold his property for $6,000 to one Alexander Sifford, an ailing schoolteacher from Susanville, who came to Drake's ranch to drink the soda waters of Drake's Spring, and wound up, as Drake had, falling in love with the place. Sifford and his family moved there and began the work to improve the ranch. Drake disappeared and died in 1904. In 1908, Sifford renamed the ranch Drakesbad, Drake's bath, in his honor. It was in no small part due to Sifford's championing of the area that Lassen Volcanic National Park came into existence in 1916.

It's a beautiful story, but all that fades to insignificance beside the note in the Guidebook that says hikers are sometimes able to secure meals there. That possibility is enough. It creates a destination. So off I go. The miles pass uneventfully and easily. At length, I can see Little Willow Lake a few hundred yards ahead.

Standing next to the lake, I see a hiker. He leaves his daypack on the ground and walks quickly toward me. He has hiked up from Warner Valley Campground, and in the maze of trails, the PCT Hiker Trail, the PCT Horse Trail, the trail to Willow Lake, the trail to Terminal Geyser, and a dirt road that crosses the area, has become disorientated. From the junction of the horse trail and foot trail he has headed south and is now, to his consternation, visiting Little Willow Lake for the second time. I show him the map in my Guidebook pages and point in the direction I am going. He allows as how he would like to tag along.

His name is Steven and lives in Salt Lake City. He grew up in Santa Barbara, California, and lived there during the time I attended the University of California campus in nearby Goleta. He remembers, as a child, frequenting the hamburger stand where I worked putting myself through college...small world. He comes yearly to a family reunion over at nearby Lake Almanor. Today he wanted to get away from it all, so he took his camera and headed to Drakesbad and the Terminal Geyser. His wife teaches biology at the University of Utah, and he, having supported her while she was in graduate school, recently went back to school and got his Master of Fine Arts. He is an artist now, a painter, using canvas and latex household paint. I ask him if he knows the name Rabo Karbekian, a fictional character of Kurt Vonnegut, who makes his first appearance in *Breakfast Of Champions* as the controversial, minimalist painter of *The Martyrdom of Saint Anthony*, a huge blue household latex-covered canvas with a single, vertical band of yellow day-glow tape on it. In a later novel, *Bluebeard*, Vonnegut ruins Karbekian's life by having all of his paintings self-destruct, a problem with latex adhering to canvas. Steven laughs, showing his familiarity. He says paints are better these days. He adds that he has two six-packs of ice-cold Sierra Nevada Pale Ale (a thru-hiker's friend) in an ice chest back at his car. On we travel.

We arrive where the trail forks, one going to the campground and parking lot, the other to the guest ranch. He tells me he will get his car and drive up to the guest ranch. I head for the ranch, looking for dinner. Enquiry locates the camp hostess, Billie Fiebiger. She tells me that dinner is served from five to seven PM, and that if I show up a few minutes after seven, she will see what she can do. I check my watch and head out to the parking lot looking for Steven. It is four-thirty.

In a few minutes he shows up and hauls a cooler out of his car. Here, near the edge of a huge meadow in the middle of Hot Spring Valley, we sit in large, comfortable chairs and watch a group playing volleyball. The time passes amiably in conversation and silence.

Ultimately, Steven checks his watch and says it is seven o'clock. He packs up, wishes me well, and heads off down the dirt road to Chester and Lake Almanor and reunions and kids. I move off toward the restaurant. Nervously trusting my pack to a nearby tree, and feeling a little awkward, I step inside. Billie is there and seats me over to one side. The restaurant is full of cheerful diners. I sit down and direct my attention to the small loaf of French bread that is quickly placed in front of me. It is a family-style dinner, that is, there is no menu. So all guests receive the same meal. The waitress, a young girl perhaps in her mid-twenties, tells me what the meal will be. She is from Germany and has come over with another friend to work for the summer. She says she is here to polish up her English a bit, so I ask her to repeat the menu. It rolls across her tongue, through my mind, and out into the animated dining room. She brings a wine list, and I wait, outwardly patient, for dinner.

Within a few minutes, the cooks and waitresses all gather at a table nearby. One is holding a couple of small cakes with a single burning candle on each. Billie announces that the couple is celebrating their 50th wedding anniversary. I stare shyly. They appear to be in their late seventies, and frail. Holding hands, they smile quietly at each other. Words are inadequate in explanation of what happens next. They seem so comfortable in each other's presence, so happy, so complete…so filled with love, that a wave—as tangible as the sudden drop in air pressure and utter calm when the eye of a hurricane travels over a land, moments before tortured and lashed—rolls through the room. Silence descends over a dining room that was, moments before, noisy and boisterous. Then the whole room, as if seeing the most marvelous sunrise, or a total eclipse of the sun, audibly catches its collective breath, applauds, and moves on.

At last dinner arrives, and I stare in amazement. The waitress's words come back. The meal consists of baked Alaska salmon, drizzled with a capered Béarnaise sauce, with lentils and tomatoes on a bed of escarole (I've never heard of escarole). I stare at it for two seconds and dig in. Thinking that this dinner is going to cost a fortune, I decide to go all out, and order a glass of Talbot Sleepy Hollow Chardonnay (I liked the name) at a mere $8 the glass. The dinner is so delicious that I have to consciously keep myself from sucking it down like a string of spaghetti and then licking the plate. I ask for another roll of French bread to prolong the inevitable. At last dessert comes. It is flambé of white peaches and some kind of Italian sweet cheese on a piece of angel food cake. I hold my napkin to my face, expecting my salivary glands to squirt like a fountain out onto the table. I cannot describe how delicious was the whole.

I sit there for a long while. No one seems to pay me any attention. At last Billie walks by and I ask her for the protocol—do I wait for a check or just go up to the cashier? She smiles and says, "The dinner is on me...just tip the waitress good." I am momentarily speechless, and suppressing the powerful urge to make Oliver Twist's near-fatal mistake by saying, "Please sir, I want some more," at last thank her profusely.

Having tipped "good," I head for the door, looking back at the old couple, still lost in each other and the candlelight. Fifty years! My father died not long before his 50th anniversary. As a surprise, we had been planning a party such as this, but it was not to be. Though many years past, the loss suddenly feels again fresh and raw. I myself have been married for thirty-four years and wonder if I will look similar in sixteen years...or if I will even be alive. My eyes mist unashamedly as I step out into the cool of the evening.

I will find out later that Drakesbad seems to be a hit or miss deal. Many skip it altogether. Of those who stop by, some are invited to shower or soak in the hot springs, others told there is no food for them. Some pay more than they anticipated for a lunch that seems woefully pedestrian, while others have a great breakfast and lunch too. Ones and twos seem to fare better than groups, but other than that I can offer no advice to travelers and intrepid serendippers, and tell myself that perhaps there *is* some advantage to looking old and pathetic.

Outside, I shoulder my pack and head down the road to Warner Valley Campground. It is nearly dark. A car drives slowly up and I hear a voice. "You look tired, can I offer you a lift?" It's only half a mile or so to the campground, and I am more tipsy than tired, but I readily agree. I look at the driver. He is wearing a khaki shirt with some patches on it. One says *Camp Host*. His nametag announces that he is Brian Thomas. From Texas and retired, he and his wife are the campground hosts. I ask him how it all works, and he says that I can stay in any open site...for $15, or I can set up my tent at his site and avoid the fee. Sitting at a table outside his travel trailer we swap stories of life and retirement, and have a few more beers. The night lengthens. At last, well past "hiker midnight," I turn in.

In the middle of the night, I arise to answer the call of nature and notice that the sky has clouded up. By four o'clock it begins to rain, and I struggle to unfurl the rain fly. Of course the rain last only a few minutes, so I begin to rouse myself and am on the trail shortly after five o'clock. My goal is the Old Station post office. It is Saturday and the post office closes at three o'clock. I must make the 23.5 miles by then to retrieve my food parcel, or wait until ten o'clock on Monday, when next it opens. And so I plow on.

The day passes uneventfully, if you don't count the smoke in Grassy Swale, the flames on the ridge above Swan Lake, and helicopters coming and going...but that's another story. As the day wears on, barely stopping to drink water, I begin to think I am going to make it. At two-thirty, I begin to look for the road that shortcuts into town. Minutes later, just as I come to a road, I see a hiker across the road and halfway up a hill. It's Richard E, and figuring that he is headed to town, I sprint on after him. In a few minutes I catch him. He says he is not going into town after all, so I hurry on.

The trail winds behind a fine home on the top of a nearby hill, and then begins a long traverse around a ridge. I can see the town below. With a sinking feeling, I begin to see that I have a problem, but there's no going back. Three o'clock comes and goes; the trail goes on. Finally, more than four miles later, at four-fifteen, I hit Highway 44, a quarter mile from Highway 89, and nearly four miles past the post office. Tired and pissed off, I look at my map carefully, and it comes to me. I remember seeing a small sign and a fence at the road where I saw Richard. I blew right by the shortcut to town!

Eluded by the silver lining, I walk up to the gas station/mini mart on Highway 89. I am seriously dehydrated, since in my haste I have barely slowed for water since this morning. At the mini mart I wind up drinking two V8s, an apple juice, and a quart of milk. Sitting outside in the shade, feeling painfully bloated, I finish off the milk, yet still feel thirsty. I walk back into the store, buy a tomato juice and talk with the proprietor, Mary. I tell her of my plight, and she calls the postmistress, seeing if she can somehow intervene. No luck. The post office is closed and that's that. On the bright side, Sunday will be my first zero day since South Lake Tahoe, two weeks ago. On the down side, it will no doubt be noon or later when I reach the trail on Monday.

Yogi's *PCT Handbook* has a note that there is a trail angel in the area who will pick you up etc., but the number is in the closed post office...seemingly a catch-22. So Mary calls the motel in town. The store, restaurant, motel, laundry, and post office are all next to each other. She discovers that there are no vacancies, a family reunion has taken up the whole motel. She tells me that a mile up the road is the Rim Rock Ranch Resort, and a call to them holds a room for me while I walk up the road drinking my tomato juice.

The following morning I reserve the room for an additional night, and carrying my clothes, head the three miles to the restaurant and laundry, thumb out to passing motorists. Within a few minutes a minivan speeds past me, then swerves to a stop a couple of hundred yards up the road. I jog up the road and jump in. The driver, Georgie Heitman, says that she is the local trail angel on her way back from delivering hikers to the trailhead, and that even though I didn't have a pack, I looked like a thru-hiker. Ah, too obvious again! She takes me to her home, where my clothes go into the washer. She makes a phone call to the postmistress at home, who, caught just in the act of leaving for the rest of the day, says my re-supply box will be in the store, as long as I have ID. It's good to have connections! Things are looking up! Georgie takes me to the store, and then to the motel, where I cancel my night's stay, collect my gear and head back to the Heitman's home.

Dennis, Georgie's husband, has some errands in Burney, and Georgie has something she is doing with the neighbors, so I while away the morning in a hammock, drinking ice cold beers and reading a spy thriller. At one o'clock, Georgie comes back and invites me to lunch with the neighbors. They have been clearing trees and brush from around and in the creek, actually an irrigation ditch, that is their water supply. We walk a few hundred yards, across the creek and through a field, to the neighbor's house. Sandwiches, beers, fresh-baked brownies, and watermelon make a veritable feast. I feel a bit guilty, since I could have been working too, but Georgie decided not to tell me about it...mercifully.

By three o'clock my clothes are sun-dried, and I begin to feel antsy. Georgie offers to drive me back to the trail, so at four o'clock I am hiking up and out onto Hat Creek Rim. So much for my zero day. As many as thirty waterless miles may lie ahead, and I aim to get some of them done by tonight. By day's end, I am nearly ten miles up the trail and setting up my little shelter. The sun lies low on the horizon, and Mount Lassen's slopes glow red-gold as day acquiesces to night. Far to the north, the lonely sentinel of Mount Shasta stretches to the sky. The sun edges behind a mass of dark, billowy clouds. Their edges glow brightly...clouds with a silver lining...for the finding.

THE SHORT STORY OF O

"There are many who had rather meet their bitterest enemy
in the field, than their own hearts in their closet."
(*Lacon*, Charles Caleb Colton)

"Don't remind me of my failures. I had not forgotten them."
(*These Days*, Jackson Browne)

I've dealt with my ghosts, and I've faced all my demons
Finally content with the past I regret
I found you find strength in your moments of weakness
For once I'm at peace with myself
I've been burdened with blame, trapped in the past for too long
I'm moving on
(*Moving On*, Rascal Flatts)

This is not a love story, nor does "O" readily and cheerfully submit to the whims of those who come to know her. It is a story of heat and humidity and sweat, of brush and insects and snakes, of overgrown trails and over-logged mountains, of little water and too many dirt roads, and of cheerless, viewless forest. Section O, from Burney Falls to the highway near Castella, is 82.4 miles long and gets more bad press than the Mojave Desert, nearly a thousand miles back down the trail… and not, perhaps, without reason.

It begins, sadly enough, with me immediately losing the trail, or rather, not finding it. At 8:15 AM, Amjed, manager of Shasta Pines Motel in Burney, drops me off at the kiosk at the entrance to Burney Falls State Park. I chat with the ranger awhile, finally getting instructions to the trail. She tells me to head over to the parking lot and look for a sign. I walk to a parking lot and do not see a sign, so I walk further along the road, pass some houses, and find myself back out on the highway. Knowing the trail crosses the highway, I head towards Burney. About a hundred yards pass. I decide this is stupid, so I cut cross-country back down toward the creek, where the trail must be. Within a couple hundred yards, I hit a fine trail and take it to the west. After ten minutes or so, I become indecisive and head back the way I came. In fifteen minutes I meet a lady who is jogging towards me. I ask directions, and she says she thinks if I continue back to a parking lot, I will find a bridge. Crossing the bridge there is a sign that tells of the PCT.

I walk back to the parking lot, down a bit to the bridge, but see no sign. Becoming irked, I head back the way I originally started. In a mile I come to a PCT junction and a bridge, which I cross. To further frustrate me, the trail heads back towards the falls, only now on the opposite side of the creek. A mile or so passes and I come to a junction with a sign pointing towards the creek. I set my pack down behind a tree and follow the junction. In a few hundred yards the trail starts down towards the bridge. There is the sign, as plain as day. I have now come in a complete circle, more than 3 miles out of the way!! Now I *am* pissed.

I look carefully at the map, see the idiocy of my ways, shrug, and continue towards Lake Britton. It is now heading on towards ten o'clock. The trail hits the end of Lake Britton and crosses the dam, then starts up and along the ridge top. There is a fine view of the Pit River, six hundred feet below. Within two miles I come to the first of the very few on-trail watering holes, Rock Creek. The day is getting hotter and hotter, so I stop for a while, filling my water containers and soaking my feet. But I don't stay long.

Now the trail begins to work its way up and across the slopes. I run into the first logging evidence, crossing what will turn out to be a vast array of skid roads, logging roads, jeep trails, and the occasional paved road. In this section, the trail passes mostly through private land...land that apparently has been and still is being logged as fast as the chain saws can run. The miles between Rock Creek and Peavine Creek, my next water stop, pass through thoroughly logged area.

By 1999, Section O was apparently all but impassable. One thru-hiker wrote in July that it was "really ugly and depressing," and that eventually, confronted with nearly impassible trail about thirty miles into the section, he took one of the myriad logging roads that stitch the area like the web of a schizophrenic spider, and hitched to McCloud. By the end of that summer, considerable trail maintenance had been done and brush, clearcut debris, and blowdowns had been erased to such an extent that thru-hikers' journals of 2000 commented on the fine condition of the trail. This first section seems a prime candidate for one of those areas, for everywhere are piles of slash slowly eroding away into mulch, downed trees and stumps. Mercifully, the trail is clean and clear, although the first of the brush begins to push its way onto the trail in the clearcut areas.

I cross road after road. In fact, it will turn out that in the first 41.8 miles of the section, from Burney Falls to just below Grizzly Peak, where the trail starts down into the steep, unlogged canyons of the tributaries of the McCloud River, I will cross a road of some kind no fewer than forty-five times.

The trail plunges into heavy, dreary Douglas fir forest. Days ago, I went through similar forest, and more than once, impiously longed for a clearcut...longed for a view of sky and hill, or any view to somewhere... anything other than lifeless ground littered with dead branches and little else. But the effects here are less than I might have wished for. The open spaces yield only trails littered with impenetrable brush and a view of mundane, more distant hills, checker-boarded with their own clearcuts. At least there is sunlight, hot as that may make it.

But nothing good seems to last long in Section O. It receives more precipitation that one might expect and is more humid than one might like. And all the clearcuts allow the sun to work its magic. The chaparral grows here like no other place on the trail, with the possible exception of the impenetrable chamise forests near Anza, 1,300 miles back down the trail. By the year 2002, only two years after all the fine trail maintenance work, journals again begin to remark on the thick brush conditions.

By the time I walk fifteen miles, my legs have become hacked and scratched, and blood slowly oozes from a dozen places (I carry no long pants). A short respite as the trail crawls through viewless forest, down and then out and up from Peavine Creek, is the only reprieve, and a temporary one at that. The growth along the creek is so thick that access is difficult. I am able to scramble down and filter a few liters of water at the mouth of a culvert, just where it goes under a road. I have lunch, sitting in the dirt on the side of the road.

Eventually I head out, and up out of the canyon. Suddenly the brush bursts into a huge swath of open land, marching down the canyon. Parallel sets of towers, two abreast, swoop down and up and disappear into the distance. The electricity cracks and pops and makes me feel odd...like the electricity is running up and down my spine or like having drunk way too many cups of too-strong coffee. I pause long enough to take a picture and hack my way back into the brush. This green tunnel of head to toe foliage is far different, I suspect, than veterans of the Appalachian Trail[1] are used to.

Within a short time, I break out into the open again. This time there are two sets of intersecting roads, just at the base of another one of California's multiple Red Peaks. I pause a few minutes to photograph some tenacious wildflowers that are hanging on into the summer heat, then cross the road and head into the brush. Within a hundred feet, just by chance, I catch a glimpse of the trail a couple of feet in front of me. There, gliding by, is the last three feet of a four-foot rattlesnake. My foot freezes in mid-air, and so do I, as the snake disappears into the brush. It's color is muted, although the diamond pattern on its back is plain, and the rattles are strangely pale, almost white, and translucent. It looks unlike any other I have seen on the trail. I wonder if it is a Pacific rattlesnake. And *now* I'm

---

1 The Appalachian Trail runs 2,100 miles from Georgia to Maine

paranoid. I move around the slopes of Red Peak, trying to use my hiking poles in a futile attempt to push brush aside so I can watch the ground. I have uttered more swear words today, most likely, than the total since I left the Mexican border.

In less than a mile, the trail opens up, and I come to a series of springs along the hillside. Only four miles ago, I filled my containers at Peavine Creek. The Guidebook mentions a trailside "bog", but it turns out to have a number of clear pools of cold water, so I take advantage and camel up for the twelve-mile distance to the next water at Moosehead Creek.

Now the trail explodes out of the brush!! Views at last! To the northwest is Grizzly Peak, around whose slopes the trail winds. Less than ten air miles away, it lies nearly double that by trail as I now head due north for five miles before turning west. Here the trail parallels one of the major logging roads, 38N10, right on the edge of the rim. It meanders in and out of the damnable brush, but for the most part is relatively open. To the west is a vast series of canyons…all part of the Pit River drainage. I can hear the sounds of chainsaws floating up from below, ripping through the quiet. Occasionally there is the sound of a large truck. I watch for several minutes, looking for a glimpse of movement, but see nothing. They sound far away.

At long last, the trail begins its arc to the west, and I begin to look for a place to spend the night. Since I filled up at the little trailside spring, less than ten miles back, I have plenty of water to carry me through. A dry camp will do fine. I find a small flat on a ridge top, sheltered by some trees, and not too far from the logging road I have been flirting with all day. Just more than twenty-five miles long, this day, which started out in anger and continued on in frustration and pain, punctuated by swearing…and the first rattlesnake I have seen since Bird Springs Pass more than seven hundred miles ago, finally comes to an end. A leisurely dinner, a deep breath, a wee dram of the fine scotch I had buried in my pack back in Burney, and it all passes. The worst is over, isn't it? As if to answer my question, some huge piece of equipment invisibly passes by on the road above. Sounding for all the world like a reptilian monster from an old science fiction movie, its volume and pitch rises and falls, disappears, reappears and finally fades into the distance. At last a cool breeze blows across the ridge. I stare at the sky for an hour. Finally, on this 100th day of my journey, I fall asleep. Tomorrow is a new day.

The day breaks cloudlessly upon me. I am up and at it early, anxious for whatever the trail has to offer, although hoping for an easier day than yesterday. It's going to be another hot one. Yesterday the temperature reached the mid-nineties, and it was humid. I expect no less today. Within three miles or so, I come to the springs that are the headwaters of Moosehead Creek. I drink all I can hold and fill a container. It is only a bit more than 14 miles to the next water, Deer Creek.

The trail winds in and out along this east-west running ridge. Every once in a while, Mount Shasta comes into view. The first good view I can remember was from the Hat Creek Rim, more than sixty miles back down the trail, where, in pastel hues, it loomed far to the north. Now, at last, it looks close. Then the trail swings to the south side of the ridge. Grizzly Peak rises ahead. The Guidebook mentions an alternate route to the up-and-down slogging of the trail around the south slopes of the peak. It suggests a road walk, which takes one to the summit of Grizzly Peak, then back down to the trail. By trail it is 2.6 miles, by road, 2.9. After the misery of yesterday, I figure I owe myself a treat, so I choose the road. Besides, one can never tell when a passing car might stop and offer ice-cold refreshment. And so, thirteen and a half miles into the day, I come to Grizzly Peak Road and off I go.

The walking part of this day's story has no really happy ending. Not a single car passes, so fantasies of an ice cold Sierra Nevada Pale Ale evaporate far more readily than does the sweat from my body on this humid day. And the makers of roads have no constraints like those of the makers of the PCT. In many places the road is far steeper than the trail, and the going tough. It doesn't take long though, and I am on the summit of Grizzly Peak.

The view is fantastic...it's why I'm here. If you draw a line from the summit of Mount Shasta to the summit of Lassen Peak, it runs almost exactly through where I now stand. To the southwest, fifty miles by air and five days of walking, is snowy Lassen. Twenty miles to the northeast and 8,000 feet higher, Shasta dominates the world. The middle part of Shasta is covered in clouds, so only its top and base are visible. Cumulus clouds now dot the sky here and there, and to the east some tower into cumulo-nimbus storm clouds. I spend a long lunch hour taking it all in. Although from Shasta it is only a bit more than seventy miles by highway to Ashland, my first stop in Oregon, this westward trend of the trail continues all the way to the Trinity Alps and Marble Mountains, then waggles up and through the Siskiyou Mountains to Oregon, and so is still 250 miles by trail. At last I saddle up and head down to meet the PCT. This extra 0.3 miles was worth it! The highlight of this section, it makes it all worthwhile...I hope.

Back at the PCT the trail begins a ten-mile downhill run into the canyons of the McCloud River. And now comes the second half of the short story of O. The trail enters the realm of the same dark, eerie, Tolkienesque forests that haunt the end of Section M and the beginning of Section N, the middle and north forks of the Feather River. The trees are old growth and huge. Miles and miles of shadowed trail wind through forest whose canopy screens so well that no understory plants can grow. The ground is littered with gray...gray logs, gray needles, gray branches. An eerie silence covers the forest, and I suddenly long for the brushy slopes of yesterday. It reminds me of Tolkein's Great Mirkwood forest of The Hobbit.

> "It was not long before they grew to hate the forest...and it seemed to offer less hope of any ending. But they had to go on and on, long after they were sick for a sight of the sun and of the sky, and longed for the feel of the wind on their faces."

At any moment I expect to see great, dark, dense spider webs tangling the trees about me. I hold a fear of spiders from a childhood experience with a black widow, and as juvenile as it is, a shiver ripples through me at the thought.

Nearing day's end, I reach Deer Creek. I am now in the six or seven mile stretch that has "nonexistent" camping space, according to the Guidebook. And it seems as though, in these forest-clogged, steep walled canyons, it could easily be true. I am beginning to run on empty and become increasingly vexed with the thought of walking into the dark, looking for a place to be. Water, however, is no longer a problem, as a number of creeks are crossed during the remaining thirty-eight miles to civilization. I fill one container and head on down, hoping to find some place to spend the night...soon.

Within two miles I find a place, just off the trail, that with a little judicious gardening, is large enough and flat enough (barely) for an old man to lie down. It has been hot all day and still is. And here come the mosquitoes. I set up my little tent, which of course makes it all the hotter in this squalid, breezeless den. Listening to the mosquitoes merrily humming around my tent, I lie naked on my ground pad until it finally becomes cool enough to put on my silk long johns. By midnight it is cool enough to slip into my bag. And so ends the second day of Section O, nineteen and a half miles further on.

Day three dawns, I think...for there is little evidence to prove it so. Trusting my clock, I break camp, anxious to make as many miles as possible on this day, thus ensuring an early arrival in Castella tomorrow. In a bit over six miles, I come to a long bridge spanning the McCloud River. On the other side, I see Richard E and Porter down among the rocks at the river. I last saw Richard as I blew by him heading into (or so I thought) Old Station, five days ago. Porter, I have not seen since I went in to Chester and he went on by a week ago. We catch up on news of the trail. They have been there for a good bit, so within minutes they pack up and leave. I stay a while longer and follow.

Now the up and down begins as the trail contours around canyon after canyon, gradually gaining the 1,500 foot elevation and 1,300 foot drop to Squaw Valley Creek, my nominal destination for the day. And now come Les Mouche, the flies. These little buggers are a real piss-off. It's certainly not the first time I've seen them; in fact they are quite familiar. I had some experience with them in the Sierra Pelona, a thousand miles ago. Then in the lower oak forests of Sections M and N they made a re-appearance. Now here they are in full force. And what is worse, they confound the very place I live in the Sierra Nevada foothills. Throughout the year from spring through fall, these little bastards swarm about your face. They seem to be attracted to moisture and heat, and fly about eyes and mouth and nostrils, and ears too. The usual method of clearing them away is to wave a hand in front of the face, not palm outward as in a greeting, but palm down as waving to cool oneself. This is known locally as the "Mariposa Greeting." Hiking with poles makes shooing them away a problem, one that I partially solve by holding my handkerchief by a corner and periodically slapping myself in the face with it. Personally, I would much rather contend with mosquitoes.

Squaw Valley looks uninviting, so I keep moving. At long last, the trail heads up and out of canyon land, toward Girard Ridge, away from the flies. The end of the day finds me twenty-one miles further along. On the very edge of Girard Ridge, Mount Shasta looms due north no more than fifteen or so miles away. I set up camp and watch the mountain change through shades of yellow and gold, and finally deep red as the sun gives up and retreats below the horizon.

Tomorrow there remain but a dozen miles to Highway I-5 and Castella. It's a little cooler tonight, and mercifully, a ridge-top breeze keeps the mosquitoes at bay. The morning finds me up and on the trail before dawn. Civilization calls. Within a few miles I come to Girard Ridge and the first view of Castle Crags, the Sacramento River, and the Interstate. Shortly thereafter I run into Richard and Porter, just starting out for the day. We hike together, and leaving forever (or perhaps at least till Oregon or Washington) the dark forest, arrive at the paved frontage road shortly before noon.

Heading toward the overpass, we try to decide what to do. The Castella post office, a couple of miles south, has my re-supply parcel. Richard's is also there, while Porter's is in Dunsmuir, four miles to the north. Dunsmuir sounds like the better deal, since it's early in the day, and one could find restaurants and motels...and restaurants there. Castella boasts only a post office, gas station, and a mini-mart, albeit a great one. Still wondering what to do, we come to the underpass and find the Spiritmobile just getting ready to leave. Spirit readily agrees to take us, first to the Castella PO, then to Dunsmuir, before she heads up the road toward a meeting with her husband in Etna.

We pile in. The post office is just closing for lunch, but the postmistress consents to re-opening for Richard and me. That done, we sit outside with Spirit and two other thru-hikers, Salamander and Juniper, drinking ice cold drinks. After a bit, we drop the ladies off at the Castle Crags State Park campground and point the Spiritmobile toward Dunsmuir. Good-bye Section O!!! Town awaits.

THE ART AND ARTIFICE OF YOGIING

I arrive at Parks Creek Summit, mile 1539.4, Section P, northern California. It is heading on towards evening, after nearly twenty-four miles, on this, the second day out of Dunsmuir.

At the road, a trailhead for an easy and popular three-mile walk to the Deadfall Lakes, there are several parked cars. I sit down to rest a spell. Richard and Porter stayed at the lakes when I left, so they are somewhere behind, but probably not far. Nearby, a lady and her teenage son are sorting equipment in the trunk of their car. We strike up a conversation, and like most people, they are amazed and intrigued by a thru-hiker's story. I ask her if she has any extra water. (I have decided to yogi these folks, and that is my gambit.) She does, and so it begins. For a few minutes we talk about hiking, and magically she asks what I find hardest about hiking day after day, week after week. Among the things I tell her is how it's pretty hard to deal with the same old food, day after day. She immediately brightens and produces a huge bag of grapes. Would I like them? Of course, I would.

They are waiting for her husband, who walked with them to Upper Deadfall Lake, then disappeared. She allows as how he might have taken one of the two other trails, which drop five hundred feet down to another parking lot at Deadfall Meadows, a mile west on the road. I tell her that I would be glad to sit here and keep an eye out for him, if she wants to drive down to see if he is there. She and her son leave to look for her husband.

Almost immediately, Richard and Porter arrive. I pull out the bag of grapes (which, seeing them coming, I had secreted in my pack) and grandly wave it before them. Needing no second invitation, they sit down in the dirt next to me. I tell them that I was faced with a real moral dilemma—whether to tell them about the grapes or not. But I wasn't really, for the smile that lights up a thru-hiker's face when confronted with delectable treats is nearly as valuable as the treats themselves. We sit there enjoying the grapes. In no time at all, the car returns, no husband. We talk a bit more and out comes a box of freshly baked brownies. She is certain no one else will eat them. "No, really, we couldn't" is not in our vocabulary, nor is hesitation our *modus operandi*. We dig in. I had never before considered how delicious might be the counterpoint of chocolaty brownies astride sweet and tart green grapes. No more than ten or fifteen minutes pass when hubby shows up. We all chat a few more minutes. They pile into their car and disappear.

A couple of dayhikers return to their car and start to sort through their gear. They set up a portable table and take out a large green ice chest. Richard and Porter decide to cross the road and head up the trail a little bit...looking for a campsite. It's late in the day and clouds are building. Not so distant thunder warbles across the ridges. As Richard and Porter start to leave, I tell them I will be along in a bit. I am on a roll.

There are some who look upon yogiing as begging, as taking advantage, as something less than honorable. I have seen it described as trying to get something from someone using guilt or trying to make them feel sorry for you. As getting something you wish you had brought, but were too lazy to carry. And I suppose that it could be so construed...in its basest form. Named after the antics of Yogi Bear, a cartoon character of the 1960s, it carries the connotation of getting the goodies by hook or by crook.

"Yogi Bear is smarter than the average bear.
Yogi Bear is always in the ranger's hair.
At a picnic table you will find him there,
Stuffing down more goodies than the average bear.
He will sleep till noon.
But before it's dark,
He will have every picnic basket in Jellystone Park.
Yogi has it better than a millionaire.
That's because he is smarter than the average bear!"

But yogiing has a history far more illustrious than the mere tale of a clever bear, an ancestry far more noble than creative lunching. Its roots lie in the almost inviolable ancient laws of hospitality, which required people to offer food, shelter and protection to those who were traveling. A protection, without which, traveling would well nigh have been impossible in those distant times, for a traveler was largely at a stranger's mercy where he journeyed and had few legal or political rights. The Bible admonishes: "Be not forgetful to entertain strangers: for thereby some have entertained angels unawares." (Heb 13:2).

But the tides of history ebb and flow, leaving a much-altered landscape in their wash. In 1847, Henry David Thoreau built his small cabin on the wooded shores of Walden Pond and contemplated a world he felt had gone irrevocably awry. A world where "we live thick and are in each other's way, and stumble over one another, and I think that we thus lose respect for one another," where people wasted their lives in the throes of voluntary servitude, acquiring land and chattels that, even so, were far easier gotten than gotten rid of; whose appetites were base, and whose intellectual pursuits were, at the very least, trivial. A man rarely at a loss for words, he would, I suspect, stand mute and aghast at the direction and distance we have traveled since he walked the hills and thought the world a shallow, crowded place.

Sixteen years later, in 1863, John Muir, that paragon of wilderness travel, sent a poem to friend Emily Pelton entitled *In Search of Breakfast*. Wandering and botanizing in the Wisconsin River valley, he learned that "strolling men of wily looks...and garments much awry" sometimes had difficulty in the finding of adequate fare. He speaks of mollifying one Jacob Wise with "kindly divers questions," thus obtaining the requisites of milk and bread, and at the same time, laying the ground rules of yogiing.

Thirteen years after that, in 1867, he left Wisconsin for a trip to South America. From Indianapolis, Muir took a train to the border and crossed the Ohio River into Louisville, Kentucky. Speaking to no one, he navigated his way through the city with a compass, bearing nothing but a rucksack, a couple of books, a plant press, and a few dollars for the journey. He eventually made his way to Florida, and everywhere along the way, he was greeted and taken in, and for the most part made welcome and provided for. Even though the Civil War was but newly over, and poverty, hardship and suspicion blanketed the land, human kindness was freely given and graciously accepted.

I think that Thoreau, who never traveled more than a few miles from his Concord home and survived largely on the generosity of others, may have judged his brothers uncharitably. For shallow and base though they may have seemed, in them Muir still found, lying close to the surface, the instinct to trust and aid a fellow human, but thinly plated by the armor necessary for those violent times, an armor readily penetrated by "kindly divers questions."

But the world has grown an even rougher place in the years since Muir's travels, and strangers on the road, especially scruffy, unfettered thru-hikers, whose wily looks cannot help but appear dangerous in times of serial murder, when paper angels adorn milk cartons throughout the land, and every day the news bears tales more desperate than those the day before. Still, the milk of human kindness flows, if sometimes sluggishly...sometimes needing assistance. And so, to me, yogiing is not only an act of getting, but an act of giving as well, of providing people with the chance to be as thoughtful and kind and generous as they no doubt yearn, yet fear to be.

I approach the couple and ask them if they have any water they might spare. They do, and the conversation begins. Mark and Jenna live in nearby Weed, a half an hour to the northwest. Seated at their little folding table they celebrate the end of a lovely summer's day. They have plenty of extra water, so I fill my last empty Platypus water container.

Jenna is a teacher. I, myself, spent twenty-five years in the profession, so we chat awhile about schools and kids and life. Then they offer a soda and salami and cheese. I sit on the bumper of their SUV, and we discuss the world and ask and answer kindly divers questions.

At last, I tell them that I have friends camping out along the trail across the road a ways, and that I should be moving on. They ask if I would like to take some cold drinks and string cheese along. And of course, I would. I make a sincere offer of remuneration, knowing they will decline. They do.

Giving them heartfelt thanks, I saddle up and head across the road and up the trail. Not far past a rock quarry, Richard and Porter hail me from some trees. Having already set up camp, they are preparing dinner when I arrive with still ice-cold fruit drinks and the cheese. It's late in the day, and the sun, partially covered by towering cumulus clouds, rides low on the horizon. Across the canyon, lightning flashes and thunder bounces across the peaks. Rain threatens but withholds as we celebrate the rekindling of the ancient laws of hospitality and share the milk of human kindness.

JEFFERSON IS A STATE OF MIND

A shiny blue pickup truck zooms by spewing gravel and dust. Within yards, the driver hits the brakes and slides to a stop. He backs up and the passenger door flies open. "Quick, get in," he yells! A bit dazed, I comply. Looking at me, he barks, "The laws of the State of Jefferson require citizens to render aid to those obviously in need...and you are obviously in need." I don't have much time to wonder just what it is about my appearance that would lead one to such a conclusion, for he immediately reaches into the back and, with a toothy smile, brings forth two cold beers. Ah...so the need was obvious. The truck lurches forward. It's a bit after eleven AM. I have hiked nearly eighteen miles this morning to make it into the little community of Seiad Valley, heart of the State of Jefferson.

The story of the State of Jefferson is fascinating, if obscure. It really began in 1819 when John Quincy Adams, then U.S. Secretary of State, and the Spanish minister drew an arbitrary line along the 42nd parallel, the boundary between California and Oregon. Beginning in the 1850s and running up until 1909, there were several attempts to re-draw those lines, attempts that included plans for a State of Jefferson in Oregon, a State of Klamath in northern California, and a State of Siskiyou that incorporated parts of both states. Needless to say, none of the plans came to fruition, but a spirit of independence, carried down from Jeffersonian ideals, that the best government is the one that governs least, remained in the psyche of the inhabitants.

The plan gained new impetus in the early 1940s. From October through November 1941, meetings were held that included mayors, town councils, the governors of both Oregon and California, boards of supervisors and chambers of commerce. A rally was held, and both Time and Life magazines sent reporters and newsreel photographers. Stanton Delaplane, a young reporter for the San Francisco Chronicle, was sent to cover the hoopla and in 1943 garnered a Pulitzer Prize for his series of articles. The news and magazine coverage was set to be aired on December 8,1942, however, the events of December 7 changed all that. On December 8, the Jefferson Territorial Committee issued a news release saying that in view of the outbreak of war, the State of Jefferson would cease all activity. And so it was. Even so, signs still remind visitors and passers through that the State of Jefferson is hereabouts.

The pickup sprints down the road and within moments we round a corner and pass another hiker. Looking up, I barely have time to notice and identify E.G. from Wisconsin. Evidentially she does not have the appearance of obvious need for the driver scarcely notices her as he speeds by. She disappears before I have time to think, let alone suggest to my host that he pick her up. We're still a ways from Seiad Valley, so I feel guilty that I am riding and she not. It's a feeling that will pass.

I quickly finish the first beer and start the second. My host apparently has had a head start on me. Within minutes he is dropping me off at the Seiad Valley store. He smiles that big, goofy smile again and roars off into the distance. It is eleven-thirty in the morning. Hello civilization!

⸺⸻⸺

This odyssey began six days ago in Dunsmuir. Morning found me awake early and ready for whatever the day had to offer. The night before, Melonee Davis, owner and proprietor of the Dunsmuir Inn Bed and Breakfast, told me that breakfast would be ready about eight-thirty. It was only six o'clock though, and I doubted that I could wait. At six-thirty, I walked the three blocks to the center of town. At the Cornerstone Bakery and Café a crowd of hikers was preparing to make short work of the kitchen supplies.

Richard and Porter were seated inside. I traveled with them the day before, but they stayed at the Motel 6 across from the bed and breakfast. I had hoped they would stop by and pick me up when they went to dinner last night, but alas, they did not. Wicked, Paparazzi, and Captain Mike were also there.

I told them all that Melonee had arranged for her friend Bill, a local, to take us all back to the trailhead at nine o'clock. We breakfasted and went our separate ways, only to congregate on the B&B porch at the appointed time. Right on the hour, Bill pulled up. We piled our gear into the bed of his pickup and crowded in where we could. Captain Mike's pack was nearly immovable. A huge watermelon rode primly in the top. Bill unloaded us at the trailhead, and off and up and up we went.

The trail crossed up and over the eastern edge of the crenellated granite summits of Castle Crags, then turned west along the southern perimeter. It was heading on towards ten o'clock and already the temperature was in the high 80s. This was but a hint of the heat to come. The trail crossed a number of washes, some with water, some not. At Sulphur Creek, I caught up with Porter and Richard. On a large rock next to the trail were bags and bags of foodstuff. I examined them, more out of curiosity than out of intention to add to my pack weight on this hot July day.

There were eight full one-gallon zip-lock bags. Two had some kind of rice mixture, but the other six had pellet-looking contents that I thought might be textured vegetable protein. Next to a twelve-inch diameter blue plastic tub, there was a large note, reading: "To whoever finds this, we brought to [sic] much food and couldn't carry it out. The green pellets are horse food. Hope you enjoy. Good luck on your journey. Please don't trash my forest." It was signed, "The Forest Nymphs." The irony of being asked not to trash "my" forest by someone on horseback who had just abandoned twenty pounds of garbage was not lost on subsequent hikers, who had adorned the note with messages of their own. Many were less than polite. Some suggested anatomical impossibilities or crimes against nature; others questioned ancestry and intellect. One of the more polite ones said: "Pack it in, Pack it out, Dumbass. That's the rule!!" signed "The Forest Trash." Even though I have previously made clear my feelings about horses in the mountains, my own comment added to the dwindling free space on the paper will remain uncatalogued, although it may have mentioned the horse and the rider who rode in on it.

By the end of the day, I was 5,000 feet higher than when I started and seventeen miles further along. After winding around and through canyons all day long, the trail at last hit the first of a series of ridgelines that it would follow until it dropped down into the Klamath River canyon, nearly one hundred twenty-five miles up the trail, where this story begins. There was a slight breeze blowing across the slopes... for which I was thankful. Winding in and out of granite-filled gullies on that day, my little thermometer peaked at 104°F... the hottest day I had seen since the Mojave Desert, a thousand miles ago. Just off the trail, I found a small area, barely able to contain my sleeping bag, and set up camp. After a quick meal, I worked my way over to a minor peak on the ridge.

To the east, Mount Shasta loomed among the clouds. The air was soft, and rock and sky and clouds melded in pastel hues of salmon and blue. Only Mount Shasta itself broke above the shadow of the coming night. The brilliance of the fourteen-thousand-foot peak slowly dimmed as it absorbed the darkness exhaled by the forest below. I made my way back to my shelter as day gave in.

It was a tiring day, but exhilarating, because the trail had become a trail once more. Gone was the damnable brush and dismal forests of Section O that had dogged my steps the past four days. The myriad roads had faded once more into the trees, and the sounds of Tyrannosaurus-trucks and stingingly angry chainsaws had given way to the wind whipping across the ridge. The rock had become sharp and crystalline, and the views once more expanded out to fill the world. Disorientation receded. The trail was once again a beckoning path to unknown horizons.

The next evening found me camped with Richard and Porter beyond Parks Creek Summit, whose tale I have already related. I had camped not far from them the night before and caught up with them early in the day. A marvelously beautiful sunset, filled with clouds and thunder, marked the end of the day. The next morning I left early, as usual. When all is said and done, it will have turned out that I do not see either of them again, as I outpace them to the Oregon border and other events unfold.

The day progressed as the trail wound along ridges, descending, strangely enough, to passes, rather than ascending to them, as one used to hiking in the Sierra might expect. In the afternoon I reached Scott Mountain Summit, a relatively well-traveled road along an historic route. As I was sitting at the edge a parking lot cluttered with a number of empty vehicles, feet resting up on the trunk of a tree, I was startled into awareness as a car drove up. The driver, headed out towards a nearby campground, stopped to chat. He readily offered up a couple of ice cold beers, which I should have declined, having miles to travel yet, but did not. We passed an hour in amiable conversation, then he headed to his camp, and I up the trail for a wearisome 1,200-foot climb. By the end of the day I was a long thirty-plus miles from where I started. The next day a twenty-seven mile jaunt brought me to Etna Summit. Late in the afternoon I was standing at the Somes Bar–Etna Road with my thumb out and headed for town.

Within minutes I was picked up by Devin, a local high school teacher. He and his son had been out fishing and were headed back to town. He told me a story of two sheep being killed by a mountain lion only a couple of days before right at the edge of town. The mountain lion was seen the next night on the football field of the high school. This news will turn out to plague me for several days as I head out of Etna and up the trail. More than once the hair on my neck would stand up and shivers run up and down my spine, when for no apparent reason, I suddenly felt watched.

Devin dropped me off at the motel, the only motel in town. To my dismay, the proprietor told me she had not a single room. They were booked for days in advance by a highway crew working on road maintenance. She offered me a cold soda and some chips, but I didn't stay long. It was getting late, and I had no idea where I would be spending the night. I went down to the grocery store. There I ran into Captain Mike and Paparazzi, who said that back down the road a ways was a place to stay. I found the building, a long, brown, two-story structure down near the motel I had just left. A sign out front proclaimed CCTG. It stands for Campus California Teachers Group. I met Ruth Ford and Thomas Lindstrom, the founders of this non-profit organization that trains people to be volunteers in Africa and Central America. Their building contains a huge kitchen, computer rooms, laundry, showers, and a number of dorm rooms that sleep two or three people. Students come there from all over the world for six months at a time, to learn how to make a difference in parts of the world where a difference is there for the making. They were between semesters, so they threw open their doors to thru-hikers.

Two nights there and I was on the trail again. The Spiritmobile magically showed up to take seven of us back to the trail. At one o'clock in the afternoon, we sat at the trailhead and shared one of the two watermelons Captain Mike was carrying. By evening I was eleven miles up the trail, camped on a windswept saddle and watching the twinkling lights of Yreka, more than twenty-five miles distant. Another twenty-five mile day carried me through the Marble Mountains and to another nameless saddle on the slopes of Huckleberry Mountain, eighteen miles from Seiad and 4,600 feet higher. With a little judicious gardening, I was able to eke out a small campsite. At first light, I was on the trail and running. In about fourteen miles I came to Grider Creek Campground and the series of roads leading to Seiad and this story's beginning.

—————⇒✦⇐—————

Back now to the story resulting from the shiny blue pickup. Distracted, dazed, and mildly inebriated, I walk around the Seiad Valley store making a few purchases, get my re-supply box from the post office and fiddle around a bit. Then I go into the restaurant and order breakfast. No, not the Pancake Challenge. Five pancakes, each as big as a plate and weighing a pound is not my idea of breakfast pleasure, free or not. I had known all along that I was not up to said challenge. I am nearly done with a more moderate breakfast when E.G. walks into the restaurant. She sits down next to me and says, "How did you get here before me?" I tell my story of "obvious need," thinking she, too, will find it humorous. Instead, she exclaims, "Yellow Blazer! You're a Yellow Blazer!"[1] I am momentarily taken aback, then my hackles are raised. Showing rare restraint, I do not say what flashes through my mind...thoughts that include the adjectives sanctimonious and condescending, and nouns that dog breeders are familiar with. Instead, I finish my orange juice, and standing, reply: "So this is how you make friends in Wisconsin, is it?" and walk out. Not much

---

1 Yellow Blazing is a term brought west by hikers on the Appalachian Trail. It means getting a ride instead of taking the trail.

later she finishes whatever town chores she has and by early afternoon has disappeared up the trail. One thing I can say about E.G., she is a hiker! Three days from now I will see her again, briefly and at a distance, in Ashland, as she hits town and is out again the same day. And that's as nice as I can be.

By mid-afternoon, there are six of us sitting outside the Seiad Valley Café, Wildflower and Pacman, GT (German Tourist), Fritz and One Gallon, and myself. We are surrounded by boxes and boxes of re-supply goods. GT keeps bringing out goodies and passing them around. She has a huge supply of chocolate, Swiss of course. We are chatting and passing the afternoon. Within a few minutes another hiker comes out of the trees and across the parking lot. He says his name is JoHobo (until recently, Hobo Joe) and that he has hiked from Mexico, although it turns out absolutely no one has seen him before. This, of course, means nothing since there's lots of people you might or might not run into on the trail. His gait is a bit unsteady and his speech slurred. He admits to having drunk an 18-pack of some beer or the other. Then, feeling inexplicably sleepy, he went over to the creek and lay down in it to beat the heat. Unfortunately, he fell asleep and is now lobster red on chest and legs. He heads over to the store and comes back with another six-pack. Although unknown to any of the present hikers, he talks the talk and knows the places. His claim to fame is that he is, most likely, the only hiker to have been arrested two times on the trail...both for drunkenness. The first was in San Diego, before he had hiked a single foot on the PCT. He doesn't tell much of that story, but the second, at Cajon Pass, more than 1,300 miles ago, is a story worth the re-telling.

Coming out of Crowder Canyon, he made his way past the McDonald's and across the freeway overpass to the Del Taco fast food restaurant in back of the Shell gas station. Having lunch and a six-pack, he decided it was such a good idea that he had another six-pack, and went to sleep on one of Del Taco's outdoor tables. The restaurant manager, suspecting him of some less honorable itinerancy than that of a thru-hiker, called the police, who took him to Apple Valley, thirty miles away. There he spent the night in jail. The next day he was cut loose and spent the day trying to get a ride back to Cajon Pass. His problem was that he had cached his pack, including valuables, in the brush near the freeway overpass below McDonald's, and he was worried that his two-day absence would end in tragedy.

It didn't, and lo these many days later finds him in Seiad Valley, once again inebriated and most likely not for the first time since Cajon Pass. He has a number of interesting tales to tell, and we would all, no doubt, be more inclined to participate in his conversation if we too had drunk twenty-four beers this day. I will learn much later that although he has taken a number of interesting side trips, he will finish the PCT in Canada, not by taking the Glacier Peak detour,[2] but by the original route, making the dangerous crossing of the now bridgeless Suiattle River.

The afternoon passes amiably, and as day ends, we have a final meal in the restaurant. When I arrived this morning, I assumed most people would be staying at the Mid-Valley RV Park, adjacent the store-restaurant. I checked in, paying my seven dollars for a shower and a spot on the ground. By the end of dinner, everyone else has decided to press on and camp further up the trail rather than spend money for a piece of ground that is elsewhere free. I decide that since I have already paid, I will stay...bad move. It turns out the "ground" is a small fenced area that also houses the propane tank. This would, of itself, not necessarily be a bad thing, but traffic and bright lights and people coming and going until the wee hours all conspire to mar the evening. To top it off, at one AM, someone on a four-wheel ATV cruises through...passing no more than five feet from where I lay.

The next morning finds me up and out in the pre-dawn darkness. I walk the mile down the highway to where the trail starts up. And *up* is the operative word here, for the trail, heading up out of the 1,450 foot elevation of the Klamath River Valley, goes up 2,000 before it hits the ridgeline, and another 3,000 after that.

The next day, precisely at noon, I cross the border into Oregon. The only thing to mar the day was the necessity of sharing the small, slimy, shallow water sources of Kangaroo Springs with a number of salamanders. At the border, I celebrate the passing of 1698.8 miles with a libation. Only a mere 952 miles remain. I hurry on towards Ashland.

---

2 A nasty series of storms in the winter of 2003 made a detour necessary due to trail damage and a half-dozen potentially dangerous fords where bridges were washed out, particularly the 150 foot bridge across the Suiattle River in Washington.

SKIN DIVING THROUGH OREGON

Oregon is beautiful country, I guess. But things have changed. More than 1,700 miles of trail lie behind me, and now only 900 are left. In Oregon, for the first time, I have begun to have momentary, shy, sly thoughts of a destination beyond that of this glorious day. In addition, the PCT through Oregon is not a difficult trail. The terrain is kind, no huge gains and losses of elevation. The miles flow by seamlessly. And then there are the interminable forests. I liken it to skin diving. You take a deep breath and sink below the surface. Swimming around among the kelp, you stay as long as you can, then burst through the surface to once again gulp precious air. Land is there, rising above the water. In Oregon and southern Washington, hiking the PCT is a similar experience. For days there is little hint that you are making progress...other than tick-marks on the Data Book pages. Then, all at once, you break into the open and there it is, a beautiful mountain rising above its surroundings. Maybe it's the Three Sisters, or Mount Jefferson, or Mount Hood, but there it is. To make up for this dearth of views, the trail winds around and over the slopes of these solitary island peaks, giving up a close, personal, marvelous view. Then it's back into the kelp for two or three days...or more.

But now there is some small hint of urgency; a destination is in mind, if not in sight. High mileage days become easy...too easy. A reading of the dozens of on-line journals shows that injuries are common in Oregon. Shin splints, stress fractures, foot injuries, plantar fasciitis, and the like are uncommonly common. I, myself, will wind up at the end of a thirty-six mile day with foot problems that will dog me 700 more miles and for nearly a year after the hike is through.

———⟫●⟪———

Editor's note: The manuscript was incomplete for the section from Ashland, past Crater Lake, the Three Sisters, Jefferson Park and Mount Hood to the Columbia River. In 2005, No Way Ray covered this 428 mile distance in about 19 days. The weather is good, the terrain mild and the hiker is able to make a lot of miles every day, typically twenty-five to thirty miles. With winter approaching, thru-hikers hurry on toward the Canadian border before the snows come.

———⟫●⟪———

Columbia River—

At long last, nearly twenty-six miles into the day, I arrive at the trailhead at Eagle Creek. In the parking lot there are at least a dozen cars. I have seen people here and there along the trail, so rather than take the

5.2 mile trail walk, I cast my fate to the winds, pull out my Tyvek ground sheet, fold it so that it exposes *PCT Hiker, To Town Please!!* and walk towards Highway 84, half expecting E.G. to pop out of the woods, yelling "Yellow Blazer, Yellow Blazer!" The gods smile, and within five minutes I am tucked into the back of a small pickup careening down the freeway. I am dropped off in the middle of Cascade Locks, in fact, right outside the door of the Salmon Row Inn. In less time than it takes to clear your ears when coming up from forty feet of water, I am drinking a glass of Walking Man Pale Ale, fresh from the tap. It's so tasty that I have another.

In the end, and considerably mellowed from the pounding of the long, downhill day, I head outside to scout out the town and find a place to be. I walk east along the main (and only) street, still feeling more than a little dazed. I pass by a big SUV-type vehicle that is parked on the street. Next to it are several people, engaged in animated conversation. As I pass by, one of the women hails me. Holding out a hand, she says, "Sir, I'd like to buy you dinner." In my hand she thrusts a twenty dollar bill. How does the old joke go? What's the difference between a thru-hiker and a homeless person? Silnylon. I thank her sincerely and walk on. I guess I've still got the old and pathetic bit going for me. Later in the evening, I will relate the story to The Walking Heads. Rainbo exclaims, "You took the money? I wouldn't have!" I explain that here was this person who wanted to do good, who took the chance to talk to someone who looked for all the world like a derelict (and could have been a dangerous lunatic), and so who was I to nay-say? So what if I probably had more money in my pocket than she did. It's the thought that counts.

I wind up at the Econo Inn at the far east end of town. For a mere forty-five dollars a night, I stay, and take a zero on the next…my first since Ashland, an entire state ago. Within a hundred yards of the motel can be found a grocery store, a restaurant (with bar), a laundromat, an ice cream parlor, a hamburger stand (try the blackberry milkshake!), a convenience store, and the post office…and The Salmon Row Inn.

Early in the morning, I wake up and prepare to leave Oregon. The Walking Heads have stayed at the other end of town, at the Best Western. They said they would be having breakfast at the Char Burger Restaurant, next to the motel, so I pack and head out. I arrive at the restaurant at six-thirty AM, a half hour before it opens, so I sit and watch the early morning traffic cross the bridge into Washington. The restaurant opens…no Walking Heads. It turns out they decided to have the breakfast buffet at the motel…something the more econo-oriented Econo Lodge does not offer. I spend a leisurely hour, watching the river flow by, then head out and up to the bridge entrance. I display my two quarters toll to the attendant.

She waves me on through, saying, "Watch out for the traffic." At only a few minutes after eight AM, I reach midway on the bridge, 2,155 miles from Mexico. The sign says, *Welcome to Washington*.

——————

Editor's note: During the winter of 2006-07, Ray certainly would have written about his hike through the state of Washington. The PCT route here travels 500 miles along the east side of the chain of volcanoes that is the Northern Cascades. It passes Mounts Baker and Saint Helens, the Goat Rocks Wilderness, Mount Rainier, and the Pasayten Wilderness to finally arrive at the Washington-British Columbia border with Canada. Eight miles further, the hiker arrives back in "civilization" at Manning Park, BC. Ray completed his PCT hike on August 29, 2005.

THIS IS THE END

There is nothing you really have to do
Nothing you have to say
There nothing you really have to have
Nothing you have to know
There is nothing you really have to become...
However, it helps if you remember
That fire burns, and when it rains, the earth gets wet

(Zen Saying)

Trail mile 2,648, just 15 miles from the Canadian border—
On a ridge high above Hopkins Lake, I run into a hiker. I ask her about a place to camp for the evening. She says that the lake has some good sites, but it is a ways off the trail. But...she says...I can always camp at Hopkins Pass. I make the switchbacks down to the pass, going by the lateral to the lake. Unfortunately, the pass is merely a rockpile, with utterly no possibility of camping. I head on down on a long traverse of the steep slopes of Blizzard Mountain.

It is heading toward dark, and I begin to become alarmed. I am not carrying a light source sufficient for night hiking. Ultimately, just before it becomes too dark to see, I come to a sign telling me that Frosty Lake is somewhere ahead. Looking at the map, I discover I have missed a junction. Back a hundred yards, I see where the PCT, which had been going north, made a sharp turn back to the southwest. Back at the junction, I set my pack down and begin to tromp up the hillsides, through the brush, in an attempt to find a campsite. After several minutes, I find a place upslope, just large enough to put up my tent.

The weather has become more and more threatening throughout the afternoon, so I hastily set up my tent. I fix dinner and crawl into my bag. Some time later, I am rudely awakened by a fierce snort and a huge crashing in the brush. It turns out that I have set up camp smack in the middle of a deer track. The deer, running into an unexpected barrier, evidently leapt twenty feet through the air, to land in the middle of the bushes, crashing through until it could again reach its accustomed track. This continues to occur at odd intervals throughout the evening. Finally I fall asleep, the wind a song in my ears. By two AM the wind is humming through clenched teeth; it starts to rain. At five AM, I hastily pack and head down the trail. It's less than six miles to the Canadian border.

I arrive at the border at 7:28 AM.[1] It is raining steadily. There is no one there, save me. Clouds swirl across the ridges both east and west. To the west, a swath of forest has been cut, making an odd looking cut, up and across the mountains. For some reason I seem emotionless, neither elated nor deflated. It seems as though the trip is not yet finished. I realize that it is still eight miles to civilization and the real end, but that is not the source of these feelings. I have a small container of fine scotch, carried from Stehekin, so I toast the trail. Holding my camera at arms length, I attempt, with mixed results, to photograph myself and the border. I tarry long enough to dismantle the obelisk and sign into the register. The rain continues as I head on up the trail. Civilization calls.

$$\Longrightarrow\!\!\!\triangleright\!\bullet\!\triangleleft\!\Longleftarrow$$

Manning Park, British Columbia—

Sitting in the bus, headed towards Vancouver, a host of emotions well up in me, so strong and so complex that they are, for the moment, indefinable. It is so overpowering that I put my head into my hands, and resting my arms on my knees, try not to move. Besides a profound fatigue and sensory overload, I recognize the emotions of joy, sadness, relief, frustration, anger and despair as they wash through me. My hands become wet, and to my amazement, I find that my eyes are running water like a faucet. It's not crying exactly, for there is no catching of breath, no sobbing...just tears.

I try to analyze my feelings. Part is pure relief. I am truly tired of walking. It is more difficult than most realize, to get up and walk all day long, every day, in fair weather or foul, whether you feel like it or not. And it's not just that I'm an old man and can't cut it. I have heard many, far younger and more robust than me, say the same. That's because it is more mental than physical, this long distance walking. And so I feel no shame to be profoundly glad to be done.

Another part I recognize as something I described long ago and so many miles away, when I spent that solitary night at the empty house of Jack Fair, as a bubble of emotion, equal parts joy and sorrow. I have completed the journey that I set out upon, and I am filled with joy at its completion, and even though I am so glad to be done, I am also filled with a profound sadness that I am leaving, heading back into that other world. The sadness is partly a sense of loss, like that of a dear friend or lover, that leaves a hollow, aching void so far inside that, though it be stored safely, to be brought out and gingerly sampled on those long nights when

1 August 29, 2005

sleep eludes and thought ranges where it will, it remains untouched for a lifetime. Trapped halfway between joy and sorrow, I feel a great pressure in my face. My facial muscles are clenched hard in a smile and tears stream down my face. It is truly an overpoweringly odd set of sensations.

And that is not all. There is an undercurrent, like a sub-sonic speaker, creating an indefinable itch, a tension in the neck and shoulders. It's fear...and anger. I am afraid that I will not be able to hold on to what I've found these solitary months along the trail. That I will, all too soon, be once again trapped by the non-essential, embroiled in the unimportant, snared by responsibilities of living in a world where others must be taken into account. I fear that in the coming weeks it will all become fuzzed and gossamer. I will become more and more entangled, like a freeway driver in rush hour traffic, until all that seems real is the shouting and the honking, the grimacing and the groaning. Frustration flows through me like an electrical current, a drumming, barking madness that causes desert winds to cease and stars to dim, though nights be clear. Life on the trail is quiet and uncomplicated. Its pace is measured. Most decisions concern only the immediate future, where will I have lunch? How far will I walk today? Will the weather hold until evening? In strong counterpoint lies the life to which I am returning, where the pace is frantic, decisions complex and numerous, the wants and whims of others muscling in and taking over...directing.

In truth, I am afraid to go home, frustrated that life will again become complex, knowing I will once again fall into the old games, watch my physical conditioning diminish as my stomach line swells. I realize it sounds like I am returning to Hell after a five-month tryst in Heaven...this is certainly not the case. I live a relatively stress-free, peaceful life. I am surrounded by mountains and forest. I have no immediate neighbors. I could go for days seeing but one or two people...but don't confront me with the facts. Sitting here on the bus headed for civilization, I am surrounded by a noisy crowd...uncomfortably close to more people than I have had to deal with for months, it seems. Cars blast by...everything is moving too fast and there is simply too much. I'll get over it, though I'm not certain, right at this moment, that I want to.

The voices all around me fade into the background. I hear the roar of wind as it streams past the bus. It sounds like the winter wind that rushes up the canyon in which I live, announcing, "Here I come, ready or not." And like a child in the Japanese game of hide and seek, silently I yell back "maada dayo, maada dayo"...Not yet...I'm not ready yet...Don't hurt me. The bus rushes on.

SUNSHINE AND SHADOW

Sunlight on granite.
Crystal water laughs its life.
No clouds. No Way.

Late in summer, the weather becomes increasingly unstable over the High Sierra. Moist warm ocean air collides with granite. Afternoon thunderstorms release the energy. The clouds roil over the ridges. Sunshine and shadow play on the ragged white blocks. The trees and wildflowers bow to the wind as they welcome the season's scant moisture.

The vivid light and the tumultuous weather marked the time No Way Ray best loved being in the Sierra. Hunkered down in the lee of a rock or cozy in a tent, he would watch the light show with pure delight.

On May 15, 2006, No Way Ray died doing the one thing he loved best. Although death came far too early in the best part of his life, he had never wanted to become old and frail and dependent. Such a high cost for freedom.

On the previous evening, we had camped on a ridge top, the one east above the damaged bridge on Deep Creek. He had been hoping for good sunset photographs. Morning came. The image I keep in my mind's eye is his face with crinkly smiling eyes peering out of the sleeping bag with the first light of dawn touching the tent wall behind his head. He was totally excited about another day of wildness and exhilaration, sweat and pain, uphill and downhill, sunshine and shadow on the mountains.

Stone Dancer

October 12, 2006
Mount San Jacinto 10,834 ft.

No Way Ray says,
"These are books whose reading are worth the time."

Albanov, Valerian. *In the Land of White Death*. The Modern Library, New York, 2000. 205pp.

Ballard, Angela and Duffy. *A Blistered Kind of Love: One Couple's Trial by Trail*. The Mountaineer's Books, Seattle, Washington, 2003. 264pp.

Brewer, William. *Up and Down California in 1860-1864*. University of California Press, Berkeley, California, 2003. 586pp.

Browning, Peter. *Place Names of the Sierra Nevada*. Wilderness Press, Berkeley, California, 1986. 253pp.

Childs, Craig. *Soul of Nowhere: Traversing Grace in a Rugged Land*. Sasquatch Books, United States of America, 2002. 229pp.

Gisel, Bonnie Johanna, ed. *Kindred and Related Spirits: The Letters of John Muir and Jeanne C. Carr*. The University of Utah Press, Salt Lake City, 2001. 394pp.

Jardine, Ray. *Beyond Backpacking*. Adventure Lore Press, La Pine, Oregon, 1992. 504pp.

—— *The Pacific Crest Trail Hiker's Handbook*. Adventure Lore Press, La Pine, Oregon, 6th ed, 1998. 373pp.

Krutch, Joseph Wood. *The Voice of the Desert*. William Sloane Associates, New York, 1969. 223pp

Leopold, Aldo. *A Sand County Almanac*. Oxford University Press.

Margolis, Hal. *Trekking Along: The Pacific Crest Trail Through Southern California*. Silogram Corporation, Beverly Hills, California, 2003. 464pp.

Meegan, George. *The Longest Walk: An Odyssey of the Human Spirit*. Paragon House, New York, NY, 1988. 402pp.

Continued on next page

Muir, John. *My First Summer in the Sierra.*

—— *John of the Mountains: The Unpublished Journals of John Muir.* Linnie Marsh Wolfe, ed. The University of Wisconsin Press, Madison, Wisconsin, 1979. 459pp.

Mueser, Roland. *Long Distance Hiking: Lessons from the Appalachian Trail.* Ragged Mountain Press, Camden, Maine, 1998. 180pp.

Ormsby, Waterman L. *The Butterfield Overland Mail.* The Huntington Library, San Marino, California. 1991. 179pp

Ross, Cindy. *Journey on the Crest: Walking 2600 Miles from Mexico to Canada.* The Mountaineers, Seattle, Washington.1987. 310pp

Rosseau, Jean-Jacques. *Meditations of a Solitary Walker.* Penguin Books, New York City, New York, 1995. 54pp

Smith, Genny Schumacher, ed. *Deepest Valley: A Guide to Owens Valley.* Genny Smith Books, Los Altos, California, 1978. 233pp.

Sutton, Ann and Myron. *The Pacific Crest Trail: Escape to the Wilderness.* J.B. Lippencott, New York, 1975. 239pp.

Acknowledgments

After No Way Ray was killed, making this book available for you to enjoy has been the work of many generous people. I want to thank Pinhead, Mother & Smother, the Tornado Twins, the three curmudgeons from Newport Harbor High, Kevin & Andrea, my Rabbitstick family including those four real men, my hiking partner Gottago, and the dauntless Flint Dragon. Ever important to Ray and me have been our family: mothers, children and grandchildren.

Meadow Ed, thank you for your words, poet's spirit, and good chow.

Another delight of this project has been the way that wonderful people have shown up to become members of the publishing team, Sophia and Rudy Wisener, Caroline Root, the computer wizards, and many other published writers, including Cody Lundin, Paul Campbell, Susan Alcorn and Tamara Wilder.

Special thanks as well for the encouragement of Liz Bergeron and her staff at the Pacific Crest Trail Association, and from the whole PCT hiking community.

About the Editor

Alice Tulloch and Ray Echols eloped in 1970. Her wilderness experience began at age 4 and includes hiking in all the same mountains and canyons as Ray. They have two children and two grandchildren. She is a retired civil engineer, and for twenty years has been a wilderness skills instructor. Since Ray's death in 2006, she has continued hiking the PCT and other trails, covering 1,850 miles in two summers.

Her trail name is Stone Dancer. This refers to the nimbleness needed for crossing rocky streams and talus slopes. It also represents what it takes to return to joy after one of life's greatest challenges. She is available for presentations on this book and other aspects of the wilderness experience. Contact her at info@tuolumnepress.com.

Give the gift of

A THRU-HIKER'S HEART
Tales of the Pacific Crest Trail

To your friends and fellow outdoors-lovers

If your local retailer does not have copies of this book in stock, additional copies can be obtained at our website on-line

www.tuolumnepress.com

or by sending $18.95 plus $4.00 shipping per book
(California residents please add $1.52 sales tax per book)
to

Tuolumne Press
PO Box 273
Mariposa, CA 95338

Make your check payable to Tuolumne Press

For additional information;
info@tuolumnepress.com
209-742-6963